Chaucer at Large

MEDIEVAL CULTURES

SERIES EDITORS

Sponsored by the Center for Medieval Studies at the University of Minnesota

Volumes in the series study the diversity of medieval cultural histories and practices, including such interrelated issues as gender, class, and social hierarchies; race and ethnicity; geographical relations; definitions of political space; discourses of authority and dissent; educational institutions; canonical and noncanonical literatures; and technologies of textual and visual literacies.

Volume 24
Steve Ellis
Chaucer at Large: The Poet in the Modern Imagination

Volume 23
Edited by Barbara A. Hanawalt and Michal Kobialka
Medieval Practices of Space

Volume 22
Michelle R. Warren
History on the Edge: Excalibur and the Borders of Britain, 1100–1300

For more books in the series, see pages 197–98.

Chaucer at Large

The Poet in the Modern Imagination

Steve Ellis

Medieval Cultures, Volume 24
University of Minnesota Press
Minneapolis
London

An earlier version of chapter 2 appeared as "Popular Chaucer and the Academy," in *Medievalism and the Academy,* vol. 1, Leslie J. Workman et al., eds., Studies in Medievalism 9 (Cambridge: D. S. Brewer, 1999), 26–43; reprinted with permission of Studies in Medievalism. An earlier version of chapter 3 appeared as "Chaucer, Yeats, and the Living Voice," in *Yeats Annual* 11, Warwick Gould, ed. (New York: Macmillan, 1995): 45–60; reprinted with permission. Excerpts of poetry from *Punch* in chapter 5 reprinted with permission of Punch Ltd.

Published by the University of Minnesota Press
111 Third Avenue South, Suite 290
Minneapolis, MN 55401-2520
http://www.upress.umn.edu

Library of Congress Cataloging-in-Publication Data
Ellis, Steve, 1952-
Chaucer at large : the poet in the modern imagination / Steve Ellis.
p. cm. — (Medieval cultures ; v. 24)
Includes bibliographical references and index.
ISBN 0-8166-3376-2 (alk. paper) — ISBN 0-8166-3377-0 (pbk. : alk. paper)
1. Chaucer, Geoffrey, d. 1400—Criticism and interpretation—History.
2. Chaucer, Geoffrey, d. 1400—Influence. 3. Middle Ages in literature.
4. Medievalism—History.
I. Title. II. Series.
PR1924 .E466 2000
821'.1—dc21 00-008464

Printed in the United States of America on acid-free paper

11 10 09 08 07 06 05 04 03 02 01 00 10 9 8 7 6 5 4 3 2 1

To

Tony Davies,
verray, parfit, gentil

and

Mark Storey,
dulnesse ys of hym adrad

"our Dan . . . lies closer to the national heart than we wot of"

Rudyard Kipling, "Dayspring Mishandled"

Contents

Acknowledgments

It is a pleasure to thank those people and institutions who have provided me with help and advice in the process of writing this book: Geoffrey Bird, Brenda Carter, Valerie Edden, A. S. G. Edwards, Julia Fitzsimmons, Warwick Gould, Anne McDermott, John McDermott, Joanna Porter, Terence Porter, Anne Running, Tessa Sidey, Stan Smith, Michael Spender, Yvonne Truscott, Kathleen Verduin, Cosetta Veronese, David Wallace, and Ruth Webber. I am extremely grateful to the staffs of the University of Birmingham Library, Birmingham Reference Library, British Library, BBC Written Archives Centre at Caversham, and BBC Broadcast Archives at Brentford. I must also thank the English departments at the universities of Bristol, Wales at Lampeter, and York for opportunities to develop my thoughts in invited papers or lectures, as well as the New Chaucer Society, at whose Congresses in 1994 (Dublin) and 1996 (Los Angeles) I gave papers drawing on some of this material. My dedication highlights two colleagues whose support and benevolence have been crucial for my work, but their names stand as proxy for all those colleagues at my home university, both in the English department and beyond, who have made it such a pleasant place for me to work.

Introduction

This book is an attempt to trace Chaucer's various manifestations in modern culture outside the academic arena. My concentration on the twentieth century represents the first occasion that the relevant material has been treated in any sustained manner, since although much has been written on different aspects of Chaucer's reception in later historical periods, attention has been largely confined to pre-twentieth-century responses to his work, and to the Middle Ages more generally. The reasons for this relative absence of attention will be amply treated in what follows, but one obvious difficulty in getting any kind of overview of the modern field is the extremely diffuse nature of the subject: this book considers such things as novelists' and poets' responses to Chaucer; children's versions of his work; modern translations; adaptations of his work for stage, television, radio, and film; and the marketing of Chaucer's "heritage." Issues that I return to throughout include the serviceability of Chaucer for modern constructions of Englishness; the nostalgia that Chaucer's work seems to prompt for perished models of community, order, and simplicity; and, of just as much significance as these requisitions on him, the perhaps surprising absence of Chaucer from the modern agenda in areas where one might expect to find him. As I remarked above, Chaucer's impact in the present century is varied and diffuse, and it is not easy to see where it consolidates and centers itself, so to speak; this not only creates problems for the literary cartographer but also bespeaks ways in which his work has been marginalized and even patronized. To take an obvious parallel, and one returned to below: if we want to "find" Dante in the modern period, there are several key places where we might start, such as the work of T. S. Eliot, or Pound, or Seamus Heaney. This is hardly the case with Chaucer, and the quest for him is for a more elusive figure and constitutes in some ways a more intriguing enterprise.

The structure of this book is roughly chronological, and in several chapters I have sought to arrange the material around an event of particular significance. I begin with a prefatory chapter on the late nineteenth century, featuring the Morris and Burne-Jones Kelmscott Chaucer of 1896. My investigations into Chaucer's popular standing in the modern period in chapter 2 take off from the Chaucer quincentenary celebrations of 1900, and I then proceed to W. B. Yeats's engagement with Chaucer in 1905–6, when Yeats's promotion of a renewal of oral literature, associated with his founding of the Abbey Theatre, looked to Chaucer for inspiration. Chapter 4 then considers the discourse of "children's Chaucer," of particular prominence in the Edwardian period, before chapter 5 continues the story with a discussion of Chaucer's exemplary "Englishness" and the ways in which this was pursued by writers like Masefield, Woolf, and Chesterton in the period following the First World War. Although this arrangement provides a chronological anchorage to the book, in several of these chapters the discussion in fact ranges widely from the late nineteenth century to the present day. With chapters 6 and 7 I attempt a broader appraisal of the types of interest modern poets and novelists have taken in Chaucer, followed by a consideration of modern Chaucer translations. Chapter 8 takes us on into the post–World War II period and to the versions of Chaucer offered on film, television, and the stage, before chapter 9 conducts in part a recapitulation of some of the concerns of this century in examining the way Chaucer has been characterized in modern historical fiction. With chapter 10, my conclusion, I continue the discussion in these latter chapters about how Chaucer has been received in nonacademic discourse in the 1980s and 1990s, and also consider in more detail a theme that has run throughout; that is, precisely the lines of communication that can be drawn between a prolific academic interest in Chaucer in the twentieth century (and its changing fashions) and the less scholarly manifestations treated in these pages.

The scope of this book is an ambitious one, therefore, and although my primary focus is British culture of the twentieth century, I have also drawn on plentiful American examples. I am aware that a good deal more might be done, and that the material of chapters 6, 7, and 10 in particular might in each case form a book-length study in its own right. One of the aims of what follows, however, both in the main text and in the sizable endnotes, is to begin a process of data collection and classification, in combination, to be sure, with a recurrent and consistent interpretative procedure. The result is a book offered to Chaucerians, students of twentieth-century literature, and nonspecialists alike, and a contribution to whatever sexcentenary celebrations Chaucer's work will trigger in the year 2000.

1

Kelmscott Chaucer

The most celebrated Chaucerian product of the nineteenth century is also, it has been argued, one of the least typical: Derek Brewer has spoken of the "isolation" of the Kelmscott Chaucer, and of how the "Romantic medievalising" it signifies is at odds with the predominant interest in Chaucer's humor and realism that characterizes Victorian responses.[1] William S. Peterson has noted more particularly how the Chaucer of Edward Burne-Jones's illustrations is "more gaunt and solitary, more inward-looking . . . and more visionary" than the common image of the portly and worldly Chaucer that derives from portraits in the Ellesmere manuscript and in Hoccleve's *Regement of Princes;*[2] indeed, in figure and apparel, Burne-Jones's Chaucer is not too dissimilar from the Pre-Raphaelite (and more specifically Rossettian) Dante, though his features are rather less gaunt and aquiline. Whether "Romantic medievalising" is the right context in which to locate the Kelmscott volume (and its "isolation" means that Brewer spends little time substantiating this context in his survey of Chaucer's critical heritage), there is no doubt that many of the qualities we shall see attaching to Chaucer in this present study—his gregariousness, his urbanism, his "man-of-the-world" status—find no echo there.

The volume does, however, pick up on one conspicuous strain of nineteenth-century thinking about Chaucer—that is, Chaucer's standing as a "nature poet." Its opening illustration, to the "Prologue" of the *Canterbury Tales,* shows Chaucer knee-deep in a garden of flowers, standing beside a large well and a bird-filled tree. We far more often find the Chaucer of the "Prologue" in illustrated editions in the vicinity of the Tabard Inn or on the road to Canterbury, whereas the Kelmscott illustration suggests the Chaucer of the dream-visions (the *Parliament of*

Fowls in particular) interpolated, as it were, into the later work.[3] The Burne-Jones illustrations are far more interested in presenting Chaucer as the poet of Nature than as the poet of human nature, and in this they tend to absolutize the recurrent association between the poet and "leaves and birds, of which he was the greatest lover ever known," as an anonymous essayist of 1859 puts it; another essay of 1871, "The Descriptive Poetry of Chaucer," parallels Chaucer and Burne-Jones as landscape colorists, while an 1886 piece refers to "Chaucer's pre-Raphaelite and truthful delineation of Nature."[4] The two last comments promote Chaucer in this respect, however, on the basis of falsely attributed works, namely Lydgate's "Complaint of the Black Knight" and the anonymous "Flower and the Leaf," respectively.

Indeed, the establishment of an accurate Chaucer canon toward the end of the nineteenth century means in effect the demise of the Chaucer of Pre-Raphaelite botanizing and the relative absence of the "nature poet" from twentieth-century accounts. As well as the two poems already mentioned, other works that would support this profile and that were regarded as Chaucer's until well into the nineteenth century include the "Cuckoo and the Nightingale" and the "Court of Love." Robert Bell's edition of Chaucer's *Works,* published in 1854–56, accepted all these poems as authentic, whereas by the time of the revised edition of 1878 they had been relegated to the apocrypha; in his introduction to this revised edition Skeat also strongly contests the ascription to Chaucer of the fragmentary Middle English translation of the *Romance of the Rose,* following the rejection of the translation as Chaucer's by Bradshaw and subsequently by F. J. Furnivall and Bernhard ten Brink.[5] Thanks to the work of these scholars, a good deal of consensus had been reached toward the end of the nineteenth century in defining an accurate Chaucer canon,[6] but what one might label the flower-and-leaf Chaucer survives in the circles influenced by Pre-Raphaelitism. In spite of Furnivall's scorn, for example, Swinburne never withdrew the ascription to Chaucer of the "Court of Love," referred to as "Chaucer's most beautiful of young poems" as late as the 1906 printing of his book on William Blake (first published in 1868), and the fourth edition of Malcolm Bell's monograph on Burne-Jones (1898) promotes the "Cuckoo and the Nightingale" as one of Chaucer's most influential works for the painter.[7]

Bell argues for Chaucer as Burne-Jones's most important literary source, "the author that first captured his fancy and held it longest,"[8] though this seems to be a fancy based on everything but the *Canterbury Tales:*

> The artist shared with Chaucer his passionate love of birds and flowers, and lavished them with a tender hand over his work; in especial, like the poet, he delighted in the English flower, the rose. . . . his great work, *The Legend of the Briar Rose* [at Buscot Park, Faringdon], is quite an apotheosis of the beloved flower. (105)

Chaucer's delight in the rose can only be a reference to the *Romance of the Rose,* for which, as Bell says, Burne-Jones made "a large number of designs" at various stages of his career (104). We know that Chaucer did make a translation of the *Rose* (referred to in the "Prologue" to the *Legend of Good Women,* F version, line 329), but already in Burne-Jones's time, as we have seen, doubts had been raised that this was the Middle English version that has partially survived. The issue can hardly be said to be settled today,[9] but that Burne-Jones was committed not only to accepting the translation as Chaucer's, but also to indulging a pretense of its being an original Chaucerian work rather than a translation, is suggested by his manner of handling the text in the Kelmscott illustrations. This is seen most clearly on pages 312–13 of the volume, where the concluding scene to the *Rose* symmetrically balances the opening illustration to the *Parliament of Fowls* across the two-page spread, and where the same poet-figure (the "Chaucer" introduced in the volume's opening illustration) features in each. Burne-Jones actually told a correspondent that he had set the opening scene to the *Rose* (where the dreamer falls asleep) "in Chaucer's bedroom" with "his spirit going out at a door."[10] Such devices stamp Chaucer's authorship on the *Rose,* as does its position in the Kelmscott volume, where it precedes works like *Troilus and Criseyde* and all the dream-visions (its doubtful status is signaled in many modern editions by its being included as the last piece in a quasi appendix).[11] Although the Kelmscott volume does not avail itself of the Chaucerian apocrypha already noted, and although Morris was concerned to reproduce a correct canon of Chaucer's works by following the text of Skeat's six-volume Oxford Chaucer of 1894,[12] one could say that the bias in favor of a poet of romantic medievalizing, as traced above, remains intact and is sealed by the choice of which works to illustrate. Some of the most famous examples of Chaucer's comic realism—the tales of the Miller, Reeve, Shipman, Friar, Summoner, Pardoner, and Nun's Priest and the "Wife of Bath's Prologue"—are not illustrated at all, while the dream-visions and a doubtful work like the *Rose* are heavily illustrated.

Peterson is responsible for propagating the myth of some fundamental objection on Morris's part to Burne-Jones's approach to illustrating Chaucer, arguing that the former saw Chaucer as "a cheerful realist whose value to modern readers lay chiefly in his portrayal of medieval life and manners" (236). Elsewhere for Peterson, Morris's Chaucer is a "sturdy medieval bard" and not the "poet of courtly love" revered by Burne-Jones (247), and this leads him to speculate that "their radically differing conceptions of Chaucer's poetry must have led to some very lively discussions between [Burne-Jones] and Morris" (252). Duncan Robinson quotes Burne-Jones's letter to Swinburne in which he does admit to "abstain[ing] from decorating certain of the *Canterbury Tales*" in spite of Morris's "urgency" that he might do something with tales like the Miller's; Morris "ever had more robust and daring parts than I could assume," Burne-Jones adds. However, as Robinson comments, "in fairness it should be added that Morris himself concentrated on the romance aspect of Chaucer's poetry."[13] In fact, there is very little evidence that Morris went to Chaucer's poetry for things other than those emphasized by Burne-Jones, however tempting it might be to link the robustness and "sturdiness" of his own person with similar Chaucerian features. It is, however, not so much the romance or nature poetry aspect of Chaucer's work that provides a common interest, but Chaucer's depiction of the classical world. Malcolm Bell talks at some length of Burne-Jones's interest in and pictorial reproduction of Chaucer's "half-Pagan, half-Christianized" treatment of classical antiquity, of "Dan Cupido and his mother Saint Venus,"[14] and for both Burne-Jones and Morris one could argue that the most significant work by Chaucer is the *Legend of Good Women*, that series of repetitive stories from antiquity of doomed love and amorous martyrdom; repetitive to the point of boredom (it has been maintained) for the Chaucerian narrator himself, but enabling that graceful homogeneity of treatment that characterizes both Burne-Jones's illustrations and Morris's own narrative poetry.[15]

The *Legend of Good Women* did in fact provide an early Chaucerian bond between the two men. When Morris moved into Red House in Bexley Heath in 1860, twelve embroidered hangings inspired by the poem were projected for the decorative scheme, and in 1863–64 Morris and Burne-Jones collaborated on both a *Legend of Good Women* embroideries scheme for Ruskin and on a similar series of cartoons for stained-glass windows.[16] The *Figure of Chaucer* pencil drawing, now in Birmingham, is related to this latter series, illustrating the famous lines on the poet's devotion to the daisy recorded in the "Prologue" to the *Legend* (F version, lines 40–63).[17] As for Morris, his first work over which Chaucer has been claimed as a "presiding influence," *The Life and Death of Jason* (1867), is stimulated in part by the *Legend*.[18] This influence is hardly stylistic, given that Morris's decasyllabic couplets are much smoother and more lyrical in tone set against the colloquial directness that is always surfacing in Chaucer's:

> Yif that I live, thy name shal be shove
> In English that thy sekte shal be knowe!
> Have at thee, Jason! Now thyn horn is blowe!
>
> (*Legend,* lines 1381–83)

Nevertheless, the choice of the self-contained story of Jason's desertion of Medea as the final book of Morris's poem, after the previous sixteen books have recounted the legend of the Golden Fleece, enables the comparison to be made with section 4 of the *Legend,* which also recounts this desertion, and this inherited subject matter doubtless occasions Morris's well-known apostrophe to his "Master" Chaucer, which appears at the start of this final book.[19]

A *Spectator* review of 15 June 1867 talked of Morris's poem as one written "with Chaucer's strong sense of the piteousness of human life,"[20] though such a comment seems to leave out of account the caustic tones directed at "false men" ("Prologue," F version, line 486) that recur throughout the *Legend* and the prosecution of Jason himself as "evere in love a chef traytour" in section 4 (line 1659). Morris's poem adopts a far more pitying attitude to both protagonists and ends with Jason's death and the noble ceremonials that followed it. Morris's treatment of Medea is much more decorous than her popular reputation normally allows for, which derives from the crazed and barbaric witch figure described in book 7 of Ovid's *Metamorphoses;* in May Morris's words this treatment is "modern," with "the sorceress being merged in the woman [and] the brutalities of the legend softened."[21] Chaucer here certainly seems to have intervened in the tradition, given that his Medea is even "softer" than Morris's: there is no reference to any of her brutalities, including the revenge she takes on Creon's daughter and her murder of the children she has had by Jason, in accordance with the *Legend's* project to assemble a series of good women who are "saints" of love.[22]

The Life and Death of Jason then sets the tone for what remains Morris's abiding interest in Chaucer: not, as Peterson claims, on account of the latter's cheerfully realist depiction of "medieval life and manners," but precisely his detachment from this context and immersion in a world of dream and of classical and romance narrative; the phrase from the opening "Apology" to *The Earthly Paradise*—"dreamer of dreams, born out of my due time"—might have been Morris's designation of Chaucer as well as of himself (*Works* 3:1). Although the invocation to Chaucer at the start of book 17 of *Jason* does locate him within his own day and age—

> Would that I
> Had but some portion of that mastery
> That from the rose-hung lanes of woody Kent
> Through these five hundred years such songs have sent
> To us, who, meshed within this smoky net
> Of unrejoicing labour, love them yet.
> . . . O Master!
>
> (*Works* 2:259)

—the collocation of Kent, roses, and song establishes a Chaucer removed from the urban and social world of the *Canterbury Tales* and translated into customary Pre-Raphaelite territory, so that it is no surprise later in the invocation to come across a Chaucer whose "dreamy eyes" are directed once more at classical romance (in this case envisaging the story of *Troilus and Criseyde*) (2:259). Indeed, this depiction of Chaucer in *Jason* could stand alongside the opening illustration to the Kelmscott volume, discussed at the start of this chapter. Nor is there any reason to think that Morris's approach to Chaucer changed fundamentally as he got older and became involved in socialism, as we shall see. In this sense the Kelmscott volume represents a final confluence of Morris's and Burne-Jones's attitudes, rather than harboring any dissension between the two.

As Banham and Harris have stated, in the late 1860s Chaucer's work acted as a kind of "medium" through which Burne-Jones and Morris accessed a classical world that was of "growing interest" to them at this time, with the *Legend of Good Women* affording a particular fascination.[23] In Morris's curious poetic masque of 1872, *Love Is Enough; or, The Freeing of Pharamond,* the character of Love himself introduces the narrative of Pharamond's quest for Azalais by setting it in the context of other lovers' stories that he asks his "Faithful" to be mindful of; these include those of several lovers commemorated in the *Legend,* such as Pyramus, Medea, Ariadne, and Cleopatra (*Works* 9:12–13). Whatever pains Love inflicts by the way, he assures his faithful of a final bliss—"Of me a wedding-garment shall ye gain / . . . and a glorious seat / Within my household" (9:78)—which echoes a similar promise made by the God of Love of an eventual "paradys" to every "trewe lover" in the "Prologue" to the *Legend* (F version, lines 552–64). It has to be said, however, that whereas the *Legend* is a set of stories about the breaking of vows and male treachery, the prolonged emphasis on the lyricized longings of the lover and on the resolution of his love in *Love Is Enough* has far more in common with the Dante-derived mysticism of Rossetti's work, in, for example, poems like "The Stream's Secret," recently published in his *Poems* of 1870. In *Love Is Enough,* Love disguised as a pilgrim actually accompanies Pharamond on his journey (9:53ff.), evoking the situation in *Vita nuova* IX, and trappings from Dante do indeed occasionally infiltrate the Pre-Raphaelite depiction of Chaucer; as well as the overlap between their portraits, mentioned at the outset of this chapter, Burne-Jones's *Figure of Chaucer* referred to above includes in its top left-hand corner the angel-with-sundial or "Dantis Amor" motif familiar from many of Rossetti's paintings, and more particularly from the decorations to a wooden settle installed in Red House in 1860.[24]

However, whereas for many twentieth-century poets an interest in Dante has frankly eclipsed one in Chaucer, as we shall see, no one could maintain that this is the case with Morris, even if, by dwelling so heavily on Chaucer the love poet, there is a Dantesque cast to his enthusiasm. In his most famously "Chaucerian" work, *The Earthly Paradise*

(1868–70), Chaucer is represented directly both at the beginning and the end of the poem; in the address to Chaucer in the "Envoi," the "pity of love" theme is again prominent:

> . . . For thou, sweet-souled, didst never stand alone,
> But knew'st the joy and woe of many an one—
> —By lovers dead, who live through thee, we pray,
> Help thou us singers of an empty day!
>
> (*Works* 6:333)

Here Morris picks up on Chaucer's role not as a poet-lover himself (as in Dante's case), but as a narrator recounting the loves of others and not daring to become personally involved because of "myn unliklynesse," as the opening of *Troilus and Criseyde* puts it in book 1, line 16. Here Chaucer the storyteller is again important to Morris, but although *The Earthly Paradise* is often compared to the *Canterbury Tales* (as a collection of stories told in turn by individual narrators), the substance of these narratives again more often evokes works like the *Legend of Good Women* than the *Tales* themselves. Thus the first story that Morris gives for the month of June is that of Alcestis, the heroine of Chaucer's "Prologue" to the *Legend* (*Works* 4:89ff.); the final tale, "The Hill of Venus," recounts at one point a vision of a familiar cast of Chaucerian lovers—Pyramus and Thisbe, Ariadne, Phyllis, and Dido (6:296). The opening line of the prefatory "Apology" to the poem, "Of Heaven or Hell I have no power to sing" (3:1), seems to pick up directly on the opening to Chaucer's poem, where the narrator also argues that these transcendental realms are beyond the range of his personal experience and that knowledge of them can only be derived from "olde bokes" (F version, line 25). The well-known opening to the "Prologue" of *The Earthly Paradise* conjures up Chaucer's London, but hardly the London of the *Canterbury Tales,* rather that of a dream-vision escape from modernity:

> Forget six counties overhung with smoke,
> Forget the snorting steam and piston stroke,
> Forget the spreading of the hideous town;
> Think rather of the pack-horse on the down,
> And dream of London, small, and white, and clean,
> The clear Thames bordered by its gardens green.

We then come across Chaucer himself writing bills of lading in the port of London (3:3).

Although *The Earthly Paradise* is set "mid such times" (3:3) as these of Chaucer's appointment as customs controller, the narratives that follow are not grounded in this urban context. Rather, the "Prologue" to the poem follows the wanderings of "certain gentlemen and mariners of Norway" in search of the earthly paradise in the western seas (3:3); at one point they cut across Edward III's fleet in the English Channel prosecuting the war against France (3:14–22). Continuing westward, they eventually find not the paradise they are seeking but an island long inhabited by a similar set of refugees, this time not from Northern Europe but from "nations who dwelt anciently / About the borders of the Grecian sea" (3:3). This confluence between north and south enables Morris in what follows (the poem consisting of tales told alternately by individuals from the two communities) to draw both on Scandinavian saga literature and on the Greek-Latin tradition; this sense of producing a kind of compendium of pan-European classics is an ambition that obviously distinguishes the poem from a work like the *Canterbury Tales*.

In fact, it is not altogether easy to see what Chaucer's relevance is to all this, nor why he should be presented at both the beginning and the end of the work. The retreat from modern industrialism at the opening to the small, white, and clean London of the Middle Ages is, as we have seen, only a stage in a further retreat from history altogether to the "happy islands" (*Works* 3:6) where the tales are told; though this is not the paradise the wanderers are seeking, the narratives themselves become a paradise substitute, a book of pressed flowers from that visionary "flowery land" (3:81). The opening of *The Earthly Paradise* sets out in topographical form the relation of Chaucer to Morris that we have discussed; that is, Chaucer acts as a conduit of the classical tradition to Morris, and the concluding envoi to Chaucer sees him as patron of the poem and, more particularly, as we have seen, of those tales that tell of the "joy and woe" of lovers from antiquity (6:333). Clean, white London with its "clear" Thames is a foretaste of the "clear green water and the quays" and the white walls of the Grecian city on the happy islands (3:3), as if both Chaucer and Chaucer's London represent a preservation and mediation of the classical world.

The differences with the *Canterbury Tales* itself, and with the setting of this work in a fourteenth-century social context, are marked. For example, there is very little individual characterization of the tellers in Morris, and certainly none of that dramatic interaction between them that is staged in the Canterbury links; as either wanderers (of Norway) or elders (of Greece), they are simply mouthpieces of dual narrative traditions. The *Canterbury Tales* is a kind of storytelling competition fraught with rivalry and (as we have increasingly learned to see) social division; by contrast *The Earthly Paradise* is a regularly ordered and uninterrupted sequence, with two tales allocated to each of the months of the year; this sense of regularity, together with the absence of dramatized narrators and the fact that the wanderers have been prompted to flee Europe because of the plague (*Works* 3:8–9), invites comparison with Boccaccio's *Decameron* rather than with the *Tales*. Perhaps a more immediate comparison is with Longfellow's *Tales of a Wayside Inn,* the first part of which appeared in 1863 and which itself has analogies with the *Canterbury Tales*. Rather than the noisy and bustling Tabard, however, Longfellow's inn, like Morris's tale-telling venue, is set apart from the contemporary world:

> A region of repose it seems,
> A place of slumber and of dreams,
> Remote among the wooded hills!
> For there no noisy railway speeds,
> Its torch-race scattering smoke and gleeds . . .[25]

The tale-tellers in Longfellow, too, have very little individual characterization, and the work further anticipates Morris by its inclusion of saga narrative, in this case in the form of the "Musician's Tale." It is significant that Longfellow's response to Chaucer, to judge from the sonnet he elsewhere addressed to him, also locates him in a completely nonurban, nonsocial context: he is "an old man in a lodge within a park," whose *Canterbury Tales* evokes "the note / Of lark and linnet, and from every page / Rise odours of ploughed field or flowery mead."[26]

The Earthly Paradise, like the *Canterbury Tales,* opens in spring, though the prefatory verse to March, the month when the first tale is narrated, evokes another pre-*Tales* episode rather than the celebrated opening to the *Tales* itself, namely the roundel sung by the birds at the end of the *Parliament of Fowls* saluting the arrival of the sun and the death of winter (*Works* 3:82; compare *Parliament,* lines 680–92). Thereafter, as noted above, it proceeds in an orderly, patterned manner through the cycle of the months of the year, that pattern of renewal and decline in its varying beauty becoming itself the "earthly paradise" in lieu of the phantasm of immortal youth sought by the wanderers. In this sense of its being an ordered totality, Morris's poem contrasts with the rather more "unstable" and unfinished character of the *Canterbury Tales,* though it does very much anticipate the effects of wholeness and totality produced by the Kelmscott Chaucer, as we shall shortly see, where the illustrations and general design of the volume have what one might call a stabilizing force. The tensions or contradictions that do exist in *The Earthly Paradise* are not, as noted, the social or "multivoiced" conflicts that characterize Chaucer's *Tales* and that have been identified by critics like Paul Strohm; in these areas Morris's poem proclaims its homogeneity.[27] Rather, tensions arise from the attempt to welcome the winter months into the pattern and to acquiesce in the rightness of death's place in the cycle, while the melancholy "Epilogue" reasserts the wanderers' quest to refute death altogether (*Works* 6:327–29). The somber lyric openings to the final two months' narratives, those of January and February, also suggest the despair of winter and the poet's own complaint to love (*Works* 6:65, 175) and indicate that the final "Envoi" to Chaucer as the patron of lovers in their "joy and woe" has some personal import for the poet (6:333).[28]

Diana C. Archibald has written well on Morris's attempt in the Kelmscott Chaucer "to impose unity on the book" and how this "undermine[s] the richness of the text itself," particularly of that "cacophony of vibrant, distinct voices" that makes up the *Canterbury Tales,* although Archibald does not consider the relation between this enterprise and the rest of Morris's work.[29] She points out how Morris's own beliefs in what he called the "ideal book" demanded that "every part of the book . . . typeface, spacing, margins—must work together to produce a seamless whole if that book is to meet the 'ideal'" (172), and how in the Kelmscott volume the illustrations, typeface, and decorative borders "blend unobtrusively to produce a harmonious, complete object of art" (173). With regard to Burne-Jones's contributions, what Archibald calls "the monolithic choice of chivalric subjects for the illustrations" tends to nullify the diversity and polyvocality of the *Tales* (178), and in looking at the "Knight's Tale" illustrations in particular, she argues that the statuesque harmonies of the passive rather than active scenes that Burne-Jones feels an affinity for conjure up an "unreal stillness" (176–77).

To these homogenizing factors one might add the recurrence in the Kelmscott illustrations of the same "Chaucer" figure, even in works, like the *Romance of the Rose,* that are not his own creation, as remarked above; and the formulaic bedchamber location, a frontally presented recessed box with everything arranged at right angles, be this the chamber of Lucretia (from the *Legend of Good Women,* 434), of Criseyde (501), or of Chaucer himself (see the illustration to "An A. B. C. of Geoffrey Chaucer," 223; again it should be noted that this last poem is a translation, from Guillaume de Deguilleville, rather than original to Chaucer). What one might see here as an elision of historical difference extends to a more general aspiration to the timeless; for example, the illustrations to the beginning and end of the "Clerk's Tale" (127, 139) portray a Griselda as maidenly and youthful at the time of her final reconciliation with Walter as she was before he married her, though this arguably endorses the theme of her unchanging constancy. However, where a figure is ineluctably marked by time, as in the case of the old hag in the "Wife of Bath's Tale," she yet maintains a statuesque body arranged in elegant *contrapposto,* in keeping with many of the other Burne-Jones figures (112). If these elements further emphasize the unified harmony that Archibald remarks upon, one should add that one area of conspicuous turbulence that recurs in illustration after illustration is in the treatment of vegetation: here we have a fondness for strange, writhing tree forms, often set in bare, almost lunar landscapes, as if the emotion and action suppressed in the depiction of the protagonists have been transferred to the natural setting (for a particularly graphic example, see the second illustration to the "Squire's Tale," 156). In these settings, the illustrations have been held to "anticipate the work of the Surrealists,"[30] though a more suggestive parallel might be with work actually contemporary with the Kelmscott volume; for example, the expressive contours of the setting that the forlorn Griselda wanders in (136) are not dissimilar to the swirling lines of sky and water that form the background to Edvard Munch's *Scream* of 1893, more particularly in its lithograph version.

The classical, elegant decorum of the Kelmscott Chaucer, therefore, with its ordering and repetitive design, tends to remove Chaucer's works from the bustling social world they are grounded in, and this removal might be summarized in one final illustration, that to the *House of Fame* on page 467, where the frenetic interchange of shipmen's and pilgrims' stories, "of werres, of pes, of mariages, / Of reste, of labour, of viages, /

Of abood, of deeth, of lyf," and so forth (lines 1961ff.), is personified as a series of sinuous, bedraped maidens politely whispering to each other. Archibald ends her essay expressing some surprise that the Kelmscott volume in its refinement and costliness should be so at odds with Morris's socialism,[31] and, as we have seen, Peterson tries to suggest Morris's frustrations that the illustrations did not endorse his supposed view of Chaucer as a "cheerful realist"; further, Morris is supposed to have held no truck with the "sophisticated teller of French and Italianate tales who most interested Burne-Jones," a conception opposed to his own picture of the "sturdy medieval bard."[32] But what we have seen here of Morris's response elsewhere to Chaucer would confirm his satisfaction with the Kelmscott volume as an appropriate embodiment of the poet's work, and Peterson's comment in fact goes counter to Morris's own sustained appraisal of Chaucer in his lecture "Feudal England" (1887):

> The court poet, the gentleman, Chaucer, with his Italianizing metres, and his formal recognition of the classical stories; on which, indeed, he builds a superstructure of the quaintest and most unadulterated mediaevalism, as gay and bright as the architecture which his eyes beheld and his pen pictured for us, so clear, defined, and elegant it is; a sunny world even amidst its violence and passing troubles, like those of a happy child . . . a world that scarcely needed hope in its eager life of adventure and love, amidst the sunlit blossoming meadows, and green woods, and white-begilded manor-houses. A kindly and human muse is Chaucer's, nevertheless, interested in and amused by life, but of her very nature devoid of strong aspirations for the future. . . . the world is fair and full of adventure; kind men and true and noble are in it to make one happy; fools also to laugh at, and rascals to be resisted yet not wholly condemned. . . . Look at all the picture, note all and live in all, and be as merry as you may, never forgetting that you are alive and that it is good to live.[33]

Here Chaucer is a "gentleman," a literary and artistic sophisticate attentive to the elegant architecture and natural beauty of his surroundings; interested, to be sure, in the picture of fourteenth-century life and manners, but in a detached and ironic way; certainly not, *pace* Peterson, the sturdy hail-fellow-well-met figure we shall have ample occasion to inspect elsewhere in this study. In "Feudal England" Morris goes on to suggest that if we require more attention to questions of social class, we should turn to a poet who is a "corrective" to Chaucer, namely Langland, whose work not only "in *form* at least belongs wholly to the popular side" but also "seems to me to show symptoms of the spirit of the rising middle class" (23:52). I have already drawn attention to Paul Strohm's work in these pages and to his analysis of Chaucer's poetry as exhibiting a "deep implication in urgent social contests of the time" (*Social Chaucer*, xiii); in particular, the attentiveness of the *Canterbury Tales* to incorporating the voices of what Strohm calls "previously excluded or underacknowledged ranks and groups," such as the mercantile and professional classes, and assimilating these within a more flexible social order,[34] paints a rather different picture from that of Morris's gentleman-aesthete, sunning himself on the social sidelines. For this latter figure, however, one might indeed claim that the Kelmscott Chaucer is an ideal expression.

Strohm himself acknowledges the limits to Chaucer's social inclusiveness, noting particularly the fact that there is no voice representing the peasantry within the *Tales* and no dwelling on the political implications of the Peasants' Revolt of 1381.[35] When Morris turns his attention to this event in *A Dream of John Ball* (1886–87), he seems to offer to fill this gap in Chaucer by conflating the modern narrator (who is taken back to the Middle Ages in a kind of dream-vision) with a Chaucerian persona who interests himself in the peasants' grievances and is described as broad in the belly and as habitually looking "on the ground, as though [he] sawest a hare"; exactly the description, of course, that the Host gives of Chaucer in the *Tales* (VII.695–702).[36] *A Dream of John Ball* has an avowedly autobiographical opening and talks of Morris's career as a socialist lecturer; when the narrator later represents himself via the Chaucerian parallels, it seems that he is simply playing on the actual physical resemblance between himself and the Chaucer of the Hoccleve portrait that several of his friends, including his biographer J. W. Mackail, noted: "The resemblance . . . extended to physical features: the corpulent person, the demure smile, the 'close silent eye.'"[37] Certainly, the gesture toward Chaucer in *John Ball* can only point up the difference between Morris's socialist beliefs and interests and an author whom Morris regarded as largely indifferent to the political issues of his own day, as we have seen.

There are, then, crucial distinctions we have to make before regarding Morris as a "modern Chaucer," to use a label that had a certain amount of currency in Morris's own day,[38] just as there are definite limits to Morris's nostalgia, however powerful, for the civilization of the Middle Ages. The sense of this period as one of communal unity, with that unity being sealed in Chaucer's work, is not an uncommon response in the nineteenth and twentieth centuries, as in this comment from 1886: "[Chaucer] combined the speech of the Norman gentleman with the Saxon poetry of the people; he turned himself to the people, and he did more than any other man in history in the admirable task of binding together the classes of the nation."[39] Morris himself never fell for this appealing idea, however. Although he accepted a greater integration between different social classes in the medieval period[40] and of course, crucially, the superiority of medieval craft in which the artist could take an individual delight that was not possible in an age of machine design, he was aware that the period could not function as a utopia: "Those who produced it [medieval art] were not free; they were serfs, or gild-craftsmen surrounded by brazen walls of trade restrictions; they had no political rights, and were exploited by their masters, the noble caste, most grievously."[41]

The paradox that the highest achievements in artistic beauty occurred "in times that were worse than these, when there was less courage, kindness, and truth in the world than there is now,"[42] means that the socialist vision of *News from Nowhere,* while in some ways reproducing Morris's visualization of the Middle Ages, is not a simple "return" to that period. The inhabitants of Morris's utopia wear apparel that "would have served very well as a costume for a picture of fourteenth-century life," and London as a place of pretty houses and gardens clinging about the river reproduces the picture of Chaucer's garden-city London that Morris determinedly clings to at the opening of *The Earthly Paradise* and elsewhere.[43] But, as we have seen, in Morris's poem this London is a staging post toward the earthly paradise, not the venue for it, just as in *News from Nowhere* it provides a kind of setting for the socialist state, but not a definition of it. And the last thing Morris would have regarded Chaucer as being was "the poet of the people," to take another phrase from Dawson's lecture referred to earlier.

In these respects Morris's view of Chaucer is less naive and even gullible than many of the responses we shall come across in the following pages. Although the passage quoted earlier from "Feudal England" refers to several simple and recurring tropes—Chaucer the child, "sunny" Chaucer, "merry" Chaucer—Morris is also aware of a poet who is other than a bluff or innocent realist, and of one working consciously within classical and European literary traditions. Mackail suggested that over and above the possible physical similarity between the two poets, they shared a "natural piety," or "steady and almost stolid dutifulness, which has been the saving strength of [the] nation"; in this they were both "typical Londoner[s] of the middle class."[44] This is a comparison that seems not to have occurred to Morris himself, with his picture of a relaxed, gentlemanly Chaucer who did not represent the middle class, and Morris acquiesced in the views of a German student who wrote to him suggesting that the influence of Chaucer on his work had been overstated.[45] In short, Morris seems to have regarded Chaucer as composed of gentleman, aesthete, and connoisseur in equal measure; in this sense, Burne-Jones's opening portrait of him in the Kelmscott volume writing elegantly at his book in contemplative retirement must have gratified Morris.

Although the Kelmscott Chaucer is of course one of the most celebrated modern responses to the medieval poet, we can return to where we began by emphasizing that the Chaucer that Morris and Burne-Jones offer us is an uncommon one in the modern period. We shall return to the volume in looking at the case of W. B. Yeats in chapter 3, but in many cases twentieth-century reactions to it castigate Morris for making Chaucer, in the words of Alfred Noyes, "too much of a post-Keatsian" and for imputing "his own 'dreaminess' and brooding melancholy to a poet who was as wide awake as a thrush looking for his breakfast."[46] Noyes, however, has his own masculinist agenda of "Englishness" to pursue, a theme we shall return to in chapter 5.

2

Popular Chaucer

In the opening chapter we looked at the gentleman-aesthete profile attached to Chaucer in the Pre-Raphaelite response to him and at the resulting Kelmscott volume that only his modern equivalent might indeed be able to afford, but we now turn to a consideration of Chaucer's broader currency outside the academy in the modern period and to more popular images that attach to him and his work. In the late nineteenth century and the earlier part of the twentieth century there is some difficulty in distinguishing between an academic interest in Chaucer and that represented by a more general readership, whereas such a distinction becomes entrenched as the century progresses. The Chaucer Society, set up in 1868, gradually coordinated the work of a number of formidable scholars in England, Europe, and the United States, but F. J. Furnivall's hopes in founding it were to rectify the "pitiable indifference" of the general reading public to its "second greatest English poet"; a poet who was, moreover, "the most gracious and tender spirit, the sweetest singer, the best pourtrayer, the most pathetic, and withal the most genial and humourful healthy-souled man that England had ever seen. . . . When will our Victorian time love and honour him as it should? Surely, of all our poets he is the one to come *home* to us most."[1] The situation in 1873, when Furnivall is writing, sounds scarcely better than it did in the first half of the century, when we hear that "Chaucer is considered as a rude sort of poet, who wrote a vast while ago, and is no longer intelligible. . . . Chaucer is nothing but old Chaucer or honest Geoffrey"—an indication of a neglect that, considering Chaucer is "one of the great poets for all time," affords "no parallel in the history of the literature of nations."[2] Furnivall himself, while spearheading an enormous amount of archival and manuscript research aimed at establishing a reliable Chaucerian text, canon, and biography, had a disarmingly "unacademic" manner, announcing inter alia that Chaucer "ought to have been caned" for the "lame" conclusion to the *Book of the Duchess* and admiring his subject's "eye" for "all the points of a woman—no man knew 'em like Chaucer."[3] Such a brisk appraisal of the good things of life is doubtless one aspect of the "healthy soul" Furnivall attributes to Chaucer.[4]

The work of the Chaucer Society was obviously crucial in gradually promoting the poet's work to a wider audience; we noted Skeat's debt to it in chapter 1, and the landmark Oxford Chaucer of 1894 would have been impossible without it. Thomas R. Lounsbury opened his magisterial *Studies in Chaucer* of 1891 with the suggestion that Chaucer "has been more read and studied during the past twenty years than during the previous two hundred"; Lounsbury refers to a growth in interest on both sides of the Atlantic, represented by the frequent reprinting (up to 66,000 copies) of Richard Morris's 1867 Oxford edition of a one-volume "General Prologue," "Knight's Tale," and "Nun's Priest's Tale."[5] One might argue that the first two decades of the twentieth century in particular were a kind of golden age of Chaucerian interest. It is then that we get a noticeable proliferation of books on Chaucer published in England aimed at the general reader; works like F. J. Snell's *The Age of Chaucer* (1901), the Rev. W. Tuckwell's *Chaucer* (1904), E. W. Edmunds's *Chaucer and His Poetry* (1914), Grace E. Hadow's *Chaucer and His Times* (1914), and the Rev. J. O. Bevan's *Chaucer and His Tales* (1915). A rather more celebrated book of the period than these (though with a similarly uneventful title), George Lyman Kittredge's *Chaucer and His Poetry* (1915), enthuses about Chaucer's fame being "never so widespread or so splendid as at the present day"; Kittredge, an eminent professor at Harvard, also salutes Chaucer as a genuinely "popular" poet, as if to forestall objections that the growth of Chaucer's popularity is restricted to the American campus.[6] We also find in the Edwardian period in particular, as we shall see in chapter 4, a large number of retellings of Chaucer aimed at children.

Fame and popularity are, however, relative, and one might judge their extent by considering the Chaucer quincentenary celebrations of October–November 1900. These included an exhibition of manuscripts at the British Museum, the commissioning of a bust of Chaucer for London's Guildhall, and, on the traditional date of Chaucer's death itself, 25 October, the unveiling of the Chaucer memorial window in

Southwark Cathedral by the poet laureate, Alfred Austin (Austin's accompanying peroration will be considered in chapter 5).[7] On 23 November the Whitefriars Club held a Chaucer dinner at which both Furnivall and W. B. Yeats spoke, while the Royal Society of Literature provided a series of memorial lectures.[8] The celebrations were very much London-based, and there is little evidence of much commemoration in the country at large; the Birmingham *Daily Mail* of 25 October, for example, is far more interested in the other historic events Chaucer has the luck to share his death-date with, though there is an enthusiastic appraisal of the poet in the Birmingham *Daily Gazette*'s editorial (for the absence of celebrations in Canterbury, see chapter 10).[9] Even in London, however, there are newspaper complaints that the tribute as a whole was "slight," with wishes that "it had been taken up with greater enthusiasm"; the same writer, though acknowledging the work done by the Chaucer Society, compares this relative lukewarmness with the fervor aroused by the recent Burns centenary of 1896 (as far afield as "the colonies and even in America"), which had the poet's "worshippers flock[ing] from near and far" to various celebrations in Scotland.[10] Although, as already noted, the next two decades were to see a proliferation of books that would spread Chaucer's appeal, it was suspected that this was a dissemination wide but not deep: Alfred Noyes, writing in 1929, bemoans the reliance on "stock quotations" in referencing Chaucer and scoffs at a "leading newspaper" for recently attributing one of these—"a verray, parfit gentil knyght" ("General Prologue," line 71)—to Spenser.[11] In 1941 Percy Van Dyke Shelly again acknowledged that Chaucer "has come to be read by hundreds where tens read him before," but again laments that this reading is limited to the same excerpts from the *Canterbury Tales*.[12]

It might therefore be suggested that the increase in general books on Chaucer primarily shows precisely that: the growth in number of his popularizers, rather than of a serious public following. There is undoubtedly a sense in which Chaucer is a popularizer's dream: a poet whose work (at least in the *Canterbury Tales*) is regarded as accessible, cheerfully realist, and "English," but who is divided from the public awaiting him by difficulties of language and an unfamiliar historical context. Across the tantalizing space that separates him from the general reader there is every enticement to build bridges. It is a commonplace in books aimed at this audience to express amazement that Chaucer has not yet come into his rightful inheritance, and that "the most genial and humourful healthy-souled man that England had ever seen," to repeat Furnivall's phrase, is still short of company. Thus G. K. Chesterton's *Chaucer* of 1932 opens by expressing "a personal conviction that [Chaucer] could be an extremely popular poet; that is, could produce the same effect on many other normal or unpretentious persons" as on Chesterton himself.[13] Much of the rest of the book is an attempt to define Chaucer's "normality" as a standard English characteristic, and we shall return to this in some detail in chapter 5. One element in it, however, is "that particular sort of self-effacing sociability which has . . . made the English gentleman the best companion in the world" (201). With the term "gentleman" here Chesterton is referring to bourgeois rather than aristocratic values; indeed he will later jokingly invest Chaucer with the tag of "Something in the City," as if he not only writes for the "normal" Englishman but even embodies him as he goes about his nine-to-five business (208). Here at any rate is Chaucer's (potentially enormous) constituency: "The ordinary modern Englishman will considerably enlarge his mind by reading Chaucer. . . . I do believe, as Dryden did, that it would be a good thing to make Chaucer an ordinary possession of ordinary Englishmen" (226). The unashamedly masculinist rhetoric of this is maintained throughout, though Chesterton also finds fault with Chaucer for displaying that weakness of the "clubable fellow" or "man's man" in putting comfort and sociability before political commitment (205–6).

Versions of the theme of Chaucer as "manly," or a "man's man," or occupying a "man's world" are constant in general appreciations of him. Thus the *Canterbury Tales* is seen as "the work not of a man of letters, but of a man of action. Chaucer has received his training from war, courts, business, travel—a training not of books, but of life" (John Richard Green, writing in 1874, with a rather different emphasis from that of his contemporary William Morris).[14] The widespread respect for what another writer calls Chaucer's "thoroughly healthy and practical mind" (perfectly in accord with that of the "man in the street") is often accompanied by implicit or explicit attacks on a modern imbalance toward aestheticism or bohemianism on the part of writers; however, Chaucer was "at all times eminently sane . . . [and] free from that not uncommon accompaniment of genius, viz. an uncontrollable irregularity of thought and expression."[15] As Lounsbury put it, we do not have to apologize for Chaucer "on the ground that, being a genius, he was incompetent to perform the ordinary duties of life."[16] This idea of Chaucer representing a "healthy" balance (we have already seen how frequently this adjective, like "manly," occurs in connection with him) is often used in presenting his candidature as the Englishman's birthright; that is, in offering to suspicious English tastes a poet who has nothing excessively "poetic" about him, and even at times an air of philistinism.[17] Henry Dwight Sedgwick, whose *Dan Chaucer* of 1934 is a sustained rhapsody on Chaucer's prescriptive Englishness (discussed in chapter 5), insists in his opening pages that Chaucer was "primarily a human being . . . and but secondly a poet," a point anxiously repeated two pages later: "Chaucer was primarily a man and an Englishman, before he was a poet."[18] Frank Hill, in the introduction to his translation of the *Tales* of 1934, notes how Chaucer offers "common sense, simplicity, ready companionship." In this, Hill adds bluffly, "he knocks the nonsense out of poetry."[19]

Even Chaucer's bawdiness, though we find regulation apologies for it in the Victorian and early modern periods, comes to have almost a healthy quality compared with "the modern problem novel or play, which are for ever suggesting vile things which they fear to speak out"; the same writer adds (though the bacteriology of the parallel is doubtful), "Chaucer is as fresh as a May morning, and his influence kills all hurtful things as the sunlight purifies garbage."[20] Noyes also recommended the study of the Wife of Bath's "healthy" coarseness to "some of our slimier moderns," and Frank Hill argues that "the frankness of Chaucer can hurt no-one, children included," even recommending the poet to parents as a sourcebook for instruction to children on the "facts of life."[21]

As the century progresses, Chaucer's bawdiness ceases to be a "problem" and even assumes center stage in the more popular appreciation of him, as we shall see, leading to the rather disheartening spectacle of *Canterbury Tales—the Musical* as a major stimulus of that appreciation. Many of the more responsible general books of the earlier period do, however, like Chesterton's, bring out the range of Chaucer's intellectual and literary interests while still promoting his qualities of "good sense" and "ordinary" affability—a kind of *mens sana in corpore sano* archetype. There is, however, an inevitable slide into a picture of a cheery, unintellectual, uncomplicated, convivial English Chaucer who is identified solely with (parts of) the *Canterbury Tales;* the Chaucer, in short, of merrie England. "At heart," we are told, Chaucer was "the plain English *bourgeois* . . . with all the qualities of a full-fed animal, leading an open-air life," or in Burton Rascoe's preposterous *Titans of Literature* (1933), "a fat little man, accustomed to drinking great quantities of ale and wine." (Rascoe suggests that "not all of Chaucer is entertaining or valuable to us now. Perhaps we could easily do without all his work except the *Canterbury Tales,* and some parts of these are uninteresting to us.")[22] The relentlessly picturesque *In the Days of Chaucer* by Tudor Jenks (1904) presents us with a "simple-hearted, broad-minded, very human Englishman, with immense relish for all kinds of life," the spokesman of the "merry, hearty, coarse England" of his time.[23] Though Jenks does not deny Chaucer's fondness for reading, even quoting the poet-at-his-books passage from the *House of Fame,* lines 652–60 (104), the early works are seen as aberrant and bookish in the worst sense, so that "one passes, in coming from his earlier poems to the famous pilgrimage, out of an old museum into the freshness and light of a crisp spring morning" (175). Chaucer's major work is a direct transcription of the heady life around him, a life, moreover, that reunited Chaucer with his early experiences as a child in his father's tavern (the fanciful idea that John Chaucer was an innkeeper descending to Jenks from Furnivall):[24]

> To the tavern came the knights and their esquires, the merchants and the prentices, the buyers and sellers of cloth and wool, the courtiers and the monks, the minstrels and jugglers [Jenks is particularly keen on these last, who are liberally sprinkled through his pages]; and all passed before the keen eyes of the boy who was to paint them so vividly for us of five hundred years later.[25]

This immersion in, and transcription of, "life" itself (compare the essay on Chaucer's "tremendous gusto" in Margaret Willy's *Life Was Their Cry,* 1950)[26] leads many writers to scoff at the idea that the *Canterbury Tales* shows any textual indebtedness, particularly to "foreign" authors, a point pursued in chapter 5.[27]

Where Chaucer is not bawdy or "merry," he can be seen as the rather more restrained "cheery," or cheerful. "The world's only great cheerful poet," Hill calls him,[28] pointing out that there have been other great poets, and other cheerful poets, but that no one else has combined the two; nor is Hill held up in this opinion even when he quotes from the "Go, litel bok, go, litel myn tragedye" stanza of *Troilus and Criseyde* (V.1786–92). In Marchette Chute's *Geoffrey Chaucer of England* (1946), the emphasis on Chaucer as a poet of delight and happiness is pervasive; thus a "typically Chaucerian sense of happiness," already present in the *Book of the Duchess,* is fulfilled in *Troilus and Criseyde:* "In spite of its bitter ending the total effect of *Troilus and Criseyde* is undeniably one of happiness"; the world of the poem, despite its palinode, is one "that no reader can believe is false and wretched. If it had been, Geoffrey Chaucer could never have loved it so."[29] Here the bluffly amicable "Geoffrey Chaucer of England" is not only the book's title but its trump card, as if anyone "of England" who allows himself to be known as Geoffrey is by definition sanguine. Thus the "whole discourse" of the Wife of Bath is "one whoop of satisfaction over the fun she has had" (250). The tendency to read into Chaucer a befitting but simplified image of Chaucer takes several forms, including W. H. Thompson's persuading himself (in *Chaucer and His Times,* 1936) that he could see the characteristic of "mischievous merriment" in the Hoccleve portrait.[30]

Some key qualities, then, in this popularizing dissemination of Chaucer in the twentieth century are common sense and empiricism, happiness and fellowship (sometimes inebriated), emphases usually reliant on particular passages from the *Canterbury Tales* alone (such as lines 31–34 of the "General Prologue"). Such qualities, often promoted as the prime constituents of English character, indicate Chaucer's centrality within the national culture. And yet, as we have already seen, with all these qualifications of the "Father of English Poetry" to become "an extremely popular poet," in Chesterton's phrase, voices have been raised suggesting that Chaucer is not really "getting through" to the general reader, or that reader through to Chaucer, and arguably less than ever in the second half of the twentieth century. The language difficulty is obviously an important factor here, though by no means the only one; what we need now to consider are the lines of communication between the academy, poets and novelists, and the wider reading public.

Writing arising from the 1900 celebrations thus suggests some reservations about the archival endeavors of the Chaucer Society: that the new trawling of "facts" relating to Chaucer's life and to the chronology and editing of his work is in danger of overwhelming appreciation of the work itself, or that "there seems to be a gulf fixed" between "those giants of energetic research, commentary, and criticism" who have done this work and the "general reader."[31] Percy Ames, in making this last observation, points out the need for "middlemen" interpreters to close this gulf, and as we have seen there was no shortage of books aiming to do this over the next few decades. Yet Shelly can complain in his polemically entitled *The Living Chaucer* of 1940 that with the advances in Chaucerian scholarship, "and with the outpouring of scholarly books and articles that has accompanied it, there has been no increase, but on the contrary a decrease, in Chaucerian criticism. I am thinking of literary criticism written by a poet or a critic rather than by a specialist, and addressed to the general reader and the lover of poetry rather than to the scholar."[32] What is wanted are not simply general books on Chaucer, but books written by authors of some prestige whose own creative work also perhaps shows Chaucer's importance; yet here Shelly can muster only a thin rota of names in the present century with a few articles between them: Sir Henry Newbolt, Alfred Noyes, Aldous Huxley, Virginia Woolf, and John Masefield (their interest in Chaucer to be considered in chapter 5 of this volume). Only Chesterton has "had the courage to write a book upon Chaucer," and even of the other authors listed Masefield's "brief paper" is far from satisfactory.[33] Shelly indeed suggests that scholars have simply been allowed to monopolize Chaucerian territory and that modern writers have avoided Chaucer because they feel "overborne and awed by learning" (20).

If this is the case then one might add that academics themselves have occasionally felt the responsibilities of "communication." Lee Patterson has noted how a series of notable scholars produced books in the first half of the century,"none of [which] makes any real use of the massive historical detail that scholarship had succeeded in accumulating about Chaucer's poetry. In fact, there is in these books by eminent and powerful scholars a marked tendency to devalue scholarship itself."[34] Patterson suggests that for these scholars there are in fact two Chaucers: "one is the fourteenth-century writer whose every word requires elaborate annotation, while the other is the purveyor of God's plenty . . . who speaks with an immediacy that obviates the need for interpretation" (18). Patterson's list of relevant works includes Kittredge's *Chaucer and His Poetry* of 1915 and John Livingston Lowes's *Geoffrey Chaucer and the Development of His Genius* of 1934, a book he considers in more detail. Turning rather to Kittredge's book, we can indeed see how it shares in the popularizing discourse we have been considering. Thus it opens with an insistence on Chaucer's nearness to us because of his interest in an unchanging human nature: "for he knew life and loved it, and his speciality was mankind as it was, and is."[35] The works are constantly seen in a modernizing context: thus *Troilus and Criseyde* "is the first novel, in the modern sense, that ever was written in the world" (109), and the *Canterbury Tales,* in the famous "roadside drama" hypothesis, are seen as soliloquies of the various dramatis personae who compose the pilgrimage party, with the "General Prologue" as the "first act"; Chaucer is thus a kind of anticipation of Shakespeare (154–55). The Wife of Bath again owes nothing to textual tradition, and everything to Chaucer's own imaginative grasp of "life" and its drama, being "one of the most amazing characters that the brain of man has yet conceived" (188–89). As we saw above, Kittredge took pleasure in Chaucer's popular standing (108), and his book is a contribution to that standing in its insistence that what is needed to "understand" Chaucer is not a knowledge of medieval traditions and contexts but an interest in human nature and characterization, especially as this has developed since Chaucer's day in the drama and the novel. In this he rebuts the Chaucer of birds, flowers, and natural scenery, which as we have seen is part of the Pre-Raphaelite interest ("these things are amiable and charming, but they are matters of every day") and updates Chaucer by making him sound like a prototype Joseph Conrad: "The supreme genius knows how to seize the moment of intensest self-revelation for each of his characters" (179).

Patterson obviously feels that scholars like Kittredge are slumming in offering a Chaucer stripped of detailed historical substance, and indeed a transhistorical emphasis—not only in terms of Chaucer himself, but in Kittredge's emphasis on the similarities between the late medieval and early modern periods—is present throughout *Chaucer and His Poetry.* But as we have seen, each of what Patterson refers to as the two Chaucers, one an object of scholarly excavation, the other much more popularly applicable, has pressing claims in the modern period, a situation that academics of the earlier part of that period are at least prepared to recognize. Derek Brewer ends his two-volume survey of Chaucer's "critical heritage" in the year 1933, after which, he argues, "the professional criticism of Chaucer by salaried academics . . . dominates," a criticism almost exclusively directed at others within the academy. Brewer displays a nostalgia for the criticism written in the period leading up to the mid-1930s, which, while nevertheless showing a "professional competence," "retains an air of almost innocent pleasure in and zest for literature, a certain elegance of style, an appeal to the educated 'common reader,' which, though not entirely lost in more recent years, are hardly marked characteristics of the modern 'Chaucer industry.'" After 1933, the implication is that the "industry" goes one way into ever greater specialization while the common reader goes another, parting company both with it and with Chaucer, and Brewer, like Shelly, notes the dearth of modern commentary on Chaucer in general periodicals, written by and for nonspecialists, that would fill the gap.[36]

Neither Patterson nor Brewer, however, mentions one more recent figure who has in some ways attempted to cross that gap, with results that might even provide a cautionary example of the dangers of so doing, Nevill Coghill. Best known for his modern English translation of the *Canterbury Tales,* published by Penguin in 1951 (discussed in chapter 7 in this volume), excerpts from which were broadcast on BBC radio in the 1940s, Coghill "has made Chaucer's poems an open book, and a delightfully human one, for many thousands who hitherto regarded them as an academic preserve." The comment is taken from the dust jacket of the first of Coghill's two books on Chaucer, *The Poet Chaucer* of 1949, tellingly published in a series entitled The Home University Library. The other work, his *Geoffrey Chaucer* of 1956, was also published in a series aimed at a general audience, the Writers and Their Work booklets issued by the British Council, and the blurb to this latter again notes how Coghill's "writings and broadcasts have done more to make Chaucer widely appreciated in our day than the work of any other scholar." Again, however, one has to ask how much scholarship Coghill can take with him in his quest for a wide audience. His later book, dominated by the rather anodyne motif of Chaucer as "all things to all men and women," a perfect blend of the qualities of the courtier-soldier-scholar-poet held together by a temperament of "wise equability and kindliness," is an iteration of Dryden's "God's Plenty" theme that, as Patterson remarks of Kittredge's book and the rest, could as easily have been written in the mid-nineteenth as the mid-twentieth century.[37] The major "modern" note is a greater relaxation in the face of Chaucer's fabliaux and their bawdiness: Chaucer "takes joy in the created world, he grasps life affirmatively, and calls nothing that God has made unclean" (48). This note is also marked in the earlier book, where the comedy of the fabliaux—"the world of bum and bumpkin"—is saluted: "In the hands of a master the crude fabliaux of country copulatives can be turned into a subtle uproar of healthy comedy."[38] This results in the memorable statement that "the quality of this new poetry can be tasted in a single line, perhaps the funniest line in the funniest story in the world" (132)—the line being "'Tehee!' quod she, and clapte the wyndow to" (I.3740). It seems an inevitable path from here to Coghill's work on *Canterbury Tales—the Musical,* which opened in London in 1968, and which I discuss in chapter 8.

If Chaucer's present popular status is firmly down-market, we should return to the crucial issue of his scant presence in a wider literary (as opposed to academic) culture, a situation that does not help toward a less reductive appreciation of his work. Though these problems are arguably more acute in England than in America, even here voices of alarm can be heard: "Early in this century, George Lyman Kittredge published Chaucerian studies in the general-interest *Atlantic Monthly,* but today Chaucer is virtually ignored even in the semi-scholarly *New York Review of Books.* For many highly educated readers, English literature now begins with Shakespeare."[39] Although Chaucer's influence on poets and novelists in the modern period has perhaps been generally underacknowledged (and we shall review any number of cases in chapter 6 where some sort of influence has been claimed), it remains true that no one since William Morris would be likely to adopt the invocation "my master" in addressing Chaucer, and that there is nothing on him that comes anywhere near the status of T. S. Eliot's essay on Dante, for example, of 1929—an essay that must have done far more to stimulate a general interest in that author than reams of scholarly commentary. It is not that Chaucer should be lacking in interest in the era of high modernism, for example: if we turn back to Lounsbury's *Studies in Chaucer,* published on the eve of the twentieth century, we find the presentation of the poet as sophisticated, skeptical, and urbane, with an advancedly "modern" outlook on a whole range of social and religious questions.[40] Lounsbury explicitly wishes to rescue Chaucer from the popularizing and "utterly mistaken" profile of affable English simplicity, or what he calls the "sleek, well-fed, comfortable view of life" attributed to him (2:472). His insistence is rather on Chaucer the man of letters, the serious artist; for example, his experiments in difficult versification show how "supremely the artist" he was (3:294), and "he has all the self-consciousness of the creative genius of later times" (3:324). In spite of these claims, however, we find several writers taking Chaucer at what we might call the popular valuation, as in W. B. Yeats's dismissive talk about "portly Chaucer . . . upon the Canterbury roads," as if such an image precludes poetic earnestness.[41] In a separate essay on Chaucer published in 1933, Chesterton plugs away at what he calls the "geniality" of Chaucer and his work in comparison with the "study in acute agony" that the modern poet is likely to produce, at one point wondering mischievously whether that geniality does not exceed even "the rosy optimism of Aldous Huxley or the ever-bubbling high spirits of T. S. Eliot."[42] Though Eliot himself did not altogether subscribe to this idea of the "genial" Chaucer, a poet so imbued with such a reputation would hardly recommend himself to a modern on record as "hating" the nineteenth-century watchwords of "cheerfulness, optimism and hopefulness."[43]

As we shall see in the following chapter, Yeats is a particularly interesting case of a writer in whom an initial interest in Chaucer is practically exchanged for one in Dante, and we might say generally that for modernist poets the prestige of the latter figure has eclipsed the reputation of the former; it is as if the critical attack on an ingrown English tradition, which we find in the work of Eliot and Pound, has incriminated the "Father of English Poetry" within that tradition, and that modernist cosmopolitanism has been unable to interest itself in Chaucer's own cosmopolitanism. In one of Pound's later books, *ABC of Reading* of 1934, there is, it is true, a handsome paean to Chaucer and to his Europeanism, but Pound's earlier comments are often more occasional and lukewarm, seeing him as a second-best for those who cannot follow Continental models: "If you have not the tongues, seek out the leisurely Chaucer."[44] We shall investigate in chapter 5 how the purchase on Chaucer as Englishman (with all the limitations that that designation might imply)—not only in popular writing but in the work of figures like Chesterton, Woolf, and Masefield—has been too strong for others to contest.

Many of these issues will be returned to, therefore; here we might summarize some aspects of the popular response to Chaucer by looking at a specific yet representative event, the Chaucer Pageant held in Edgbaston, Birmingham, in June 1924 to raise funds for Saint Martin's Church. The program tells us that this took the form of the pilgrims gathering before the Tabard Inn, where the tale-telling actually begins: the Friar in fact tells the first tale, but the Summoner's reply is interrupted by

> a bugle call, the noise of bells, music, etc. A man enters, leading by a string a bear which dances, and coins are thrown.
>
> At this juncture the Morris dancers entertain the company. Before they have quite finished there is a cry of "Pedlar," who enters to advertise and sell his wares.
>
> The *Merchant* then suggests that they "be on their way," but before they depart *Mine Host* asks for "one of the good old English songs." The tables are cleared, and they sing "Summer is i cumen in."[45]

At this point there was an interval. Part 2 opens as "the pilgrims reassemble, and the *Wife of Bath* suggests a dance. The whole company dance 'Sellenger's Round.'" After this there is a further interruption, with the entry of no less than Richard II and the royal court; there are further dances, the enactment of the Prioress's and Clerk's tales "to please *His Majesty,*" who "desires to speak with *Chaucer,* whose 'Merry Lines' have entertained him," and as a closing act "the *King* thanks the company and knights *Mine Host* for his liberality to the pilgrims."

One notes here the dominant emphasis on the "merrie England" theme, not only in the songs, morrismen, bear-dancing, and so forth, but also in the use of the Tabard as focus throughout part 1 (the contrast with Morris's Chaucer, whose habitat is the "rose-hung lanes of woody Kent," is evident); a drawing of the Tabard with its merry clientele features on the program cover, and we have already seen (in Tudor Jenks) attempts to emphasize the linkage between Chaucer and the public house. Moreover, the presence and graciousness of Richard II implies an England that is "merrie" politically as well as culturally, the thanks to Chaucer and the (extraordinary) knighting of the Host enacting a sort of monarch-commons concordat with which to conclude. The empiricism of Chaucer's work, which, as noted above, is often to the fore in popular responses to him, is again highlighted here; the fact that the *Tales* makes use of actual locations and an "autobiographical" narrator enables that easy transit between fiction and history that happens when "Richard II" enters the pilgrims' company.[46]

Much general interest in Chaucer is indeed a disguised interest in history or topography, with the Tabard becoming at times as celebrated as any of the characters in the "General Prologue" and with the route to Canterbury being carefully traced in guidebook fashion. Thus Eleanor

Smyth's brief *Essay on Chaucer* (1924) concludes with an evocation of her visit to the Tabard, "as a Chaucer lover," before it (or rather its Elizabethan reconstruction) was demolished in the late nineteenth century, and there is a lengthy description of the pilgrims' departure from the inn courtyard, with the villagers gathering around to see them off, on their "four days' journey in April, 1387."[47] Here the "General Prologue" is being treated as an instance of actual reportage, further inviting the reader to fill out its missing historical details. The fact indeed that the map and time references in the *Canterbury Tales* are tantalizingly incomplete and inconsistent has increased the temptation they afford for subsequent consolidation; this ranges from meticulous scholarly attempts to plot the various stages of the Canterbury journey to a rather more touristic retracing of the pilgrims' steps. Thus Thompson in *Chaucer and His Times* finds it "a matter of regret that we have not more told us of the life of the journey; of the haltings and sojournings of the pilgrims; and how they refreshed the inner man." Such lacunae, however, allow the author to indulge various delicious speculations, so that his book becomes at times almost a gazetteer of pubs along the way—"some of Chaucer's company may have rested the night at the White Hart [in Rochester]," and so forth. His book ends, moreover, not at the shrine in Canterbury Cathedral but predictably with a lament for the demolished Tabard.[48] Here we might note that one of the most notable scholarly books of the 1920s, John M. Manly's *Some New Light on Chaucer* (1926), is both a symptom of and a stimulus to the empiricizing obsession of the period, in its claims that the actual "originals" on whom Chaucer's pilgrims were based, including a contemporary London innkeeper named Harry Bailly,[49] could be uncovered from the historical documents.

The "history" that emerges from writers like Smyth and the devisers of the Chaucer Pageant is a frankly idyllicized one, a time of fellowship, gaiety, and union, and writers who have conducted a more searching examination of Chaucer's age have not been slow to point out the misrepresentation of the general grimness and brutality of fourteenth-century life that is thereby offered. Thus Coulton's study *Chaucer and His England* of 1908, "a book intended for the general public," according to its preface, opens with and maintains throughout an attack on any romanticizing of the era, and its final chapters in particular offer a remorseless amassing of evidence on the corruption, sinfulness, crime, and scandal that characterize the late Middle Ages. Even so, Chaucer escapes uncontaminated, since his "incurable optimism" does indeed hold to a picture of "merrie England" that knows nothing of the horrors of war, plague, or social revolt; "Chaucer let all these things go by with scarcely more than a shrug of the shoulders."[50] The result for Coulton is therefore some difficulty in writing on "Chaucer and his England" at one and the same time, and Chaucer disappears for chapters at a stretch while Coulton details the mass of terrible conditions that the poet was indifferent to.

Thus even those with doubts about "merrie England" often seem not to doubt that Chaucer's work provides us with its essence, and nostalgia of one form or another is an obvious ingredient in the popular response to him. In G. K. Chesterton, this nostalgia takes a more searching form, and it seems appropriate to end this chapter by returning to the most stimulating of the general-readership accounts, his *Chaucer* of 1932. Both witty and knowledgeable, Chesterton avoids getting bogged down in either the archival or the picturesque; though he makes use of several popularizing tropes (Chaucer as healthy, jovial, English, and "the Father of his Country"), he also makes a far more original use of them. In deploring capitalist pseudoindividualism where every man "live[s] in the same villa and every man in a different universe," he upholds the medieval guild system as offering a fuller identity to its members than anything found in modern standardization, where "the current tendency . . . is to discuss not so much cooks as cookery and not so much clerks as clerking." This powerful response to the individualization of Chaucer's pilgrims also underlies Chesterton's nostalgia for Chaucerian community: "What [modern] pilgrimage have we on which these two different men [the Clerk and Miller] will ride together . . . and remain different?"[51] Whereas many popular accounts offer simply a retreat into a lost land of Chaucerian goodwill, Chesterton offers an active polemic on behalf of the Middle Ages, and one that raises some interesting issues of nationhood, which we shall return to in chapter 5.

3

Spoken Chaucer

Several issues raised in the first two chapters come together in discussing W. B. Yeats's response to Chaucer, a response stimulated by his acquisition of the Kelmscott Chaucer in 1905. The volume, however, took Yeats in a direction contrary to Morris's own, wherein he acclaimed Chaucer as the model of a poet speaking directly to his audience in a populist vein, at a time when Yeats himself was in search of a new "common idiom." The part played in this by the Kelmscott Chaucer, which was a fortieth-birthday present to Yeats from Lady Gregory and other friends, is apparent from a letter he wrote to Florence Farr shortly after receiving it:

> I have my imagination full of Chaucer and would like to hire a bicycle and go the journey of the Canterbury pilgrims from Southwark and Greenwich to Canterbury through Rochester. I do not see why we should not go with some harmless person to keep up appearances. . . . for the Psaltery . . . one wants changes of voice—even different speakers at times—and choral bits for singing. The danger of the Psaltery is monotony. A thing the ancients were more alive to in all arts than we are—Chaucer for instance follows his noble "Knight's Tale" with an unspeakable tale told by a drunken miller. If Morris had done the like—everyone would have read his *Earthly Paradise* for ever. By the by Chaucer in that same unspeakable tale calls a certain young wife "white and small as a weasel." Does it not bring the physical type clearly to the minds-eye? I think one wants that sort of vivid irresistible phrase in all verse to be spoken aloud—it rests the imagination as upon the green ground.[1]

Yeats's reaction to the volume seems explicitly anti-Morris not only in his contrasting the latter's monotony with Chaucerian variety, but in his highlighting the fabliau realism of Chaucer and in the stimulus the volume provides to engage with the physical world and to "do" the Canterbury route.[2] What the Kelmscott initially spurred Yeats toward was not the classicizing, refined, and decorous ideal that we argued in the opening chapter the volume embodies, but rather the reverse: a new ambition toward physicality and realism enters his own work.

The initial response was a powerful one: in a letter of 3 August 1905 he tells A. H. Bullen, "My imagination is getting so deep in Chaucer that I cannot get it down into any other well for the present" (*Letters* 457). The actual debt to Chaucer that this response then took has been traced by Ronald Schuchard, who sees Yeats's Chaucerian enthusiasms around 1905 as bound up with the inception of the Abbey Theatre and with Yeats's interest in oral verse, whether spoken from the stage, recited to the psaltery, or even disseminated through the countryside by the wandering minstrel. Yeats's hopes for the Abbey Theatre would eventually have it as, in Schuchard's words, "a sort of speech guild for culture, using its workshops to restore all the spoken arts, training minstrels and reciters for the countryside as well as actors for the stage."[3] What Yeats valued in Chaucer was a simple, vigorous, immediately apprehensible language—the "vivid irresistible phrase"—that could appeal to all social classes. Schuchard notes how during the early months of 1906 Yeats gave a series of lectures, sometimes assisted by Florence Farr, which went to make up the essay "Literature and the Living Voice" published later that year. In one such lecture delivered in Leeds in March, Yeats declared:

> If modern writers were . . . to reach the workingman, they must put literature more in touch with life by embodying the spoken art in the printed book. By making their work simpler, and by adapting the language to the spoken as distinguished from the printed work, "they would bring back to literature a great deal of the masculine vitality they found in writers like Chaucer, who wrote essentially for the ear, and in whose works the variety of the world flowed in on every page."

"Yeats told his audience that from Chaucer he had discovered the need to simplify his own work and had rewritten his plays to increase their 'masculine force,'" Schuchard continues (11), and yet it is extremely difficult to substantiate in any detail Yeats's debt to Chaucer's "masculine vitality," and Schuchard himself can go no further than pointing to a couple of phrases in the revised version of *The Shadowy Waters*.[4] In a letter to John Quinn of 16 September 1905, Yeats reports on this revision:

> I have altogether re-written my *Shadowy Waters*. There is hardly a page of the old. The very temper of the thing is different. It is full of homely phrases and of the idiom of daily speech. I have made the sailors rough, as sailors should be, characterized all the people more or less, and yet not lost any of my lyrical moments. It has become a simple passionate play, or at any rate it has a simple passionate story for the common sightseer, though it keep back something for instructed eyes. I am now correcting the last few lines, and have very joyfully got "creaking shoes" and "liquorice-root" into what had been a very abstract passage. I believe more strongly every day that the element of strength in poetic language is common idiom, just as the element of strength in poetic construction is common passion. (*Letters* 462)

Although there is no mention of Chaucer here, Schuchard is undoubtedly right to suggest that the emphasis on the "strength" of "common idiom" comes in the wake of Yeats's delight in the Kelmscott volume.[5] Whether this is sufficient to justify labeling "creaking shoes" and "liquorice-root" as "vivid Chaucerian language," which Schuchard does, is open to question, however. Admittedly "the roote / Of lycorys" does feature as an image of Nicholas's sweetness in that "unspeakable tale told by a drunken miller" (I.3206–7) that Yeats refers to in the letter to Farr.

The passage that Yeats told Quinn he was joyful over changing became in 1905:

> AIBRIC. I have good spirits enough.
> I've nothing to complain of but heartburn,
> And that is cured by a boiled liquorice root.
>
> FORGAEL. If you will give me all your mind awhile—
> All, all, the very bottom of the bowl—
> I'll show you that I am made differently,

That nothing can amend it but these waters,
Where I am rid of life—the events of the world—
What do you call it?—that old promise-breaker,
The cozening fortune-teller that comes whispering,
"You will have all you have wished for when you have earned
Land for your children or money in a pot."
And when we have it we are no happier,
Because of that old draught under the door,
Or creaky shoes . . . [6]

No one reading this passage would ever, I think, suppose that Chaucer lay behind it as an influence, without Yeats's prompting. There is, it is true, a contrast of voices here between Aibric and Forgael, down-to-earth and idealistic respectively, that perhaps gestures to the Chaucerian "changes of voice" that Yeats applauds in his letter to Farr, but it is less the extremes of Miller and Knight than the Pandarus/Troilus contrast we find in *Troilus and Criseyde*. Forgael's quest for a transcendental love, contrasted as it is with Aibric's skepticism, even in his fidelity to Forgael, does resemble the situation between the two main male figures in Chaucer's poem. A little later than the passage just quoted, Aibric utters a cautionary rejection of the visions of the "crazy herdsman":

His wife knows better.
Has she not seen him lying like a log,
Or fumbling in a dream about the house?
And if she hear him mutter of wild riders,
She knows that it was but the cart-horse coughing
That set him to the fancy.

(*Poems* 230)

This seems to me in fact the clearest Chaucerian touch in the work, prompted by Pandarus's deflating "That I se yond nys but a fare-carte," in reply to Troilus's fervent declaration that he has sighted Criseyde in the distance returning to Troy in book V (line 1162).

However joyful Yeats was over "creaky shoes" and "liquorice-root," the passage containing these phrases, as well as Aibric's speech on the "cart-horse coughing," was in fact left out of *The Shadowy Waters* when it was condensed for stage production in 1906; indeed, the whole dialogue between Forgael and Aibric enacted while the sailors are offstage was shortened considerably. And by *Later Poems* (1922), when, as I shall argue, Yeats's interest in Chaucer had become rather less populist, the short passage relating Aibric's heartburn and its liquorice-root cure was also omitted from the revised narrative poem.[7] How far both these alterations suggest doubts about Yeats's commitment to a neo-Chaucerian "common idiom" is an interesting question; or rather, perhaps the question they raise is how successfully that common idiom had been integrated into the poem or play in the first place. Certainly Aibric was never as homely a character as the surprising revelation about his heartburn and its cure makes him sound. Further, Yeats's claim in his letter to Quinn that in revising the 1900 version of the work he had now made "the sailors rough, as sailors should be," is hardly borne out by the language we hear them speak, whether in the poem version of 1906:

> We joined him for his pay, but have had none
> This long while now; we had not turned against him
> If he had brought us among peopled seas,
> For that was in the bargain when we struck it.
> What good is there in this hard way of living,
> Unless we drain more flagons in a year
> And kiss more lips than lasting peaceable men
> In their long lives?
>
> (*Poems* 225)

or in the acting version (first published 1907), where the sailors speak in prose:

> Little pay we have had this twelvemonth. We would never have turned against him if he had brought us, as he promised, into seas that would be thick with ships. That was the bargain. What is the use of knocking about and fighting as we do unless we get the chance to drink more wine and kiss more women than lasting peaceable men through their long lifetime? (*Plays* 320)

Certainly Yeats's sailors make a fair shot at picturesque swashbuckling, but compared to Chaucer's "roughs" they seem measured company indeed.

At the conclusion of "Literature and the Living Voice," Chaucer, who has not been mentioned at all in the body of the essay, enters as its crowning argument in a formulation very similar to that in the letter to Farr: "William Morris, who did more than any modern to recover mediaeval art, did not in his *Earthly Paradise* copy from Chaucer—from whom he copied so much that was naive and beautiful—what seems to me essential in Chaucer's art." By falling into a "monotonous" lyricism that was designed for a cultivated readership, Morris missed out on developing a vigorous orality in his work:

> Had he accustomed himself to read out his poems . . . and to gather an audience of average men . . . he would have been forced to Chaucer's variety, to his delight in the height and depth, and would have found expression for that humorous, many-sided nature of his. . . . all the old writers, the masculine writers of the world, wrote to be spoken or to be sung.[8]

Judging from the evolution of *The Shadowy Waters,* however, and indeed from Yeats's work as a whole, it is a moot point as to how extensive Chaucer's influence was. Chaucer's variety and common idiom inspired Yeats, yet there were marked limits to just how "common" he was able or was prepared to become, and his notion of the popular life seems rather more decorous, sanitized, and picturesque than Chaucer's and lacking in any fabliau elements. When the "rough" sailors talk about draining flagons and kissing lips in Yeats's poem one is reminded of a passage in a late essay in which he talks of certain youthful infatuations: "I remember praying that I might get my imagination fixed upon life itself, like the imagination of Chaucer. In those days I was a convinced ascetic, yet I envied Dowson his dissipated life. I thought it must be easy to think like Chaucer when you lived among those morbid, elegant, tragic women suggested by Dowson's poetry."[9] And Yeats then quotes lines from Dowson's "Villanelle of the Poet's Road": "Unto us they belong, / Us the bitter and gay, / Wine and woman and song." If Chaucerian life is being equated with nineties decadence it is hardly surprising that we should not immediately recognize it when we come across it in Yeats. It is possible, however, that a poem like "The Hour before Dawn" is where we should look for a "Chaucerian" reaction against asceticism in Yeats's work, a poem featuring a "rogue with a merry face" and a set of carnivalesque actions such as cursing, drinking, and pummeling, in a familiar Yeatsian dialogue between life and life's longing for death (*Poems* 302–7).

There is a good deal of rather unexamined usage of the term "life" throughout "Literature and the Living Voice," with Chaucer coming in just at the end to set the seal on it. Moreover, Chaucer (in the final words of the essay) is one of those "masculine writers" who "wrote to be spoken or to be sung, and in a later age to be read aloud for hearers who had to understand swiftly or not at all and who gave up nothing of life to listen, but sat, the day's work over, friend by friend, lover by lover."[10] Not only is Chaucer a poet of life then, but—and this would be crucially attractive for Yeats—one whose work sets up no breach with living itself: his audience lives and listens simultaneously. As John Stevens has suggested, "There was perhaps a general expectation of 'dalliance' before, after, and perhaps even during, a reading of a love-poem" such as *Troilus and Criseyde;* the well-known frontispiece to the poem in Cambridge Corpus Christi College MS 61 "shows one couple 'commoning' as Chaucer reads."[11] Chaucer's work, then, records life and indeed promulgates it, and not only in its "rough" or homely versions: he delights in "the height" as well as the depth, the noble "Knight's Tale" and the "unspeakable" tale of the Miller, presenting, moreover, the unity that existed between them, for in the Middle Ages "the life of the villages, with its songs, its dances and its pious greetings, its conversations full of vivid images . . . ran, as it were, into a point of fire in the courtliness of kings' houses."[12] Chaucer wrote "when there was but one mind in England,"[13] a unity hankered after in the essay *Discoveries* of 1907, when "there was little separation between holy and common things, and . . . the arts themselves passed quickly from passion to divine contemplation, from the conversation of peasants to that of princes, the one song remembering the drunken miller and but half forgetting Cambuscan bold" (that is, the "noble kyng" of "Tartarye" in Chaucer's "Squire's Tale"). But today that unity, summed up in Yeats's phrase "the sanctity of common ploughland"—which may be inspired by Chaucer's picture of the saintly plowman ("General Prologue," lines 529–41)—is broken: "We may never see again a Shelley and a Dickens in the one body" (*Essays* 295–96).

That need to reintegrate Shelley and Dickens is again expressed in the preface to *The Unicorn from the Stars and Other Plays* (1908), though here Yeats admits that the idea "of bringing together the rough life of the road and the frenzy that the poets have found in their ancient cellar" has been one that "I have been capable of expressing completely in criticism alone."[14] The difficulties that Yeats had in reproducing "the rough life of the road," discussed above in relation to *The Shadowy Waters,* were mitigated by collaboration with Lady Gregory, who brought to plays like *The Unicorn from the Stars* "a greater knowledge of the country mind and country speech than anybody I had ever met with," sufficient to create "the rough, vivid, ever-contemporaneous tumult of the roadside" (*Plays* 1296, 712). Indeed, though Yeats always doubted his own talents for comedy, and consequently his ability to reproduce Chaucerian variety, he felt that the repertoire of the Abbey Theatre in toto might be such a reproduction; thus, discussing the shortcomings of the play *The Shadowy Waters,* he asks for it to be judged

> when set among the plays of my fellow-workers. . . . I write of the tragic stories told over the fire by people who are in the comedies of my friends, and I never see my work played with theirs that I do not feel that my tragedy heightens their comedy and tragi-comedy, and grows itself more moving and intelligible from being mixed into the circumstance of the world by the circumstantial art of comedy.

In short, the Abbey Theatre was "the common basket" into which "one or the other [of Yeats's fellow-dramatists] were at hand to throw a bushel of laughter."[15]

It is apparent, then, that following the presentation of the Kelmscott volume to Yeats in 1905, Chaucer is significant for what he sees as a major shift in his career, "the search for more of manful energy . . . instead of those outlines of lyric poetry that are blurred with desire and vague regret."[16] Chaucer's is a various, masculine, life-giving art that testifies to social cohesion; but the problem remains, of course, why, if Chaucer is so ideally qualified as Yeats's model, there are so few actual or apparent references to him throughout Yeats's writing, apart from the clutch referred to above in the letters and works of 1905–6. The question might be rephrased by noting the way that critics have handled the Yeats-Chaucer relationship; that is, in the few cases where they have adverted to it: thus Richard Ellmann, discussing the essays collected into *Ideas of Good and Evil* (1903) and *The Cutting of an Agate* (1912), suggests that Yeats's search therein for a literature of "unity and simplicity" leads back beyond Spenser and Shakespeare to an earlier period: "Of all the poets, perhaps Chaucer was closest to what Yeats desired because closest to the folk tradition."[17] If "of all the poets" Chaucer has this eminence, it seems extraordinary that this is the only place in his study of Yeats where Ellmann refers to him, and this indicates the powerful temptation to acknowledge Chaucer as a key presence in Yeats as well as the difficulties of substantiating it; hence Ellmann's "perhaps." Even among medieval writers, there are noticeably more references in these essays by Yeats to Dante and Villon than to Chaucer. One critical strategy, of course, is to resort to the familiar "age of Chaucer" convention; thus a statement such as "Yeats's predilection was for an age like Chaucer's when the human mind was organic and art anonymous" evades the problem of specific influence, though it raises the paradox of individualizing by Chaucer's name a so-called anonymous age.[18] We have already seen in the previous chapter what a suspect monolith the "age of Chaucer" idea is, and that historians who affect to offer it to us often end up sundering Chaucer from the age that bears his name.

Reporting on the four years 1887–91 in *The Trembling of the Veil* (1922), Yeats declares, "I thought that all art should be a Centaur finding in the popular lore its back and its strong legs"; thus, "though I preferred Shakespeare to Chaucer I begrudged my own preference."[19] Yeats resolved his dilemma by adopting his own "age of Chaucer" scenario, being, as he put it, "envious of the centuries before the Renaissance" (*Essays* 349) but for all that showing no great inclination to familiarize himself with England's major pre-Renaissance poet. Thus in the essay on Spenser, dated 1902, "the time of Chaucer" phrase (*Essays* 365) figures as a commonplace shorthand for a halcyon gaiety, passion, and beauty—"Merry England with its glad Latin heart" (Essays 377)—that survives into Spenser but is already there encroached upon by the emerging Puritan morality.

With the birthday gift of 1905 Yeats got the opportunity to put flesh onto the bare bones of such generalization, and also perhaps to overcome his preference for Shakespeare over Chaucer, and certainly, as we have seen, the result was a deep initial enthusiasm; the image of the halcyon days was realized. But there was the risk, of course, that the image would be exploded, that reading Chaucer would actually disprove, rather than confirm, the "merry England" picture, and this seems to be what gradually happened with Yeats.

For one thing, the ideal in "Literature and the Living Voice" of a literature that would not obtrude upon the actual process of living, while supposedly upheld by Chaucer and by his working within an oral culture, is, one might say, actually undermined by Chaucer's own work. Yeats suggests that readerly isolation is a specifically modern malaise: "When a man takes a book into the corner, he surrenders so much life for his knowledge, so much, I mean, of that normal activity that gives him life and strength," whereas "the old culture . . . was not at the expense of life, but an exaltation of life itself."[20] But this is the very situation that Chaucer gives us in the *House of Fame:*

> But of thy verray neyghebores,
> That duellen almost at thy dores,
> Thou herist neyther that ne this;
> For when thy labour doon al ys,
> And hast mad alle thy rekenynges,
> In stede of reste and newe thynges
> Thou goost hom to thy hous anoon,
> And, also domb as any stoon,
> Thou sittest at another book
> Tyl fully daswed ys thy look;
> And lyvest thus as an heremyte,
> Although thyn abstynence ys lyte.
>
> (lines 649–60)

And though I can find no reference in Yeats to this work,[21] a poem he does refer to, the *Legend of Good Women,* opens on a similar picture of engrossed private reading—"ther is game noon / That fro my bokes maketh me to goon, / But yt be seldom on the holyday" ("Prologue," F version, lines 33–35)—set off against the only thing that can draw the narrator from it, the beauty of the month of May.[22] The point might be made quite simply that in his emphases on Chaucer's simplicity, orality, and populism, Yeats tended to ignore the extent of Chaucer's learning and of his widespread reading in classical and medieval letters, adopting indeed an image of Chaucer practically antithetical to that of Morris and Burne-Jones.

Of course, there is no simple dichotomy between literature and living in Chaucer's work, and in a later essay of 1914, "Art and Ideas," Yeats accepts that Chaucer's celebration of the month of May is itself a bookish construct: "Works of art are always begotten by previous works of art. . . . When we delight in a spring day there mixes, perhaps, with our personal emotion an emotion Chaucer found in Guillaume de Lorris, who had it from the poetry of Provence" (*Essays* 352). Though as early as 1904 Yeats can briefly make the same point, namely that Chaucer "borrowed . . . much of his way of looking at the world" from French writers—as part of his defense of "National" writers not being confined to influences from their own country—his emphasis remains in the same essay that of the pre-Renaissance writers having direct access in their work to some unmediated "living" that modern civilization has lost: "They lived in times when the imagination turned to life itself for excitement. . . . There was nothing to draw their imagination from the ripening of the fields. . . . Everything that their minds ran on came on them vivid with the colour of the senses, and when they wrote it was out of their own rich experience." And we then have a picture of Chaucer's naked, empirical encounter with "the reddening apples in the garden" and a reference to the celebration of trees in his work.[23] If Yeats was seeking at this time "a movement downwards upon life"[24] as a reaction against an enervated, overliterate modern culture, it is natural that he should minimize the intertextual elements of Chaucer's work.

In fact, Yeats's insistence in "Literature and the Living Voice" that Chaucer wrote for listeners and not for readers misrepresents Chaucer's own frequent acknowledgments of a readership—"Turne over the leef and chese another tale" ("Miller's Prologue," I.3177)—and of reading as a private activity, mixed, to be sure, with many indications that his works were also intended for oral presentation.[25] In short, Chaucer's works are a site of tension and transition, in terms of the nature of the implied audience as of many other things, and many of the Yeats comments we have looked at tend to create a series of false coherences in him, a response that Chaucer will frequently be fated to undergo. Yeats could not have been oblivious to these tensions, and perhaps they explain the limit of Chaucer's serviceability to him in his "movement downwards upon life," forcing him to quickly revise or drop completely some of the 1905–6 formulations. Hone tells us that Yeats was again "deep in Chaucer" toward the end of 1910, when there was a possibility of his succeeding to Dowden's chair of English at Trinity College,[26] and it may be this immersion that is responsible for comments like that in the introduction to Tagore's *Gitanjali* of 1912, which offers a partly revised assessment: "When there was but one mind in England Chaucer wrote his

Troilus and Cressida, and though he had written to be read, or to be read out—for our time was coming on apace—he was sung by minstrels for a while." Indeed, Tagore's lyrics, which "display in their thought a world I have dreamed of all my life long," the work of a "supreme culture" growing out of a "common soil," are now seen as akin to the work of "Chaucer's forerunners," as if the fall into modernity that Yeats had previously found in Spenser, say, has now been located in Chaucer himself (*Essays,* 390–91). And from this time onward it is at this critical transition stage that Yeats locates Chaucer. In *The Trembling of the Veil* (1922) he lays the weighty charge of fragmenting Europe's mind and heart at Chaucer's door: "Music and verse began to fall apart when Chaucer robbed verse of its speed that he might give it greater meditation, though for another generation or so minstrels were to sing his lengthy elaborated *Troilus and Criseyde.*"[27] And in *A Vision* Chaucer is given the briefest of mentions again as a transitional figure straddling two gyres, caught between a lost "public certainty" and an emergent "private certainty."[28]

The fact that Chaucer is mentioned so rarely in Yeats's later work is rather strange, given that the newfound tensions Yeats sees in him—or at least in his age—should have increased his attraction for a writer obsessed with the idea of "the world as a continual conflict."[29] And indeed one critic has argued persuasively for the body-soul antagonism in "Sailing to Byzantium" paralleling that in *Troilus and Criseyde.*[30] Of all the poems of Chaucer we should expect this to have the greatest appeal for Yeats in the second half of his life, as his work, in Schuchard's words, "moved toward a new aristocratic form and audience,"[31] an aspiration expressed most powerfully in the essay "A People's Theatre" of 1919, where Yeats expresses his "counter-longing" to the predominant modern taste for comedy and for the realist novel, both deriving from the limited procedures of "observation and a speech founded upon that of real life." In many ways the hero of this essay is another medieval writer, Dante, who, had he written plays, "would have written from his own thought and passion, observing little and using little, if at all, the conversation of his time,"[32] and in Dante's work Yeats sees not only the quest for a heroic solitude but also the titanic struggle with that which opposed it, namely Dante's day-to-day involvement with politics, party, and the opposite sex.[33] Shakespeare, too, is a record of a similar struggle, taking from Plutarch "great dramatic persons . . . who made their death a ritual of passion; for what is passion but the straining of man's being against some obstacle that obstructs its unity?" (252). In comparison with such momentous drama, Chaucer, it seems, could now offer Yeats very little, and indeed Yeats declares that the interest in "great dramatic persons" was one "Chaucer never shared" (252). The unity of culture of Chaucer's day is still assented to (251), but given that the difference of historical phase makes this impossible for Yeats's own period, his attention will now switch to "unity of being," the quest by the individual to overcome internal antinomies, and on this Chaucer, a far less glamorous figure than Dante, has nothing to say. Yeats tends to edit completely in "A People's Theatre" the earlier Chaucerian impetus behind his plays by declaring that he, Lady Gregory, and Synge, "not understanding the clock, set out to bring again the theatre of Shakespeare or rather perhaps of Sophocles."[34] What price "literature and the living voice" now?

We should expect, then, that any echoes we hear from Chaucer in the later work, and certainly that of the 1920s, would come from a poem like *Troilus and Criseyde,* both a tragedy and, in Elizabeth Salter's words, "a poem for a cultural elite,"[35] but we might also expect much else of Chaucer to drop from favor; "portly Chaucer . . . upon the Canterbury roads," to borrow a phrase from *Autobiographies,* is not likely to feature greatly for a poet intent on remaking himself as Lear or Blake or *il penseroso.*[36] And indeed Roland Blenner-Hassett has argued that while "The Phases of the Moon" is indebted to the well-known passage in the "Franklin's Tale" on the moon's "eighte and twenty mansiouns" (V.1123–34), and while *A Vision* "depends for its calculations on the phenomenon of *Annus Mundus,*" which is treated by Chaucer (for example, in the *Parliament of Fowls,* lines 67–70), Yeats was unwilling to acknowledge his debt to a "realist" writer like Chaucer, whose "attitudes towards life, art and conduct [were] most antipathetic" to him.[37] Even where he remains influential Yeats disowns him.

What has been traced in this chapter is the suggestion that the populist force of Chaucer, which seems to have impressed Yeats so much in his initial reading of the Kelmscott volume after 1905, gave way in Yeats's later years to a more occasional interest in the aristocratic and esoteric elements of Chaucer's work, as Yeats's own antipopulism emerged. But the question has also been raised of how far, in any case, Yeats was ever committed in his earlier work to reproducing some neo-Chaucerian "life." Though Chaucer seemed to offer the whole spectrum, from the rough life of the roads to the courtliness of kings' houses, and though modernity had been a shattering of that spectrum so that we now had Shelley *or* Dickens, or Shelley *or* Burns, Yeats's sympathies in an essay like *Discoveries* of 1907, even while he appeals for a reintegration of the "whole man," remain with "the way of the bird until common eyes have lost us"; as he puts it, "if [the soul] begin to slip away we must go after it, for Shelley's Chapel of the Morning Star is better than Burns's beerhouse" (*Essays* 266–67). Moreover, even in "Literature and the Living Voice" Chaucer is only mentioned at the very end, as already remarked, to clinch Yeats's argument. In those slightly earlier essays and lectures that also campaign for a revival of the oral tradition, such as "Speaking to the Psaltery" (1902) and the first of the "Four Lectures, 1902–4," Chaucer is conspicuous by his total absence.[38] With the Kelmscott volume Yeats seemed to be offered the poet his theories were in search of, and rather prematurely he jumped at the chance, only to realize soon enough that Chaucer wouldn't "do," however much his work exposed the inadequacies of even his most enthusiastic modern disciple, William Morris.

While Chaucer might offer many different things to Yeats, from rough roadside drama to the most arcane speculations on astrology, his work hardly offers the unity of such diversity that Yeats first saw in him, and modern Chaucer criticism would stress much more the sense of his work as an arena of competing and often dissonant voices and of historical tensions that reflect changing social structures and the orality-literacy transition. Yeats came to see something of this, and indeed (to end where we began), it is practically embodied in the Kelmscott volume itself. Here we have (Yeats held) a popular, oral performer, enshrined in what is "the most beautiful of all printed books," to repeat his own description in a letter to John Quinn thanking Quinn for his share in the gift (*Letters* 451). We therefore have the rough life of the roads given all the embellishments of a special Gothic printer's type and Burne-Jones illustrations, accessible only to those who could pay connoisseurs' prices. It is no surprise that a writer presented in this way should come to have his popular status eroded, and there is something especially piquant about Hone's description of the later home the volume found for itself, in Oxford, in 1921: "One went up the stairs . . . to a room at the top of the narrow house where Yeats kept his Kelmscott Chaucer open on a lectern."[39] But as Yeats continued to explore the struggle between the summons of "the winding ancient stair" and the call of life's "fecund ditch,"[40] one wonders if he ever spared a regretful thought for that "unspeakable" tale of a miller in which, for one character at least, a study upstairs in a house in Oxford is certainly not incompatible with the most vigorous participation in living.

4

Children's Chaucer

The golden age of editions of Chaucer aimed at children is the first decade and a half of the twentieth century: between 1903 and 1914, selections from the *Canterbury Tales* retold for children by various authors appear practically at the rate of one a year, with many of these reissued in the 1920s and 1930s, after which there is a marked decline in their frequency. In this chapter I am not looking at the standard secondary classroom editions of Chaucer, often of a single tale with notes and commentary, such as the much used and reprinted Macmillan's English Classics series edited by Alfred W. Pollard; rather I am considering prose paraphrases or translations of various kinds, often aimed at a younger age group. Some of these, it is true, were intended for use in schools and can usually be identified by their severe and unenticing appearance, as with Ada Hales's *Stories from Chaucer* of 1911, directed at "upper standards of Elementary Schools."[1] On the other hand, F. J. Harvey Darton's *Tales of the Canterbury Pilgrims* of 1904 is a domestic storybook and handsomely illustrated, with a lavish cover design stamped in gold and with a jolly introduction by F. J. Furnivall.[2]

The founding work of the genre is Charles Cowden Clarke's *Tales from Chaucer, in Prose* of 1833, "designed chiefly for the use of young persons," as its subtitle says, but it was not until the 1870s, with the second edition (1870) and with Mrs. H. R. Haweis's *Chaucer for Children: A Golden Key* (1877) and Francis Storr and Hawes Turner's *Canterbury Chimes* (1878), that the fashion became established. Mrs. Haweis adapted her first book to produce *Chaucer for Schools* in 1881; *Chaucer's Beads: A Birthday Book, Diary, and Concordance of Chaucer's Proverbs or Soothsaws* followed in 1884 and *Tales from Chaucer* in 1887. An *Academy* review of *Chaucer for Children* noted that his works, "in selections of some kind or other, are now text-books in every school that aspires to give sound instruction in English"; it is clear, then, that the growth in currency of Chaucer's work in the last third of the nineteenth century, remarked on in earlier chapters, extends to all ages of readers.[3]

Having said this, the limitations on Chaucer's actual popularity, also already noted, may have something to do with unfavorable childhood experience of some of these texts. "Children's Chaucer" is usually concerned solely with the *Canterbury Tales* (although Mrs. Haweis's compilation does include some of the "Minor Poems"), and it is obvious that discretion has to be exercised in the choice of these. In most compilations (with or without the "General Prologue") one passes straight from the "Knight's Tale" to the "Man of Law's Tale," since the fabliaux are of course inadmissible; other tales then commonly included are the Clerk's, Pardoner's, Nun's Priest's, Franklin's, and Wife of Bath's (but not her "Prologue"). If this type of selection seems rather a doughty diet of childhood reading to modern tastes—for example, *A Child's Book of Chaucer* drawing on the Cowden Clarke versions published by Brodie in 1927 has solely the "Prologue," "Knight's Tale," and "Man of Law's Tale"—one must remember that these retellings are often slanted toward bringing out the romance, adventure, and fairy-tale elements in the above tales. Thus in the "Knight's Tale," for instance, Theseus's concluding "First Mover" speech, as well as other passages, can be omitted, leading us straight from Arcite's death to the happy-ever-after marriage; the tale ceases to be a "philosophical romance" and becomes a story about knights and a princess.[4] Similarly, the "beautiful lady" theme in, for example, the Knight's, Man of Law's, Clerk's, and other tales can be stressed, often through illustration; the four tales in Janet Kelman's *Stories from Chaucer* of 1906 are actually retitled "Dorigen," "Emelia," "Griselda," and "Constance" (stories told by the "Man of Land," "of Might," "of Books," and "of Law," respectively), and the illustrations to each tale by W. Heath Robinson concentrate on portraying these heroines.[5] Markedly Edwardian-type belles or Snow White look-alikes are a recurring feature of the illustration in these books during this period.[6]

Even without illustrations, such books must have found a market, and even the Brodie book referred to above was reprinted as recently as 1950. It is, however, an interesting index of changed attitudes that more recent retellings emphasize a totally different selection of tales. Thus Geraldine McCaughrean's version of 1984 includes the Miller's, Reeve's, and Merchant's tales (the former subtitled "A Barrel of Laughs") but merely refers to the fact that, as the narrator puts it, "we had . . . the trials of Constance (who seems to have converted half the known world to Christianity without me hearing tell of her before)."[7] Here the tone of jocular ignorance is part of "Chaucer's" personality throughout as "a bit of a lad," establishing his credibility with his young readers, a feature we shall return to.

Indeed, the concept of a "Children's Chaucer" genre is interestingly related to the idea of Chaucer himself as essentially a child, or as proceeding from a period in literary history of childish immediacy and unsophistication. This attitude was particularly current in the nineteenth century, when authors as various as Thoreau, Barrett Browning, Meredith, and Landor comment on Chaucer's childlike gentleness and frolicsome innocence.[8] The most sustained appraisal in this vein is an anonymous article in *Temple Bar* (1873), which ends with the following summary:

> He was as great a genius as a writer in age so young can be; and we can quite understand how the excessive finish, the troublesome self-consciousness, and the oppressive melancholy of the poetry of ages more advanced, induce many to turn to the strains of an earlier time, which, if they have all the faults, have likewise all the graces, of childhood—simplicity, sincerity, transparency, and joy.[9]

The body of the essay in fact seems more interested in detailing these faults than the graces; thus it is regretted that the "immediate, superficial, transitory" impressions of the natural world in Chaucer's work permit of no Wordsworthian philosophizing on "the deepest and most suggestive relationship that exists in the universe," that between "man" and "nature" (310, 315). Moreover,

> childhood is all eyes and tongue, and so is Chaucer. He gazes intently, and then babbles profusely. We think he will never be done. He is often tiresome. So are children. . . . he is fresh, pretty, sincere, downright, delightfully ignorant, full of indescribable charm; but we sometimes wish him in bed and that sleep was *not* "unmeet to him." (311)

The fact that Chaucer is "all eyes and tongue" leads to both garrulity and indiscretion; thus details in the "Prologue" like the Miller's wart, the Cook's "mormal," and the Knight's "bismotered" costume show

> the spirit of the *enfant terrible,* who, if anybody has got on a dirty gown, blurts it out before the whole company. He sees it and he says it, never thinking that he ought not to say it, since he does not think at all. . . . he takes about seven hundred and fifty lines to describe them all [the pilgrims], and seems to fancy that he has been very brief. . . . excessive talk is the fault of children—of grown-up children no less. Italians talk from morning till night. So do servants. (313–14)

We saw in chapter 2 (and will see again in chapter 5) how Chaucer's unembarrassed directness is for other critics part of his "manly," no-nonsense approach to the world; indeed it is not uncommon, if a little disconcerting, to come across phrases like "childlike manfulness" to describe him.[10] The *Temple Bar* essayist insists that ultimately "we must remember [Chaucer] did not talk to us of today, and it is our fault if we listen. He talked, a child, to children—the biggest, oldest, wisest, cleverest child of the company—and so he amused them incessantly" (311).

Such a piece seems to promise a delightful companion for children: not only an author who is fresh, pretty, playful, and so forth, but one who contains all kinds of mischievous revelations. It is not uncommon, however, for children's versions to edit out references even to such things as the Miller's wart and the Cook's ulcer, or at least to downplay their full offensiveness,[11] and it goes without saying that the comment on the Pardoner in line 691 of the "Prologue" is always inadmissible. In any case, Victorian versions of children's Chaucer do not really offer the poet to this audience as a figure synonymous with play or frolic. For one thing, as we have seen, there is a necessary emphasis on his rather more sober tales, and although these may be retold, as suggested above, as simple narratives of romance, the editors are generally concerned to present Chaucer as a serious moralist rather than an irresponsible child. Thus Mrs. Haweis's *Chaucer for Children* has a reassuring foreword addressed "To the Mother" in which Chaucer is held up as "a thoroughly religious poet. . . . his pages breathe a genuine faith in God, and a passionate sense of the beauty and harmony of the divine work" (xii). Mary Seymour's

Chaucer's Stories Simply Told of 1884 also presents us with a man "whose love was always on the side of good and virtue, and who hated nothing but the mean, the deceitful, and the untrue." Even if he sometimes depicted what was "loathsome," it was only so he might "hold it up to the world's repugnance."[12] Furnivall's introduction to Harvey Darton's volume also talks of Chaucer's "reverence for all that was noble and pure, his hatred of cruelty and wrong, his exposure of social evils," and so forth (xviii).[13] This latter essay is an interesting case of the attempt, one feels, to talk to two audiences at once; the emphasis on Chaucer's morality is reassuring to parents, whereas children are told that Chaucer as a boy "was a little elvish-looking fellow—as he says in his *Canterbury Tales*—as bright and quick as a boy could be, plucky and slippy at football, hockey, and other games." "Cricket was not then known," Furnivall helpfully adds. Moreover, "if any orchard-robbing or other mischief went on among his school-fellows, I doubt not that Chaucer, like Lydgate, did his share of it. But we may be sure that his brains kept him at the top of his class" (vi). Here we have a role model for lusty English boyhood, just as, in the next chapter, we shall see attempts to define Chaucer as the prototype Englishman. Furnivall begins and ends his introduction with reference to England's imperial mission and with a salute to those like Chaucer who have "handed us down the England and the language which we possess, and which we have to put and keep in the forefront of the world" (iii–v, xviii).

This note of nationalist indoctrination is in fact rare in children's versions, perhaps surprisingly so. Victorian editions do contain didactic matter, as we have seen, but generally concerned with rather broad notions of Chaucer's piety or nobility; Mrs. Haweis in *Chaucer for Children* is also keen to bring out his anti-Catholic feelings and dislike of nuns and prioresses (6–7, 23n), a point made more strongly in *Chaucer for Schools,* where Chaucer's "sarcasm" toward the Prioress is again stressed, together with the "Wicliffism and true Protestant feeling" of the "Parson's Tale" and others that make Chaucer a forerunner of Luther (x, 37n). As we move into the twentieth century, however, this type of editorial exhortation starts to diminish; indeed, we eventually arrive at children's versions with hardly any introductory "guidance" at all, as in Eleanor Farjeon's *Tales from Chaucer* of 1930, which contains solely a brief preface, mainly concerned with the technical problems of the retelling. With McCaughrean's 1984 version, we simply have versions of the tales themselves. Chaucer is now there for the jocular stories alone, with no attempt to provide any medieval context in the form of historical or biographical preliminaries. This is part of the process of wholesale modernization, abetted in McCaughrean's case, as we have seen, by the topical subtitles ("A Barrel of Laughs," "A Racket at the Mill," and so on).[14]

We have indicated how the fabliaux (or at least references to them) start to make their way into twentieth-century children's versions, a trend that reflects a more general acceptance of Chaucer's bawdiness that becomes evident in the 1930s in the work of scholars like John Livingston Lowes, and then on into the 1940s with Coghill (as we saw in chapter 2), to become today perhaps the dominant feature in the popular recognition of Chaucer.[15] It is instructive to chart the evolution of this acceptability over the last century or so. Many early children's editions simply leave the fabliaux out, especially those that claim to be no more than selections from Chaucer; others attempt at least a kind of suture where these omissions take place, as in Mrs. Haweis's *Chaucer for Schools,* where the pilgrims' applause for the "Knight's Tale" and the Host's casting around for the next speaker—"Lat se now who shal telle another tale" (I. 3109–16)—are recorded, only to be followed by the Host's calling on the Clerk and thus overleaping great stretches of unacceptable narrative (87). What this latter practice does recognize, of course, is that much of the force and significant innovation of the *Canterbury Tales* lies in the interaction between the pilgrims en route the "links"—and the problem for children's Chaucer versions in particular is to give some flavor of this: to have, if you like, the Miller's interruption to the sequence without having his tale. This problem is intensified in those versions, like William Calder's and Farjeon's, that declare themselves to be aimed both at a general (adult) audience and at young readers in particular; here the relation between omission and inclusion requires fine judgment.

Thus Margaret Macaulay's *Stories from Chaucer* of 1911 complains of the practice of giving various tales in isolation, and makes much in its preface of how here "an attempt has been made to exhibit the general scheme and conduct of the *Canterbury Tales* . . . including the Prologue and some of the conversations of the pilgrims on the road."[16] Such a procedure is hardly new, Macaulay having been here anticipated by, for example, Calder and Harvey Darton, and in any case we proceed in traditional fashion from the Knight's to the Man of Law's tales with only a fleeting reference to the fact that tales *were* told by the Miller, Reeve, and Cook (96); nor are we given any indication what these were about. In Emily Underdown's *Gateway to Chaucer* of 1912, the existence of the offensive material is acknowledged, only to be actively demoted in the customary transit from Knight to Man of Law: "The company, whose attention had wandered during the idle chatterings and rough story-telling that had taken place before, now prepared for something worth hearing, and with a sober cheer the Man of Law proceeded with his story."[17] After acknowledging the existence of the fabliaux, however unwillingly, the next stage is to give some indication, albeit brief, of their contents; thus Calder (who as we have seen has an adult audience partly in mind) gives a brief and disapproving paraphrase of the "Miller's Tale," concentrating solely on the fictitious Flood story, where we are told that John "was roused from his slumbers by a great hullabaloo which was going on below" and so cut the rope and fell; what occasioned that "hullabaloo" we are not told, nor scarcely of the existence of Alison (130–31). A similar procedure is followed in Harvey Darton, where the "Miller's Tale" is solely about a clerk tricking a carpenter, the former at the right moment crying "Water!" to ensure John's broken arm (54). With Sturt and Oakden's *Canterbury Pilgrims* of 1923 Alison finally makes an appearance, though not the amatory plotting: Nicholas takes pity on the fact that, wed to an old husband, she gets little entertainment, and arranges the trick on John so that he can take her to the fair. The cry of "Water!" occurs on the way back from their outing, when Nicholas accidentally sets fire to Alison's ribbons with his torch (37). With the Farjeon version of 1930 we achieve physical contact, though not between Alison and Nicholas, who remain dedicated simply to youthful jokes. Absolon's love interest is, however, represented, but the misplaced kiss occurs when Nicholas puts his head out at the window, the "thyng al rough and long yherd" that Absolon is startled by being the man's beard. The second time Nicholas attempts the joke he gets scalded in the cheek (47–48).

With the late twentieth century there is much less embarrassment about the fabliaux, as already remarked, though a version as recent as Ian Serraillier's *Road to Canterbury* (1979) continues to omit them.[18] The two versions current in the 1980s and 1990s, however, complete this narrative of the gradual incorporation of the "Miller's Tale." McCaughrean's retelling certainly has Nicholas and Alison physically interested in each other, though their smooching takes place on a settle underneath the barrels rather than in a bedroom; there, we are told, they "held hands and kissed and carried on" (20). Absolon once more kisses Nicholas's face, though on the second occasion Nicholas "proferred [him] the seat of his pants" (22), which seems a strangely decent indecency. Finally, with Selina Hastings's selection of 1988 we get almost the full story; the misplaced kiss does take place on Alison's "naked bottom," and the second time around Nicholas "too stuck out his bottom, letting out a vigorous fart as he did so." The accompanying illustration by Reg Cartwright shows plenty of naked flesh, though the cartoonlike format of these illustrations together with continued elisions in the narrative mitigate the full physical impact of Chaucer's story of haunchbones, holes, and things rough and hairy.[19]

A similar history attaches to the "Reeve's Tale": from early omissions and brief, unrevealing notices, to some sort of account in the 1920s and 1930s, to a more complete retelling today. Sturt and Oakden have the fracas occasioned by Aleyn stealing a kiss from the miller's daughter, though not in the bedroom; there is therefore no misplaced cradle trick and indeed, one feels, no real point to the retelling (42–43). With Farjeon we do enter the bedroom, though without the sexual element to the story the proceedings become very confused: the students move the cradle to the foot of their bed from the miller's merely as a preface to finding their way out of the room, though no reason is given for their doing this, nor for their sudden decision to go home in the middle of the night. The wife, disturbed by them, sees someone in the bed without the cradle and thinks there must be an intruder (having apparently forgotten the offer of hospitality to the students), and mistakenly belabors her husband with her stick (53). McCaughrean's version, which is surprisingly prim, also uses the intruder motif, but this time makes some sense of it. Here the students do not stay the night, but return after the household is asleep and then move the cradle from the wife's to the miller's bed. They then make burglar noises (saying "'Burgle, burgle, burgle,' in low voices") and the wife, after getting up to investigate, finds the "intruder" in "her" bed, and so on (34–35). Finally, Hastings more or less tells the tale as it is, with the students getting into bed with the wife and daughter (41).[20]

It would be interesting to see what Hastings might have done with tales like the Merchant's, Shipman's, and Summoner's, though in leaving them out she reflects the fact that these have always appeared only sporadically in children's versions. When the Merchant's does occur, as in Farjeon and McCaughrean, the crime against January is nonscurrilous, a matter of stealing pears in the latter (113), and, in the former, as Pluto says of May, "she means to make game of [January], and eat pears with Damian in the tree" (129). With Farjeon's version of the "Summoner's Tale," Thomas burps "full in the Friar's face," and the conundrum then becomes how to "divide the sound of a sigh and the smell of an onion" (103–4). It is needless to multiply these instances of suppression and accommodation, but it is clear that by the 1980s it is no longer necessary to skip certain tales on the grounds that, as Storr and Turner's *Canterbury Chimes* told its audience, "most of the badness you would fortunately not understand, and till you are older it is better for you not to understand it."[21] As a final example, Hastings presents the knight's crime at the beginning of the "Wife of Bath's Tale" emphatically: "Ignoring all her pleas, he threw her to the ground and raped her" (62), where nearly every previous children's version has talked generally about an unspecified crime against chivalry, and so forth.[22]

The two versions from the 1980s, those by McCaughrean and Hastings, represent, we might say, alternative modes of up-to-dateness. The latter does this by being open about elements previously suppressed, as we have seen. McCaughrean's version in this regard is much more diluted; her modernity consists in introducing throughout jocular, debunking amplifications, particularly in the "links," so that the narrative comes across at times like a *Carry On* film. Thus, after the Clerk tells his tale, he is knocked from his horse by a comically outraged Wife of Bath, ending up "in a cart rut like a duck in a pond" (47), and at one point the Reeve tosses the Miller's bagpipes into the river (36). This knockabout tone is underlined throughout by the narrator's own adolescent asides, as in his reaction to the "Shipman's Tale": "Personally, I would have preferred a pirate story" (36). Nor is such a tone confined to the links; witness Emily's reaction to the marriage arrangements with Palamon at the end of the "Knight's Tale": "'Urgh, do I have to? His hair's awfully thin already, and I don't like his mouth.' She had a voice like the teeth of a comb clicking" (14). We have reached the opposite extreme to the ponderous aspect of early children's versions; here everything is being treated in a spirit of light farce that can incorporate neither the serious nor the shocking. At the opening of the "Wife of Bath's Tale," the knight, on meeting the maiden, "helped himself to a kiss. The lady picked up her green skirts, and shrieked and swooped like a parrot in and out of the trees, all the way back to the Court" (50).[23]

If on the other hand Hastings has a laudable desire to tell Chaucer "straight" and not to overingratiate herself with young readers, there remains some doubt about what age group her version is designed for. It certainly *looks* like a book for young children, with the large, colorful illustrations by Reg Cartwright referred to earlier; the nature of the retellings presupposes, however, a rather more mature audience, as does the short introduction, which has none of that childlike language representing the attempt to converse with young readers that we so frequently find. As we have noted, the retellings themselves (as of the "Miller's Tale") remain a sort of three-quarters-way-house on the route to full revelation: "Not Alison's lips but her naked bottom! 'What a joke!' gasped Nicholas" (33). At any rate, Hastings's Chaucer, as in so many children's editions, is offered as primarily a poet of narrative; the "General Prologue," which, as we note in chapters 2 and 5, has had such a fascination for adult audiences in its construction of (English) character and setting, is sketchily represented and even dismembered, with extracts from it introducing each tale in turn, as also happens in Serraillier and Hastings. This obviously proceeds from the need, where only a selection of tales is given, to give notice of a few speakers rather than of the entire party, though in McCaughrean's version the descriptive details of the "Prologue" become simply more material to be used in the expanded links that, as we have seen, are this version's most singular feature. In the interests of novelistic (and even soap-opera) continuity, all the characters are kept repeatedly before the reader's eye, so that, for example, Madame Eglantine can chime in with her comment on the "Miller's Tale": "'Ooh! You've made me blush, Master Miller. Regardez, messieurs, je suis blushing!' she exclaimed, fanning her snow-white cheeks. 'By Saint Loy! What a coarse story!'" (23).

One other device used by this last version is to provide a more complete finale to the *Tales* than the Chaucerian text allows for, in the form of an epilogue describing the pilgrims' arrival in Canterbury when the plan of telling homeward-bound tales is discussed; here Harry Bailly and the Wife of Bath also announce their engagement (110–13). This desire for completion constitutes, of course, a hallowed tradition, right back to the anonymous "Tale of Beryn" and Lydgate's *Siege of Thebes,* two texts that in Harvey Darton are drawn upon to provide the scene of the arrival at the inn at Canterbury (where the principal feature is a trick played on the Pardoner by a serving-girl) and also an account of the homeward journey, largely taken up by Lydgate (who has bumped into the party in Canterbury) reciting his work (*Tales of the Canterbury Pilgrims* 296–318).[24] Harvey Darton resists, however, completing one of the most tantalizing lacunae in literature in not providing any judgment on who actually wins the tale-telling contest.

In finally summarizing a century of children's Chaucer, we are left with a junior version of some of the tropes attaching to "popular" Chaucer looked at in chapter 2: once divorced from Victorian moralizing, we see the affable, child-friendly poet of the *Canterbury Tales* offering a world of picturesque entertainment and fellowship devoid of anything much in the way of religious or social concerns. The "graces" of childhood that the *Temple Bar* writer found in both Chaucer and his age, "simplicity, sincerity, transparency, and joy," arguably remain the dominant note in the retellings we have looked at, even if Hastings's version has begun a process of undermining them. We are invited into "Chaucer's world" as a curiously innocent and dehistoricized place that exudes benignity, with at the center of it a happy, playful Chaucer marked by that "self-effacing sociability" that we have seen Chesterton enthuse over. In 1952 Regina Kelly published a fictionalized biography entitled *Young Geoffrey Chaucer,* in which the events of Chaucer's life (including some that never happened, like his studying at Oxford) are traced up until his appointment as *valettus* to Edward III. If such an account is of necessity oddly truncated, given that what we know of Chaucer's literary career almost entirely postdates this period, Kelly manages things so that the child is truly father to the man, with all Chaucer's storytelling skills in place practically in his infancy, as well as his future marriage to Philippa Roet (the romantic subplot takes off from Geoffrey's childhood meeting with Philippa, continuing through their various meetings as they grow up). "'There is naught I like better than to hear the tales you tell.' 'And there is naught I like better than the telling of them,'" the children confide to each other.[25] A little later, Chaucer is seen telling the story of the "Nun's Priest's Tale" to the Countess of Ulster's young son and subsequently regaling Edward III's court with the "Miller's Tale" (80, 144), as if the entire stretch of his career can be telescoped into this youthful period. Moreover, the young poet is actually shown his mature vocation by his childhood friend Philippa, who, at the moment Chaucer is protesting his admiration for the French poets, makes this telling intervention: "'The people of England have a tongue of their own. Why not put it into books?' was Philippa's argument" (94).[26]

Such a sentimental infantilization of literary history has doubtless been perpetrated on other writers, but Chaucer, long regarded as a child moving in a child's world, is obviously a prime candidate for such treatment. We might end this chapter, however, with a very different approach to the Chaucer-as-child trope, which sees this identity as anything but innocent and as one used by Chaucer himself as a strategy of opposition. "The remarkable and underappreciated importance of childhood to the Chaucerian imagination in general" has been discussed by Lee Patterson, who not only stresses the ubiquitousness of children throughout the *Tales* but also argues that the two tales Chaucer himself tells, "Sir Thopas" and "Melibee," properly belong to the genre of medieval children's literature. The description of Chaucer that the Host is made to give at the beginning of "Sir Thopas," as both "elvyssh" and a "popet" (VII.703, 701), points in fact to Chaucer's taking up the uncanny position of the elf-child as a mode of resisting prevalent and constricting roles for the poet, particularly in his obligations to the court. Patterson's account of Chaucer's "association of himself with what can broadly be termed children's literature" develops into a complex historical and theoretical study, and it is not surprising, perhaps, that the children's Chaucer versions I have been looking at show little cognizance of the issues Patterson identifies in Chaucer's own thinking, with most of the tales of fragment VII that he is principally concerned with—"Sir Thopas," "Melibee," and the Prioress's and Monk's tales—rarely featuring in modern children's compilations.[27] The subject raises again the issue of the marked divergence between popular and academic interests in Chaucer that we have looked at in chapter 2 and will return to in the final chapter.

5

English Chaucer

At points in chapter 2 we touched on the idea, common to several writers, that Chaucer and his works are an embodiment and even prototype of "Englishness," a theme that is pervasive enough in the popularizing dissemination of Chaucer to warrant a chapter by itself. The period when this nationalistic interest in him is most evident runs from later Victorian times to World War II, though across this span there are interesting and manifold changes in emphasis that reflect the waning of imperialistic mission. Thus one of the most resoundingly patriotic celebrations of Chaucer occurs at the height of such mission, in Matthew Browne's *Chaucer's England* of 1869, where we are presented with a Chaucer who is "every inch an Englishman . . . English in the essential objectivity of his mind, and in the directness of his touch."[1] This directness seems to be akin to what the *Temple Bar* writer in the previous chapter criticized as Chaucer's childlike indiscretion; according to Browne, however, "not to shirk anything is a pre-eminent note of the English character," and Chaucer "hits the right nail on the head at once" (1:46). Chaucer's full-blooded descriptiveness in the face of the pilgrim company and the fact that "his poetry is penetrated with the social spirit" (1:47) lead Browne to contest hotly any influence of the *Decameron* on the *Canterbury Tales;* the evasions (including plague evasion) of the former work emphasize how "the whole conception is evidently mediaeval-Italian,—cowardly, romantic, and thin," whereas with the *Tales,* "its Englishness we recognise at a glance,—the inn, the company, the good fellowship, the common purpose (so different from mere running away or retirement), the straightforward look of the pilgrims in the poet's picture,—all this is, I repeat, thoroughly English, and as peculiar to Chaucer as anything English can be" (1:86–87).

This bluffly open approach to the world and an emphatic social instinct are what have made the English "*par excellence* colonists, missionaries, gatherers together, founders of social groups," and in this sense "who is an Englishman more English than Chaucer?" (1:46–47). The colonizing purpose is, however, grounded in the "fixed centre" of the domestic hearth; the "heart of England" is truly the home, and Chaucer's "extreme tenderness in writing of children" and his insistence (in the "Summoner's Tale") that in the Englishman's home "no priest may tithe, or toll, or have predominance" show the importance to Chaucer of the nation's domestic ethos (1:249ff.). Browne deals with the most conspicuous instances of French and Italian influence on Chaucer's poetry by choosing to ignore, throughout his two volumes, any work that precedes the *Canterbury Tales*, which "contain . . . more Englishness than any other poem in the language." For this reason, he adds, Chaucer "may fairly be taken as a typical person, so that no impertinence can be charged against such a title as 'Chaucer's England'" (1:49–50). Browne does not perhaps go as far as some later writers who regard Chaucer as not simply a repository of Englishness but as originating and, as it were, patenting it; there is indeed in his account a strong sense of Chaucer as an honorary Victorian, apart from his being stained with an "indelicacy and filthiness" (1:282) that Browne does in fact devote an entire chapter to condemning.[2]

This confident, aggressive, and at times xenophobic appraisal (so dissimilar, we may note in passing, to that of Browne's contemporary William Morris, discussed in chapter 1) surfaces elsewhere in Victorian responses. Thus F. D. Maurice on Chaucer: "He has been called a Wycliffite. He is not that. He is simply an Englishman. He hates friars, because they are not English and not manly."[3] Though some writers (unlike Browne) are willing to investigate what are commonly known as Chaucer's French and Italian periods (posited as running from the late 1360s to the mid-1380s, and in which Chaucer's work is deeply indebted to writers like Machaut, Dante, and Boccaccio), there is frequently the sense that the poetry produced during these periods is merely prefatory to Chaucer's true vocation, in his so-called English period, of enshrining the national spirit in the *Canterbury Tales*, an enterprise that no longer needs the stimulation of "foreign" books but is prompted directly by the vibrant English life he sees around him. John Richard Green, in declaring that "the genius of Chaucer was neither French nor Italian, whatever element it might borrow from either literature, but English to the core," adds categorically that "from 1384 all trace of foreign influence dies away," before discussing Chaucer's subsequent career as far as his death and burial at Westminster, that center of the English constitution.[4] We have seen Tudor Jenks compare passing from the pre-*Tales* works to the *Tales* with emerging from a musty and bookish museum into "the freshness and light of a crisp spring morning," while Noyes wants an author sprung straight from the native soil rather than from literary sources, which have led critics to lay "too much stress on the foreign element in him."[5] The fact that passages from the *Tales* can yet have a provenance in works like the *Romance of the Rose* is accordingly met with by some painful head-scratching or outright disbelief.[6]

Even a scholar as respected as Kittredge tends to make a division, as we saw in chapter 2, between an essential Chaucer of (original) characterization and a derivative Chaucer of the "everyday" natural scenery of birds, flowers, and so forth, though his appraisal is devoid of any overt nationalist sentiment. Even so, it is difficult not to feel that Kittredge's position is in part a response to Legouis's 1910 monograph on Chaucer (English translation 1913), which suggests that these skills in characterization are not distinguishable from Chaucer's earlier phases and that they too proceed from a response to the created world that is essentially French, a "diffused, indefinable and yet quite certain" air of light and clarity, "precisely of the same quality as that of the Ile-de-France": "as in the case of the French *trouvères,* there runs through his work a joyousness born of the pleasure of living, and which shows itself in a partiality to sunny scenes, a constant reminiscence of spring time, may-bushes, flowers, birds, and music."[7] For Legouis, "it is wrong to speak of the French period of Chaucer's development. He is always French . . . [and] it was in his French style and manner that he painted contemporary society in England" (60–61). Chaucer's "mind was French, like his name," and "whenever he goes outside France, he also goes, in some measure, outside his own nature" (57, 60).

It is clear then that a figure like Chaucer, nourished in a European cultural context and yet often seen as voicing "Englishness" par excellence, offers ample opportunity for nationalist controversy. Legouis's claim on him as essentially French is anticipated during the nineteenth century, notably by Étienne Sandras, and it is not difficult to find a whole range of counterassertions claiming Chaucer as crucially Italian (or indebted to Italy), Irish, or even American.[8] But to claim Chaucer for England is, of course, far more common. Austin's speech at the unveiling of the commemorative Chaucer window in 1900, referred to in chapter 2, becomes typically chauvinistic:

> Was not Chaucer Controller of the Customs in the port of London, as, moreover, he was the Parliamentary representative for Kent, Clerk of the King's Works at Windsor, the confidant of rulers, warriors, and statesmen, a soldier in France, a diplomatist in Italy? In my humble opinion no man can be, or ever became, a really great poet who could not have been a successful man of affairs, a methodical administrator, a sagacious statesman, aye a victorious general, or a circumspect and impressive Archbishop. Whether it is their limited possession of the practical temperament that has hindered the Celtic race, which has produced so many beautiful poets, from producing, to speak with accuracy, a really great poet, a poet of the first class, I will not presume to say. But I believe it is because of the fundamentally practical, weighty, massive element in the English character and intellect that England has given birth to the greatest poets, and the greatest number of them.[9]

The emphasis on worldliness and practicality here is similar to that we have already seen in writers like Browne and Ames (see chapter 2 above), whereas those who wish to claim other national ancestries for Chaucer will often insist on more elusive qualities to be found in him and his work, such as the "mercurial" quality that led Furnivall to relate Chaucer to the Irish, as noted earlier, or the element of "lightsomeness" that even Browne is prepared to admit (though not dwell on), which derives "from the Italian, or perhaps through the French."[10] In G. K. Chesterton, as we shall see, we come across the interesting case of a writer wanting to press Chaucer's practical and sociable English temperament while at the same time allowing for a more remote and even mystical Chaucer, the "elvyssh" figure addressed by the Host in the "Prologue to Sir Thopas" (VII.703).[11]

Indeed, as we proceed in the twentieth century there is often the sense that Chaucer's Englishness is a less easily definable quality than that enounced in the confident declarations of Browne, Maurice, or Austin, and that it has to be approached in more indirect ways. Browne's assertions that no one could claim to be "more English than Chaucer" and that the *Tales* "contain . . . more Englishness than any other poem in the language"[12] make one wonder why Chaucer has rarely been endowed with the nationalistic status achieved above all by Shakespeare, in works such as G. Wilson Knight's *This Sceptred Isle* of 1940, where Shakespeare is hailed as "the voice of England" offering a particular message for the country in wartime.[13] The question raises once more the relative absence of Chaucer from the general consciousness that we discussed in chapter 2, and which Chesterton in particular draws attention to: "In no common English ears, as yet, does his name actually sound as a thunderclap or a trumpet-peal, like the name of Dante or of Shakespeare."[14] But the title of Wilson Knight's book already supplies part of the answer: the difficulty of extracting from Chaucer's work, for all its supposed Englishness, direct declarations of patriotism, to compare with John of Gaunt's speech on "this sceptred isle" from act 2, scene 1 of *Richard II*. Legouis, fixated on a French Chaucer, is able to point out that "there is not a single patriotic line in his work," at a time moreover when "this feeling was beginning to rise with some force in English hearts," and Ames, for all his talk of Chaucer's "essentially English" character, also confesses his "insensibility to the emotions of patriotism."[15]

Indeed, a *Times Literary Supplement (TLS)* editorial of April 1940, again entitled "Chaucer's England," does feature the poet's "message" for an England at war, though in a spirit very different from Matthew Browne or from that Wilson Knight finds in Shakespeare. For one thing, the editorial is able to make use of the absence of obvious patriotism in Chaucer to accommodate the present alliance with France: "No man in history is more essentially English than Chaucer, but in his handling of all the facts of life as material for poetry there is much of the spirit of our friends the French, to whom he was indebted for his first lessons in the art of versification. Both nations can salute the poet who belongs to them both."[16] This position in fact echoes an article on Chaucer in the same issue by R. W. Chambers: "Chaucer is the first great example in literature of that Franco-British marriage which the *Petit Parisien* the other day urged should be made indissoluble." Both Chambers and the editorial agree that another relevant aspect of Chaucer for 1940 is his genial stoicism; apart from his surviving plague and political upheaval, he was "robbed by highwaymen, beaten, wounded (twice, if not more, within three days). He lost his clerkships, but not his sense of humor. Soaked in rain, 'forgotten in solitary wilderness,' he supervised the dykes and ditches of the Thames. Yet cheerfulness breaks through."[17] In the editorial this attitude becomes an exhortation to the nation: "In this doubtful April, with its showers less sweet than icy, we find Geoffrey Chaucer more natural than nature. He is the best spring day we have had this afflicted year. His smiling acceptance of the worst the fates can do, his persistence in seeking and finding truth and beauty in perilous times, have a special message for England today."[18]

In the darkest days for England of the Second World War this, then, is Chaucer's "message": to keep smiling through. One might argue that in some ways these pieces are fine examples of what we have since learned to call spin-doctoring: they omit to mention, for example, the irony of Anglo-French warfare persisting through Chaucer's lifetime, warfare in which he was, after all, briefly a participant and prisoner; they raise suspicions, moreover, that no one would ever have thought of bringing Chaucer forward in wartime were it not for the fact that 1940, as the sixth centenary of Chaucer's birth, requires some sort of tribute. Chaucer is made, somewhat ingeniously, to "speak" to the nation, but hardly, one suspects, because he is a constant resource but because the commemorative occasion requires it.[19]

Otherwise a "wartime Chaucer" is not greatly in evidence, though one interesting occurrence is the series of verse pastiches by G. H. Vallins printed in *Punch* from the beginning of 1944 onward, presenting a portrait gallery of representative English figures, such as "The Sergeant-Major," "The Land Girl," "The Scolemistresse," "The Soldier." Many of these celebrate qualities of endurance and bravery in the face of enemy attack, as with "The Conductresse" (i.e., of a London bus): "And in the kinges werre [she] had born hir perte / With lowly patience and high corage / Whan that the bombes felle on hir viage."[20] The wartime series was wrapped up in the victory celebration issue of 9 May 1945 with a piece headed "'And Pilgrims were they Alle'":

> "Now drinketh" quod oure Host, "bi-fore ye go,
> For we are in o felawshipe y-bonde
> With men and wommen in this faire londe,
> And with hem alle that in the werre were slayn,
> Both neigh and fer, and come nat back ageyn,
> That to us alle, y-wis, were lief and dere.
> I preye yow drinke your wine, and han god chere."
>
> (398)

The emphasis on a nation's stoicism and mutual reliance is lost in the continuations Vallins produced after the war, where the focus is rather on the peculiarities of individual trades and pursuits, and where much is made of the quaint sporting terminology beloved of such as "The Cricceter" or "The Umpire."[21] We also see difficulties in keeping the notion of a (metaphorical) pilgrimage going in peacetime, and although the series continued until well into the 1950s, the complete absence of any female "pilgrims" after 1945 (they had constituted almost half the wartime number) suggests how far women had to relinquish roles of public prominence brought to them by the war.

A far better known depiction of the nation at war in terms of Chaucerian pilgrimage also dates from 1944, namely Michael Powell and Emeric Pressburger's film *A Canterbury Tale*. This opens with the reciting of the first lines to the "General Prologue" and with a view of Chaucer's party of pilgrims on the road, before the Squire watching his hawk in flight is replaced on screen by the same figure in modern soldier's dress watching an airplane. The emphasis on continuity and on the linkage with our immemorial forebears is a major theme in the film, values threatened not simply by warfare but by modern technology, so that we then move to scenes of tanks tearing along the Pilgrims' Way, or the Canterbury-bound train on its "road of steel" usurping the sound of "ring of hooves and creak of wheel."[22] One of the major departures from Chaucer is indeed the setting of the film along the Pilgrims' Way, or on what Hilaire Belloc called the "old road" from Winchester to Canterbury, and more particularly in the village of "Chillingbourne" (presumably Chilham), the final stopping place before Canterbury on the journey.[23] This enables a loving and luscious evocation of the beauties of the Sussex and Kent countryside and of its picturesque settlements and (vanishing) rural trades, a typical piece of World War II pastoral and one promoted as an object of national piety for the soldiers billeted at Chillingbourne in the film and through them for the viewer.[24] Although at the outset protagonists and audience alike are addressed by the film's voice-over as pilgrims disoriented and uncertain of destination in the troubled times of 1944, the conclusion stages a celebratory arrival at Canterbury Cathedral, where the prayers for emotional and spiritual healing of at least some of the individual pilgrims are answered.

A Canterbury Tale is clearly a nostalgic and idyllicized recreation of a Chaucerian original in which not much more than the name survives, and even that name refers not so much to Chaucer's text as to the idiomatic usage whereby "canterbury tale" has come to mean tall or far-fetched story: here the reference is to the bizarre subplot of the film in which the Chillingbourne "glue-man" pours glue into the hair of local girls in order to keep them in at night and not distract the soldiers from educating themselves in England's glorious heritage in their leisure time. Although some of the film's pilgrims do have tales to tell, these are of the typically modern confessional variety, dealing with lost love or personal disappointment and only meant for chosen intimates; certainly there is no notion of a storytelling community to appease a sense of solitude felt throughout. Like the other pieces of wartime Chauceriana already mentioned, the mood of the film, though of course Anglophile, is far from triumphalist, in contrast to contemporary filmic uses of Shakespeare, such as, famously, Olivier's *Henry V*.[25] Even the presence of an American soldier among the main protagonists, and one who himself learns to love the beauty of the old country, does not lead to any belligerent optimism in the face of the enemy, given that the enemy is understood as that of an urbanized indifference to the past as much as the specter of foreign foes, who are in fact hardly ever mentioned.

The Chaucer therefore mediated through these pieces and the England he represents are far from rampantly militaristic or managerial-administrative, as with Browne, nor do the *TLS* articles present him doing things like beating up (foreign) friars; Chaucer and England are here rather on the defensive, though "cheerfulness breaks through." In this latter instance we are back with a version of the affable English temperament that we had occasion to look at in chapter 2, and in many twentieth-century discussions of the Chaucer-England relationship the emphasis indeed lies on notions of merriness rather than militancy. A good example is Sedgwick's *Dan Chaucer* (1934), in which the author's enthusiasm for Chaucer the Englishman was briefly touched on in chapter 2. Not only was Chaucer "the first true Englishman," but the *Canterbury Tales* lays down foundational models of the national temperament, above all in the person of Harry Bailly, "the truest typical Englishman that has ever been delineated." Through such models Chaucer "had done more than any other man to make English men Englishmen."[26] This exemplary construction has therefore a gelling force, Harry being a type to which Englishmen can and should aspire; if it is objected that such a model would involve us in disliking our wives and in not having very exacting standards of intelligence, we might remark that Sedgwick himself, as an American, writes at a safe and picturesque distance from such consequences. Indeed, some of the most nostalgically enthusiastic pictures of merrie England come from American writers already commented upon, like Sedgwick, Jenks, and Chute and like Percy Mackaye (see chapter 8 in this volume). Sedgwick is clearly more in love with English personality than with England's political power, and at one point frankly accuses Chaucer of "insular nationalism" (92).

There are, as it were, two currents to the idea of Chaucer as a founding father, whether it be of the nation's literature or of its temperament and character. The first would see Chaucer as laying down models that have never been superseded, as in Sedgwick's talk of the Host as the truest type ever delineated; the second acknowledges Chaucer as father while regarding him as outstripped by his sons, notably Shakespeare, in what we might call the "Prologue motif." This latter idea is presented by Noyes, for whom Chaucer is not merely the "Father of English Poetry" but of its drama and its line of novelists, too, "above all things, a maker of preludes": "It is a gracious act of the Muses that they should have set at the head of the long and glorious pageant of English literature, this many-coloured company of pilgrims, winding through the lanes of an English April, down to England's noblest shrine." Here the "General Prologue," which is Chaucer's greatest achievement,[27] is not so much to the *Tales* themselves (which it greatly overshadows) but to the pageant composed by the subsequent writers it prompts (as in its skills in characterization). As that from which the whole tradition of English literature springs, it is important it should be kept free of the contamination of foreign sources: in Noyes's eyes a kind of Chaucerian virgin birth, divinely impregnated by the Muses with a little help from the English soil and the English weather. But Noyes is clear in his insistence that Chaucer's importance lies as much in what comes after him as in his works per se, and in this he shows none of the nostalgia for Chaucer as at once the creator of the English line and its apogee that we find elsewhere, and above all in Chesterton's *Chaucer,* which we shall consider below.

Noyes's talk of "the long and glorious pageant of English literature," with Chaucer's pilgrims at its head, is a trope picked up by a modern writer who had a recurrent interest in Chaucer, Virginia Woolf. In her book of essays *The Common Reader* (1925), Woolf traces the progress of (largely English) writing from medieval to contemporary times, a project she returned to just before her death in a barely begun work provisionally entitled *Reading at Random,* or *Turning the Page,* which "would depict the history of English literature as a continuum."[28] The first essay in *The Common Reader* is on Chaucer, or rather on the fascination that Chaucer afforded to the "common reader" in the person of Sir John Paston, whose domestic life and that of generations of his family are preserved in the famous fifteenth-century *Paston Letters.* For Woolf, Chaucer is indeed the "commonest" of poets:

> The pleasure he gives us is different from the pleasure that other poets give us, because it is more closely connected with what we have ourselves felt or observed. Eating, drinking, and fine weather, the May, cocks and hens, millers, old peasant women, flowers—there is a special stimulus in seeing all these common things so arranged that they affect us as poetry affects us, and are yet bright, sober, precise as we see them out of doors.[29]

The idea that Chaucer draws on the common stock of the life and experience around him (and "out of doors") is also to the fore in the opening essay of *Reading at Random,* entitled "Anon," where the *Canterbury Tales* is contrasted with Spenser's *Fairie Queene:* "The one is clear sharp definite . . . direct, about this real man, this real woman, here and now," whereas the other dallies and wanders in the land of the private imagination.[30] With the Renaissance and the invention of the printing press, Woolf argues in "Anon," authorial self-consciousness is born, "the man who first sees himself and shows himself to us" (385); thus Spenser "is aware of his art as Chaucer was not . . . the voice of a man practising an art, asking for recognition, and bitterly conscious of his relation [to] the world, of the world's scorn" (391). Chaucer's work is corporate, then, rather than individualistic, just as, she argues in "Anon," the drama that preceded playwrights like Kyd and Marlowe is "a common product . . . in part the work of the audience" (395).

Chaucer's work obviously "founds" subsequent literary practice in some respects; thus in *The Common Reader* his refusal to "flinch" from "the life that was being lived at the moment before his eyes" leads to an "unabashed and unafraid" realism that is willing to tackle farmyards, dung, unshaven chins of old men (as January in the "Merchant's Tale," IV. 1824–25), and the whole range of clothes, food, and drink, "as if poetry could handle the common facts of this very moment of Tuesday, the sixteenth day of April, 1387, without dirtying her hands."[31] One remembers that this essay was published at almost the same time as Woolf's *Mrs Dalloway,* with its emphasis on the "moment" of a single Wednesday in June, though Woolf admits that "being able to speak without self-consciousness of the parts and functions of the body" is one area of common experience lost to the modern writer "with the advent of decency" (29). Chaucer's "morality" in refusing to moralize is also hailed, his making "a complete model of the world without excluding the bad or laying stress upon the good"; thus his readers, "instead of being solemnly exhorted . . . are left to stray and stare and make out a meaning for ourselves. It is the morality of ordinary intercourse, the morality of the novel" (31–32). On the other hand, the modern writer has "perhaps things of greater interest to say" than the mere emphasis on narrative unfolding that Woolf sees in Chaucer, his ability to make us want "to learn the end of the story"; for the moderns "events are seldom important," and Chaucer's interest in characterization and consciousness and even his descriptive powers (he possesses not "a tithe of the virtuosity in word-painting which is the modern inheritance") are rudimentary (27–28).

Indeed, Chaucer possesses a set of simple "convictions" in the portrayal of character that permit of no problematization nor ambiguity: "We know what he finds good, what evil; the less said the better." In the matter of young women, for example, whether narrators or narrated, such as the Prioress, Emily (the "Knight's Tale"), and Virginia (the "Physician's Tale"), "they are parts, one feels, of the same personage. . . . as she goes in and out of the *Canterbury Tales* bearing different names, she has a stability which is only to be found where the poet has made up his mind about young women." Chaucer briskly lays down these solid and unadorned characterological foundations for his "building" so that he can then proceed to his real interest, which is "get[ting] on with his story" (29). It must be admitted that Woolf's estimation of Chaucer in *The Common Reader* is hardly progressive; indeed, it partakes of many of the commonplace and even patronizing attitudes toward him that feature in the popularizing commentaries we looked at in chapter 2, and it is no surprise to discover that her critical preparation for the Chaucer essay did not go much beyond such Victorian stalwarts as Matthew Arnold and James Russell Lowell.[32] In *The Common Reader,* "the surprising brightness, the still effective merriment of the *Canterbury Tales,*" is born out of Chaucer's naked encounter with the life "being lived at the moment before his eyes" (30); his natural habitat is the open air, the "out of doors," and he is never distracted by "abstract contemplation" from "fix[ing] his eyes upon the road before him" (31). He is a frank empiricist, painting the environment and the types of people who would already be known to readers like Sir John Paston (26) and presenting these in a morally unproblematic and simplified way. Paston himself (as "novelistically" recreated by Woolf) is represented as more complex than anything in Chaucer, "one of those ambiguous characters who haunt the boundary line where one age merges in another and are not able to inherit either" (33); indeed the modern element of his ambiguity is sited in the very fact of his reading. This point is taken up in the fragmentary chapter entitled "The Reader," which was to succeed "Anon" in *Reading at Random;* the creation through the printing press of the self-conscious writer leads in turn to the creation of the reader, the two enjoying a private and intimate interaction that replaces the communal emphases of the early playhouse and of pre-Renaissance literature.[33]

It seems, then, that Woolf wishes Chaucer to inhabit the realms of the pastoral and, as it were, the preliterary; others may read him, but he cannot be himself a reader, and Woolf's evident fascination with reading as an activity of both loss and gain at the time of the Renaissance and subsequently would locate Chaucer on the far side of this fortunate fall into self-consciousness. In this she shows no interest in anything by Chaucer outside the *Canterbury Tales,* and no interest in his own pronouncedly "bookish" leanings: Ovid, Dante, Boethius, Boccaccio, and so forth, are as nothing compared with the life being "lived at the moment before his eyes." Woolf's conviction of the simple clarity of Chaucer's characters in terms of presentation and moral status is based on figures like Griselda—"there is no blur about her, no hesitation"[34]—but it might have been pulled up short by, for example, Criseyde, though there is no evidence of any Woolfian interest in *Troilus and Criseyde,* in spite of the commonplace that this could be seen as the first English novel. In the idea of Chaucer's speaking directly out of communal and collective experience there is a parallel with Yeats's nostalgia, discussed in chapter 3, for a poet absorbed, so to speak, into his audience, an idea that Yeats upon consideration was forced to abandon, as we have seen. Woolf's view of Chaucer changed very little in this regard, however, and in "Anon" we may still infer that Chaucer is the "innocent" mouthpiece of a collective tradition, rather than what Woolf would define as a writer: "That babbling, child like, story telling singer, that gossip at the farm yard door, that innocent eyed, naked, alternately lustful, obscene and devout singer, who was now and again a great artist died in 147[8] (7), And with him died the part of his song that the audience sang."[35] It is ironic that Chaucer "died" with the advent of printing in the late fifteenth century only to be simultaneously resurrected in Caxton's edition of the *Canterbury Tales;* indeed, when we come across Woolf's recently emerged seventeenth-century reader in the person of Lady Anne Clifford in "The Reader," the volume she is reading is "excellent Chaucer's book." Chaucer is now retrospectively a writer; the book has, in the words of "Anon," "given him a separate existence."[36]

Woolf's final novel, *Between the Acts* (1941), the composition of which overlapped with *Reading at Random,* also shows the awareness of an English Chaucerian heritage, half lost, half retrieved. The ideas of community and kinship that his work embodies—the fact that his dramatis personae, in spite of their "immense variety," are "one consistent type" or "parts . . . of the same personage"[37]—are here applied diachronically to the pilgrim race of the English nation; in an early draft, visitors to Pointz Hall, where the novel is set, pick up a volume of Chaucer in the library, and "some felt, 'This is my England. . . . I am padding along the road; I am the Clerk; I am the Nun; I am the Knight.'"[38] In the pageant-play that is the focus of the novel, the Canterbury pilgrims winding in and out of the trees at the rear of the stage form a continuous backdrop to the scenes from different historical periods and suggest a fundamental identity underlying temporal difference; as the Reverend Streatfield puts it in his summing-up, "Did I not perceive . . . in Lady Harridan . . . a Canterbury pilgrim? We act different parts; but are the same."[39]

Between the Acts is set "in the very heart of England" (9), and its "open-air" pageant whose subject is England (47) has performers and audience drawn from the same community; moreover, in the unspoiled landscape setting of Pointz Hall ("no house had been built; no town had sprung up," 32), it echoes Woolf's talk in *The Common Reader* of the "virgin land" of Chaucer's day: "No villa roofs peered through Kentish tree-tops; no factory chimney smoked on the hill-side" (27). In spite of this, the novel problematizes rather than endorses any "timeless" theme of Chaucerian continuity. Thus the pageantry of the play has nothing of that picturesque glorification we see in Noyes's comment above, with

Chaucer's "many-coloured company of pilgrims" at the head of the national stock; Woolf's pilgrims are rather an anonymous line of diggers and delvers dressed in "sacking," and their words to the audience are blown away by the wind (48–50). Indeed, in spite of her emphasizing Chaucer's fresh portrayal of life in *The Common Reader,* Woolf nowhere enthuses about specific characters like the Host or Wife of Bath or Miller, as we have seen others do: Chaucer represents sameness rather than individuality, as we have seen, and a profound individualizing force belongs only to postmedieval writing, in Woolf's view. In her novels this force of variegation is at least as important as the values of recurrent identity and the national collective that *Between the Acts* seems at once to question and display nostalgia toward; the novel satirizes the rather cozy "communal" interpretation of the Rev. Streatfield, yet leaves open the possibility that, as Mrs. Swithin puts it, there never "were such people [as the Victorians]. Only you and me and William dressed differently" (108), just as the swallows who return to the barn every year may or may not be "the same birds" (63).

No such reservations about Chaucer's heritage (other than the fact that it is scandalously unrecognized) attach to Chesterton's *Chaucer* of 1932, a book that is by far the most stimulating of the "general readership" accounts of Chaucer (one perhaps has to wade through a great many of these to feel this forcibly) and thus worth particular attention. As we remarked in chapter 2, this work incorporates an active polemic on behalf of the social, intellectual, and religious organization of the Middle Ages, and is also singular in the sheer primacy of the position it accords to Chaucer on many different levels:

> There was never a man who was more of a Maker than Chaucer. He made a national language; he came very near to making a nation. . . . Chaucer was the Father of his Country, rather in the style of George Washington. And apart from that, he made something that has altered all Europe more than the Newspaper: the Novel.[40]

But the major emphasis of the book is not on Chaucer's primacy but on his centrality; in his work we find a "balance" (one of Chesterton's insistent terms) between the youth and freshness of the world and its maturity and sophistication, "an instant of radiant ripeness," or "flame of the highest happiness [which] flashed for a moment in the mirror of the genius of Chaucer; like the noonday sun upon a naked sword" (185). The ripe "moment" of Chaucer is seen as the fruition of medieval Catholic virtues of balance, order, common sense, comprehensiveness; everything that is opposed to the extremism, narrowness, partisanship, and individualistic excess that mark postmedieval times. The book ends with representing Chaucer's work as "the shout that showed that normality had been found," a "great voice" given "only suddenly, and for a season, to the most human of human beings" (293). "Normality" is indeed another of Chesterton's key terms; Chaucer represents the norm (briefly) revealed as the Englishman's birthright, and the whole book is, as we saw in chapter 2, a contribution to realizing Chesterton's desire "to make Chaucer an ordinary possession of ordinary Englishmen" (226).

This ordinariness that is common to Chaucer and to the family of Englishmen is defined, in the chapter entitled "Chaucer as an Englishman," as follows:

> He minds his own business; he does not talk shop; he is even content to remain under the mystical cloud of being Something in the City; he does not make scenes, and has a particular kind of limited politeness to servants; he is rather silent and yet somehow sociable. . . . he is manly; he is modest, at least in external manners; he is well-bred; he is well-groomed; he is solid and reasonable and reliable; but he has his good points, for all that. And the greatest of these is something that neither Puritanism nor the Public School has contrived to kill; he is generally fond of a joke. (208)

In this last, however, there is, as remarked above, balance; the seed of the sense of humor in Chaucer has since grown into something "extravagantly" English, like the "almost maniac laughter we sometimes hear from the Elizabethans," or the "Dickensian lunatic-asylum of laughter" (210). If the list of qualities above may appear a little tepid, especially compared with the picturesque excesses of Sedgwick's merrie Host as the English type, one must add that for Chesterton the elements of solidity, reliability, and so on are relatively minor components of a profile that also includes all the inheritance of the orthodox medieval

Catholic, above all Charity, so that Chaucer "stands clothed in scarlet like all the household of love; and emblazoned with the Sacred Heart" (275). In this he is "the last great Englishman of . . . united Christendom" (128), as well as the emergent Englishman of the modern state; once more, a point of "noonday" balance.

Though the workaday qualities are now for the modern Englishman shorn of their religious emblazoning, they remain for Chesterton an ideal standard, an ordinariness that in Chaucer himself was anything but ordinary: "A man must have a balance of rather extraordinary talents, and even rather extraordinary virtues, in order to seem so ordinary. As they say of St Peter's at Rome, it is so well proportioned that it looks almost small" (35). And again: "Some may hold, but I do not hold, that a man cannot be really original who has this huge appetite for what is normal" (208). All the elements of charity, cordiality, and fraternity in Chaucer's works must have been "normal" medieval notions, "or a man like Chaucer would never have had them. . . . he was not the sort to go digging for abnormal notions" (207). The gospel of normality that Chaucer hands on to the English is not, of course, his own discovery; by definition it must have been derived from what Chesterton calls the *communis sententia,* or common sense, that Chaucer was "pickled" in (236). And yet in Chaucer it has the force of a religious revelation, both ordinary and extraordinary, the poet taking upon himself the status of the mundane in an act that has Chesterton drawing parallels at more than one point with the Incarnation; moreover, like Christ, Chaucer is double-natured, or "duplex" (27, 95). Ultimately there is a complete fusion between individual and context that makes the quest to grant primacy to the one or the other pointless; thus of the "curious primeval kinship between England and Chaucer," Chesterton "do[es] not care whether it was something that England invented and Chaucer glorified; or whether it was something that Chaucer invented and England glorified" (214).[41]

Although Chesterton's study then prompts the question, Is Chaucer English or is England Chaucerian? such a problem raises for the author false notions of cause and effect; Chaucer "is as large as the land and as old as the nation. There is little enough in him of the mystic, in the narrow or special sense; yet it is impossible not to feel something mystical about his magnitude as an emblem of England" (214). This emblematic quality is manifest in Chaucer's response to the very land itself, above all to "a certain spirit of nonsense" harbored by the landscape, as in the name of the "little town" of Bobbe-up-and-doun that the pilgrimage passes through at the start of the "Manciple's Prologue" (IX.1–2; p. 282); England here becomes "Elfland" (and points up the Host's description of Chaucer as "elvyssh," referred to above). It is worth quoting at length from the concluding paragraph to "Chaucer as an Englishman," where Chesterton returns once more to attacking the patronizing attitudes that are his target throughout and offers a visionary climax that is, as far as I am aware, immoderately unique in commentary on Chaucer:

> There is something personal about England. . . . England is a person. And it is very like the very indescribable sort of person this book has to describe. . . . if the country called by the poets Albion could be conceived as a single figure, it would be a giant. And when I think of Chaucer in this primary and general fashion, I do not think of a Court poet receiving a laurel from the King or a flagon from the King's butler, nor even of a stout and genial gentleman with a forked beard setting forth from the Tabard upon the Canterbury road; but of some such elemental and emblematic giant, alive at our beginnings and made out of the very elements of the land. Perhaps if we were caught up by that eagle that whirled away the poet to the gates of The House of Fame, we might begin to see spread out beneath us the titanic outlines of such a pre-historic or primordial Anak or Adam, with our native hills for his bones and our native forests for his beard; and see for an instant a single figure outlined against the sea and a great face staring at the sky. (215–16)[42]

Chaucer is always there, but so immersed in the English fabric that an effort is needed to make him out. In this, Chesterton's book not only makes the greatest claims for Chaucer's significance, but also for the significance of the modern neglect of him, whereas some other discussions of Chaucer's foundational status have a less troubled and indeed progressivist view of history or plug away cozily at the continuity of merrie England. Thus Sir Arthur Quiller-Couch, "gossiping" in 1934: "It has sometimes occurred to me to wonder, when people talk of Chaucer being so racily English, if England be not (in spite of Puritans) the jolly land she is because our literature has kept her so constant to this good fellow's tradition—that the jolliness is actually Chaucer's aura inherited."[43]

If Chesterton's study gives the impression of swimming against the tide of a modern Chaucerian neglect, the fact that the most obviously "Chaucerian" literary work of the twentieth century is, with its author, now itself largely neglected points up the problem of Chaucer's "absence" from our wider culture discussed here and in chapter 2. I am referring to John Masefield's two-part poem *Reynard the Fox,* published in 1919. One of Chesterton's laments was over the increased sundering of the commonalty in modern life, the lack of common enterprise that might bring today's equivalents of the Miller and Clerk together: "The real modern problem is—what pilgrimage have we on which these two different men will ride together? I mean, of course, one on which they will ride together and remain different."[44] It is the type of question that reading the *Canterbury Tales* often prompts commentators to ask. Masefield himself in his 1931 lecture on Chaucer made a rather half-hearted comparison with the varied participants on a modern skiing holiday or Mediterranean cruise,[45] but he is perhaps on more tenable ground in *Reynard the Fox,* where the parallel offered is that of a rural foxhunt. For one thing, this does permit a more varied picture of social class, from the local squire down to the "lads" and ostlers, though, in parallel with Chaucer's "General Prologue," the emphasis remains on a fairly prosperous section of the middle classes, comprising the parson, the doctor, the major, and so forth. And everyone is, moreover, on horseback.

Like the "General Prologue," Masefield's poem starts off at an inn, the "Cock and Pye," where the hunt meets.[46] The dramatis personae are deeply indebted to Chaucer's poem, both in broad conception and individual detail; thus the parson bears unmistakable traces of Chaucer's Monk, though without the satirical intent:

> The parson was a manly one,
> His jolly eyes were bright with fun.
> . . . .
> He kept no Lent to make him meagre,
> He loved his God, himself and man,
> He never said, "Life's wretched span;
> This wicked world," in any sermon.
> . . . .
> His voice was like the tenor bell
> When services were said and sung.

And he had read in many a tongue,
Arabic, Hebrew, Spanish, Greek.

(531–32)

The doctor's son invites comparison with Chaucer's Squire:

Richard, his son, a jolly youth,
Rode with him, fresh from Thomas's,
As merry as a yearling is
In May-time in a clover patch.
He was a gallant chick to hatch,
Big, brown and smiling, blithe and kind
. . . .
To see him when the scrum was packt,
Heave, playing forward, was a sight.
His tackling was the crowd's delight
In many a danger close to goal.

(537–38)

And the master of the hunt occupies the place of Chaucer's Knight:

An old, grave soldier, sweet and kind,
A courtier with a knightly mind,
Who felt whatever thing he thought.
His face was scarred, for he had fought
Five wars for us. Within his face
Courage and power had their place,
Rough energy, decision, force.
He smiled about him from his horse.

(554)

The fact that this assembly is the prologue to a foxhunt, rather than a visit to a shrine, and that extended passages describe things like prowess at rugby might not allay the doubts of those seeking to make adverse comparisons between medieval and modern "community." This is not, moreover, a competition in storytelling, but, with part 2, in being first in at the kill. Certainly the dominant note of Masefield's "Prologue" is one of "sport"; as we see from the above passages, words like "jolly" and "merry" are frequent, and increase in number in the final few portraits that compose the hunt. Thus with Len Stokes the landowner, who "grinned round at men with jolly joy" and whose "clean blood . . . / Ran merry" (543–44); and with Pete Gurney the dairy farmer: "he was a manly English person, / Kind to the core, brave, merry, true" (547), followed by his nephew Ock:

With beer to drink and cheese to eat
And rain in May to fill the grasses,
This life was not a dream that passes
To Ock, but like the summer flower.

(548)

"He loved the English countryside," we are told of Tom Dansey, the whipper-in (551), and this affection is further highlighted throughout the poem.

Unlike the *Canterbury Tales,* there is no internal "Chaucer" figure describing the hunt, but third-person narration. However, one of the principal figures described, the huntsman Robin Dawe, bears some similarity in his traditional English qualities to the type of standard national figure embodied in Chaucer that we have seen feted by Chesterton and others:

His face was of the country mould
Such as the mason sometimes cutted
On English moulding-ends which jutted
Out of the church walls, centuries since.
And as you never know the quince,
How good he is, until you try,
So, in Dawe's face, what met the eye
Was only part; what lay behind
Was English character and mind,
Great kindness, delicate sweet feeling
(Most shy, most clever in concealing
Its depth) for beauty of all sorts,
Great manliness and love of sports,
A grave, wise thoughtfulness and truth,
A merry fun outlasting youth,
A courage terrible to see,
And mercy for his enemy.

(553)

Chaucerian elements are present in the women, too; the parson's wife is richly dressed, "stout" and "full of life," a man-eater like the Wife of Bath (531); the horse trainer's daughter Belle has the Prioress's pity for delicate animals (541); and Chaucer-type expressions invest the sisters Jill and Joan ("they were bright as fresh sweet-peas," 533) and Carrie, the beautiful daughter of the squire ("she was a very golden rose," 535).

It will be clear, I think, that *Reynard the Fox* is pervasively, even exhaustively, "Chaucerian," but it is Chaucer filtered through a narrowing, nationalist perspective. "Merrie England" is the dominant theme of the first part of the poem, and as in Chesterton's fantasy of a Chaucer composed of the very elements of the English landscape, Masefield effects a transposition of Chaucer into the rural shires and downland. The second part of the poem, describing the chase itself, is a celebration of English topography and nomenclature, with the fox's eventual escape traced in detail across the picturesque face of the land:

> The fox swerved left and scrambled out,
> Knocking crinked green shells from the brussels-sprout,
> He scrambled out through the cobbler's paling,
> And up Pill's orchard to Purton's Tailing,
> Across the plough at the top of the bent,
> Through the heaped manure to kill his scent,
> Over to Aldam's, up to Cappell's,
> Past Nursery Lot with its whitewashed apples,
> Past Colston's Broom, past Gaunt's, past Shere's,
> Past Foxwhelps' Oasts with their hooded ears,
> Past Monk's Ash Clerewell, past Beggars' Oak,
> Past the great elms blue with the Hinton smoke.
> Along Long Hinton to Hinton Green,
> Where the wind-washed steeple stood serene
> With its golden bird still sailing air.
> Past Banner Barton, past Chipping Bare,
> Past Maddings Hollow, down Dundry Dip,
> And up Goose Grass to the Sailing Ship.
>
> (578)

In *The Common Reader,* Woolf decried any identification between Chaucer and "the land" in her insistence upon the former's sense of the "uncompromising" and "untamed" spectacle the countryside then was, the fact that it "was no looking-glass for happy faces, or confessor of unhappy souls."[47] In Masefield, however, Chaucer is transposed into a timeless England of rural, and indeed historical, seclusion: even though the poem was published in 1919, there is no reference whatsoever to the First World War. In the following chapter, we shall discuss Chaucer's impact on the work of other modern writers, including those who in one way or another contest his identification with the values of Englishness.

6

Writers' Chaucer

Although most of the material considered thus far has received very little attention from critics and scholars, the same cannot be said about the question of Chaucer's influence on modern canonical writers. In this chapter, we shall review the critical industry that has attempted to establish this influence, an industry headed not so much by Chaucer scholars but by those researching modern literature and anxious to throw up new angles of explication. The subject might seem to promise a corrective to my points hitherto about the limited impact of Chaucer's work outside the academy, yet in many cases in what follows the writerly engagement with Chaucer seems far less substantial than critical ingenuity would have it. And several modern writers seem to have gone to Chaucer on what one might call the Woolfian quest of requiring a rudimentary benchmark that modern sophistication can pride itself in exceeding.

In fact, Harriet Monroe, writing in *Poetry* in 1915, claimed that the twentieth century would witness, for poets at least, Chaucer's passing:

> The urbane Chaucer for five centuries has led the poets his successors: in motive as well as technique they have been mostly of his mind, accepting his aristocratic point of view, his delight in the upper-class pageant, and almost entirely ignoring the burden-bearing poor. But perhaps Langland is like to bridge the centuries and clasp hands with the poets of the future, the prophets of the new era.[1]

For Monroe, Chaucer's inauguration of the iambic measure "opened the way for some of the greatest rhythmists who ever lived—Shakespeare, Spenser, Milton, Coleridge, Shelley, Swinburne and others," but the Whitman-led "impetus toward free verse" that is now bearing such fruit in the early twentieth century represents a return to the rougher music of Langland and his "Old-English predecessors," as witnessed by Pound's version of "The Seafarer" (336–37). This stylistic return signifies for Monroe a new epoch of social reform, as the above quotation indicates, in distinction to a patrician outlook fostered by an "irresistible" Chaucer whose "will" has been done for centuries by his successor poets (335).

With regard to writers associated with *Poetry,* like Pound and Eliot, Monroe was to be disappointed in her political aspirations for the new movement (and in her canvassing of Langland), but certainly their own attack on the native line of English verse represented by the rota of names she gives above does involve some rejection of the "Father of English Poetry." Although Pound's scattered comments on Chaucer do include enthusiastic endorsements of his work, particularly in *ABC of Reading,* where it is hailed as more "compendious" than Dante's or Shakespeare's and drawing on a "wider" European culture,[2] such remarks are offset by more negative appraisals. The measure of condescension implied in his reference to "the leisurely Chaucer," noted in chapter 2—the suggestion of a lack of earnestness or of Chaucer's not being fully the "serious artist"—is emphasized by Pound elsewhere in comparison with Dante: the latter was "positivist on his craft, in this he was a *fabbro,* and one respecting the craft and the worker. Italian poetry would have gained by following his traces, and our own would be less a mess if Chaucer had so closely considered technique instead of uselessly treating the Astrolabe."[3] Such reservations and inconsistencies have perhaps limited Pound's effectiveness as a modern spokesperson for Chaucer, as has the sporadic nature of the engagement with Chaucer shown in Pound's verse itself, where echoes of the former's "exquisite lyrics"—"Merciles Beaute," "The Former Age," "Truth"—are more in evidence than any impact from his major work.[4]

Eliot's response to Chaucer was more occasional than Pound's, though not perhaps sufficiently so to justify Derek Brewer's suggestion that he had "not a scrap of sympathy with or interest in Chaucer."[5] In his 1926 review of Root's edition of *Troilus and Criseyde,* Eliot presents himself as a watchful attender on Chaucer's recent fortunes:

> Within the last ten or fifteen years our attitude towards Chaucer has changed. . . . we are becoming aware that the whole stock

> of critical commonplaces about Chaucer must be reinventoried. . . . those who approach Chaucer in this new spirit recognize that the centre for critical judgment of Chaucer is not the "Prologue" to the *Canterbury Tales* . . . but decidedly *Troilus and Criseyde*.[6]

This switch of interest to *Troilus and Criseyde* recognizes that poem as an orthodox statement of a medieval worldview that "we are learning to take . . . a little more seriously," and in this Chaucer's poem is "a document second in importance, in its kind, only to the *Vita nuova*. It is a pendant to the latter, and the two are perfectly consistent." This consistency lies in what Eliot calls in the Dante essay of 1929 (with reference to the *Vita nuova*) "the Catholic philosophy of disillusion"; that is, not expecting "more from *life* than it can give or more from *human* beings than they can give; [looking] to *death* for what life cannot give."[7] Eliot concludes his review by quoting from lines 1807–24 from the palinode to *Troilus*, lines outlining the hero's vision from his heavenly elevation of "this wrecched world" and of the blind human lust that works within it, a position that Eliot argues is the logical consummation of "the sense of the whole poem."

Eliot congratulates Root for espousing just this interpretation in the introduction to his edition, though Root in fact makes the poem far more festive than does Eliot, recognizing its "full understanding and appreciation of . . . human values" and the fact that Chaucer's "serene Catholic temper . . . could thoroughly enjoy and understand the world, while still recognizing its 'vanity.'"[8] For Eliot, however, the poem's "sobriety and restraint are extreme," not only in the stylistic homogeneity that permits "few brilliant lines [to be] detachable from the weft of the work" but also in its "high dispassionate view" of the place of its protagonists "in a fixed and firm moral order." There is no indication in the review that Eliot finds any humor in the poem; any narratorial ambiguity in the treatment of, for example, Criseyde; any celebration, however qualified, of sexual love; indeed he states explicitly that the poem has no "romantic interest." Although he admits that Chaucer occupies a peculiarly elusive historical position that makes problems for modern readers ("difficult for a Continental because he is an Englishman, and difficult for an Englishman . . . because he belongs naturally and quite locally to the main body of European thought"), there is a sense in the review that

Eliot has Chaucer exactly where he wants him; that is, as representing a univocal Christian orthodoxy in which the tremendous tensions inherent in *Troilus and Criseyde* have been smoothed over, and wherein Chaucer becomes, in Eliot's estimation, an appendage to Dante. By heading his review "Chaucer's *Troilus*," Eliot elides Criseyde at the outset in his preoccupation with the hero's quest for transcendence.

A similarly Dantocentric view is outlined in another Eliot text of 1926, the recently published Clark Lectures delivered at Cambridge. Although Chaucer is hardly mentioned in the course of these, the conclusion to the final lecture features Eliot's "tribute" to him, in the form of his quoting the final stanza of *Troilus and Criseyde,* a stanza that begins, of course, with three lines translated from Dante; moreover, Eliot introduces the quotation with a reference to Chaucer as "that greatest of English poets."[9] This seems an astonishing piece of tokenism in view of Eliot's near-total silence concerning Chaucer elsewhere in his writing, but his adoption of Dante as his primary poetic exemplar, which becomes marked in his career from these lectures onward, occasions here this act of fulsomeness toward a writer who is regarded as Dante's English reflex, and one whose work, for Eliot, seems practically reducible to the ending of *Troilus*. Even in Dante's case Eliot consistently minimizes the diversity of styles and "voices" that goes to make up his work, particularly in the *Divine Comedy,* in his adoption of Dante as a model of "classic" austerity, uniform and unembroidered, and he seems even less willing to do justice to the pluralism of Chaucer's poetry.[10] In the *Canterbury Tales* in particular, as Paul Strohm has argued, a polyvocal ensemble of speakers and literary genres characterizes the capacity of Chaucer's work to "contain unreconciled voices," including voices of various kinds of orthodoxy that have to share their place in a heterogeneous collective with those of dissent.[11] By switching his attention to *Troilus and Criseyde,* Eliot may have felt that he was escaping from this noisy English polyphony into the European Catholic mainstream, but there is very little evidence that this represents a general movement of critical interest, as Eliot claims; indeed, the *Canterbury Tales* remains the supreme object of attention for scholars, writers, and popularizers alike throughout the early part of the century, as we have seen. Eliot's comment seems wishfully prescriptive and as much without foundation as the attempts by some scholars to argue for substantial correspondences between his own work and Chaucer's.[12]

One rehabilitation of the importance of Criseyde that has been seen as a direct response to Eliot's views is found in William Carlos Williams's long poem *Paterson* (1946–58). Gale Schricker has argued that the letter appended to book 2 of the poem and signed "La votre C." (in imitation of Criseyde's letter to Troilus, V.1590–1631) represents Williams's desire to combine in the work the "female" element, which is "empirical" and "related to the concrete world of everyday experiences," and "the male element," which "is abstract, idealistic, thinking beyond the present world to ideas."[13] Schricker argues that this is synonymous with Williams's quest for a poetry bonded in tangible locality and in the realm of the empirical, in a conscious rejection of Eliot's universalizing imperatives, and that Williams's declared admiration for Chaucer is for a poet whose pursuit of ideas always commences with "concrete physical life" and involves a celebration of the "local" (18).[14] Although Williams's scant use of literary allusion in *Paterson* is indeed part of his rejection of Eliot's flight from the local into the ahistorical textual "tradition," the few allusions to Chaucer in *Paterson* do thereby stand out the more, and justify Schricker's argument that Criseyde is "not just an allusion [but] . . . an embodiment of the difficult empirical world that Williams has always courted and felt that Eliot neglected" (23). On the other hand, the idea that the actual form of *Paterson,* with its incorporation of poetic lyric and prose passages, letters, newspaper reports, documents, and so forth, has any meaningful relation to the *Canterbury Tales*'s combination of poetry and prose is surely fanciful, even if encouraged by Williams's own declared approval of the prose-poetry mix in the *Tales.*[15] It is true that Williams prefaces one prose "report" in the poem with reference to the Host's words to Chaucer, "Thy drasty ryming is nat worth a toord!" (VII.930), adding "and Chaucer seemed to think so too for he stopped and went on in prose,"[16] but the fact that *Paterson* attributes this interruption to the character of "Sir Thopas" rather than to the Host underlines the moment as a tenuous piece of opportunism in Williams's poem.[17] Williams does perhaps appreciate rather the self-mocking elements in the Chaucerian persona, in keeping with the several instances in *Paterson* where the poem adopts a somewhat wry perspective on its own procedure and performance.

One figure whose work provides a more powerful analogy with the mixed form of the *Canterbury Tales* is James Joyce, a writer who more than any other in the modern period has been discussed in terms of a Chaucer connection. Dolores Palomo, for example, in pairing the two writers as "medieval alpha and modern omega," has argued that the "diversity of genres, voices, and styles" we find in Chaucer is reflected significantly in *Ulysses* and that both writers specialize in juxtaposing "contrasting tones and perspectives to achieve ironical and hence critical effects."[18] These common "permutations of narrative voice" (24) have been examined at greater length by Helen Cooper, who sees Joyce and Chaucer as comparable under three main headings: "naturalism, the play of styles, the use of privileged texts"; the latter's

> refusal to privilege one genre, one reading of the world, above another, sets him in something of the same position in relation to his work as Joyce: the artist as God paring his fingernails. Joyce famously, and Chaucer notoriously, are absent from their works as authoritative voices guiding their readers towards predetermined moral ends.[19]

Both authors' response to the range of Christian and classical texts that their work makes repeated use of and reference to is thus one of undermining any authoritative status such texts may claim, exposing them as "fallible narration" within a play of mixed discourse (151). In maintaining this position, Cooper reflects a good deal of critical writing in recent years concerned to argue for a "postmodernist" Chaucer, and one skeptical of the orthodoxies that such as Eliot claimed for him.[20] The argument is pushed rather too far in Cooper's suggestion that an interest in sheer contingency is as apparent in Chaucer as in Joyce in the absence of moral absolutes: to say that "the Oxford of the 'Miller's Tale' is . . . almost as fully realized as Joyce's Dublin" is utter extravagance,[21] while Bloom's wanderings through the city compose a journey theme very different from that of the Canterbury pilgrimage in their rich harvest of picaresque and "apparently casual" incident (143). Nor is there much mileage in comparing Bloom with "the pilgrim Chaucer," as Cooper does (153); indeed, the emphasis on the privatized nature of multifarious experience in *Ulysses* as opposed to the social collectivity of the *Tales* is a major difference between the two texts, and as we saw in the previous chapter, a nostalgia for Chaucerian community frequently goes hand in hand with the sense of an isolation felt to be peculiarly modern.

Distinctions between the public and the private also have to be drawn in considering a more specific Chaucer-Joyce parallel; that is, that between Molly Bloom's concluding monologue in *Ulysses* and the "Wife of Bath's Prologue." As Cooper notes, the two speakers are united by a similar egotism, freedom from moral censors, and unrestrained sexuality (149); there is also the constant justification of the instinctual drive as a divinely sent "instrument": as Molly puts it, "thats what a woman is supposed to be there for or He wouldnt have made us the way He did so attractive to men."[22] Other critics have gone further than this in arguing that the two figures constitute a "recurring archetypal character" defined in opposition to a "decadent, male-dominated, Roman Catholic society," and one evoking in her male authors fear and sympathy in equal measure.[23] John Lammers also argues that both women practice an uninhibited sexuality "in order to survive in male-governed societies" (496), however much this might lead them to adopt the ruthless characteristics of such societies; the fruits of this behavior for Molly, however, seem rather less certain than for the Wife. Any success resulting from her interest in the young clerk Stephen is left deliberately uncertain at the end of the novel, as opposed to the Wife of Bath's achieved satisfaction with and dominance over Jankyn; moreover, the Wife's independent status as businesswoman and her continuing quest for pliable partners contrast with Molly's precarious liaison with Boylan, given that her soliloquy leaves us with the sense that the "mastery" remains his rather than hers. In noting these differences, Lammers remarks on the fact that Molly "has no chance to tell her opinion publicly" (499), and once more the sense of an insecure private status, compared with the public presence of Chaucer's pilgrims, marks many of those moderns who have a tale to tell. This is the case with what is arguably the most familiar neo-Chaucerian modern genre, the "professional" or vocational tale itself, as in Margaret Atwood's *The Handmaid's Tale,* considered later in this chapter. Rather than tales told out of a communal stock to a communal audience, as in Chaucer, such works are often autobiographical confessions, life stories that in various ways tell of displacement from community. Such considerations would lead us to modify Lammers's suggestion that Molly's frailty and lack of public voice in comparison with the Wife are a specific index of the deterioration of morals and morale characterizing early-twentieth-century Ireland (499-500), and to argue that they have a more general application (see chapter 10).[24]

The Molly–Wife of Bath connection has been noted by many other critics,[25] but beyond this the titles of some of the pieces we have mentioned, "Alpha and Omega . . . " and "Chaucer and Joyce," for example, suggest a parallel viewed in terms of broad correspondence rather than detailed influence. Joyce's actual study of Chaucer seems to have been quite limited, though the two writers have features enough in common to permit the kind of suggestive comparison that Cooper's article in particular makes.[26] With other writers we are left with a more fragmentary linkage, often limited to individual texts, though there are cases where parallels with Chaucer, if not overarching, can be seen as recurrent. One such case is Henry James: over the last decade or so critics have been ever busier in revealing the bonds between these "surprising bedfellows," to use Elizabeth Steele's phrase.[27] Indeed, W. R. Martin and Warren Ober have claimed that James's very first piece of published fiction, "A Tragedy of Error" (1864),[28] is actuated by "a deliberate policy of what might be called subversion," the text subverted being Chaucer's "Franklin's Tale."[29] By calling the ship on which the returning husband is brought home the "Armorique," James lays down a clue—via a reference to the opening line of the "Franklin's Tale," "In Armorik, that called is Britayne" (V.729)—to a whole network of correspondences that unfold between the two texts. These include, as Martin and Ober argue, the absent husband, the other man, the presence of rocks at sea, the reference to the woman's suicide, "the green retreat or garden," and the northern French location (57). The authors argue that the "subversion" of Chaucer's tale lies in the lack of honor that James makes central; here the woman and her lover unsuccessfully try to murder the returning husband, and the atmosphere of deceit, brutality, and betrayal counters the emphasis in Chaucer's tale of everyone doing right by each other. In this, James not only produces a clever *jeu d'esprit* but is also making the point that the lack of idealism in his tale is "closer to life" (58).

James's clues to Chaucer's text are treated concisely and with discretion by Martin and Ober, in spite of their rather lame conclusions, which we shall return to, but their criticism-as-detection approach is open to abuse, as we see in the cases of Steele and Adeline Tintner. Both these critics see James as inviting his readers down an elaborate path of Chaucerian mystery-solving: in the words of the former, any reader who relishes "turning detective" will find many "small leads" in James's novel *The American* (1877) that will end in unmasking that work as "a re-arrangement . . . of Chaucer's *Troilus and Criseyde*."[30] While the general parallel between the two texts is, in Steele's phrase, "thought-provoking" (139)—a woman, characterized several times in terms reminiscent of

Chaucer's tag for Criseyde as "slydynge of corage" (V.825), eventually succumbs to family authority and deserts her faithful lover—the detailed correspondence Steele tries to build up rests for the most part on the flimsiest of evidence.[31] For one thing, there is no real Pandarus figure in the novel, in spite of Steele's attempts to distribute the characteristics of such a figure around the various protagonists in a process she calls "splitting"; the whole point, indeed, about Newman's courtship is its self-reliance and the contrast between his American practicality and self-belief and the curious and involved reserve of the French family circles he enters. In spite of the emphases on Newman's constancy and nobility, and on his experiencing the "happiness . . . identical with pain" of unresolved love,[32] he is clearly no Troilus figure, neither in personality nor destiny, and he clings utterly to a belief in earthly fulfillment and to his own powers of achieving it. At one point he imagines an ascent akin to that of Troilus at the end of Chaucer's poem, though his view of the earthly scene is very different: "If he could have looked down at the scene, invisible, from a hole in the roof, he would have enjoyed it quite as much. It would have spoken to him about his own prosperity and deepened that easy feeling about life to which, sooner or later, he made all experience contribute. Just now the cup seemed full" (213). It is true that these easy feelings receive a setback in the eventual loss of Madame de Cintré, but the novel ends with the restoration of Newman's good nature (344), not with a Troilus-like quest for transcendence, as Steele claims (138). It is Madame de Cintré, having retired to the Carmelite convent, who is left maintaining "the vanity of earthly desires" (308), but James makes it quite clear throughout the novel, as well as in the author's preface, that it is Newman's view of the world that interests him, almost exclusively.[33]

Adeline Tintner, an acknowledged influence on Steele,[34] organizes not an "unmasking" of James's work, but, to use her own metaphor, a "literary treasure hunt" (with "many clues on the way"), this time through the pages of James's story "Daisy Miller" (1878). Here the treasure in question is the key to that text in the form of Chaucer's *Legend of Good Women,* more particularly the "daisy theme" in its "Prologue."[35] Not only is Daisy a "martyr" to her love for Winterbourne, but she is no less than the tenth martyr following on from the nine Chaucer treats in the *Legend;* we can uncover this number from such evidence as "at the tenth mention of the word 'innocent'" in the story Daisy is reported as seated under the Velázquez portrait of Innocent X in the Doria Palace.[36] Although Tintner is able to support the martyrdom theme by reference to episodes like that in the Colosseum, where Daisy compares herself to one of the Christian martyrs being faced by the "tiger" of Winterbourne, her argument effaces the elusive qualities attaching to Daisy in its crude judgmental certainties: "she is deeply and seriously in love and is basically too shy to make this love clear" (20). Tintner is also convinced of the derivation of Daisy's proper Christian name, Annie, seeing in this another Jamesian "clue" to his Chaucerian source, in the dedication of the *Legend* to Anne of Bohemia (14; see the "Prologue," F version, lines 496–97). One is surprised after all this to find Tintner offering no suggestion as to the Chaucerian origin of Annie's middle initial, "P."

Between Chaucer scholars anxious to claim an abiding modern status for their object of study and scholars of modern literature anxious to find new interpretations of overworked texts and pressing suggestive parallels to excess, the claims for influence are likely to become inflated, if sometimes entertainingly so. There is also the danger of a certain condescension toward Chaucer in the hands of some modern critics; for example, in Martin and Ober's conclusion that the duplicity in "A Tragedy of Error" is "closer to life," a belief that depends in part on taking what they call the "openness" of Chaucer's tale on trust. Many commentators would rather see in the "Franklin's Tale" a critical exposure of patriarchal ideas of "trouthe," whereby a woman is clandestinely shuttled between men striving to outbid each other in terms of chivalric "gentillesse." However, the basic parallel that Martin and Ober suggest is intriguing, not least because it surfaces again in connection with a work that has not been seen, as far as I know, in a Chaucerian light, James's novel *The Spoils of Poynton* (1897). Here it is the young man, Owen Gereth, who is forced by the heroine Fleda Vetch to live up to a code of honor that involves him in keeping "troth" to another woman, against the interests of both himself and Fleda; as the latter tells him from out of her emotional tumult, in terms very reminiscent of lines 1478–80 of the "Franklin's Tale," "You mustn't break faith. Anything's better than that. . . . The great thing is to keep faith. Where's a man if he doesn't?"[37] Moreover, Fleda's insistence that she is prescribing Owen's conduct out of a concern for him, rather than for Mona—"I'm thinking of his honour and his good name" (111)—echoes the male claims throughout the "Franklin's Tale" that it is Dorigen's status and reputation that is uppermost in the minds of the men who would keep her to her promise (see V.1331, 1477, 1527–28). Once more, however, within this novel that treats of an exacting and self-punishing system of honor we see what Martin and Ober call "subversion," though that system is questioned in a different way from that in "A Tragedy of Error." Everything again goes disastrously wrong rather than coming out right; Mona does not act as "freely" as the other two, and by insisting on Owen's honoring his troth condemns them to misery, and the "spoils" themselves go up in smoke at the end of the novel. We also have the interesting gender reversal whereby the weakness at the core of Owen (166) is manipulated by the three women, Fleda, Mona, and his mother, who, paralleling the three male protagonists of Chaucer's tale, pass their victim around from one to another throughout the course of the novel.

What has happened in this case is that the seeming harmony of Chaucer's ending has become unraveled, and a similar process emerges if we compare another neo-Chaucerian text with its predecessor, namely D. H. Lawrence's novella *The Fox* (1922) and the "Nun's Priest's Tale." The comparison has been the subject of an interesting article by Marijane Osborn, who begins by admitting the scant reference to Chaucer throughout Lawrence's career,[38] but who then finds intriguing parallels, including March's predictive dream of the fox who will later seize her (in the person of Henry), as well as similarities of location.[39] In this case, however, the fox escapes with his capture (and kills another cock, in the person of Banford, in the process),[40] though as Osborn points out, the sense of his final victory, at the end of the novella, is not completely certain. Here, March is still trying to resist the pressure Henry has exerted throughout to "close her eyes . . . and give in to him";[41] whereas Chauntecleer did "his eyen cloos" (VII.3332) but later escapes through his own wits, March is battling against a submission that yet seems inevitable, with "sleep weighing . . . unconscious" on her eyelids (71).

Whatever the eventual outcome, Osborn regards Lawrence's treatment of Chaucer not as subversion but as inversion: "The fable is being restructured to offer a shockingly inverted conclusion for a moral allegory, one in which evil intention wins"; she then talks about this as a "realistic" conclusion, as if, like Martin and Ober, she regards Chaucer's original as innocently idealistic.[42] It is true that several analogous works we have looked at thus far have the effect of dismantling the Chaucerian closure, as if updating the original narrative for a more fragmentary and uncertain modernity. Another commentator who has discussed the relevance of the "Nun's Priest's Tale" to Lawrence, Milton Miller, sees in the comparison between Chauntecleer and the cock of the novella *The Man Who Died* (1929) the difference between an acceptance of communal life and a thirst for aloneness "that precludes any real social fulfilment."[43] These modern retellings harbor what is arguably a patronizing stance toward their originals, even to the extent of not bothering to acknowledge Chaucer as that original; a fashion indeed among modern writers to "do a Lollius" on him, as it were.

A modern Chaucerian analogue that brings together some of the themes discussed thus far in this chapter is F. Scott Fitzgerald's *The Great Gatsby* (1925). Several of the correspondences this shows with *Troilus and Criseyde* have long been recognized, though they take on a deeper significance, I would argue, in the context of other works referred to above. F. T. Flahiff, in calling attention to *Troilus* as "the true source" of Fitzgerald's design (and to Fitzgerald's acquaintance with R. K. Root, *Troilus*'s editor), notes his "playful furtiveness" as the "most tactful and evasive of artists" in not acknowledging that source, actually paralleling this with "Chaucer's creation of his pseudo-source, Lollius"; as we have seen, however, this is representative of a more general omission.[44] *The Great Gatsby* recalls Chaucer's text far more than does, say, James's *The American:* here we have the recognizable similarity of a fiercely idealistic lover subjected to betrayal, and, as Nancy Hoffman has shown, a scene like that of Daisy's invitation to tea at Gatsby's mansion in chapter 5 of the novel intriguingly echoes Criseyde's fateful visit to Pandarus's house in book III of the poem. We have the two brought together by a Pandarus-narrator figure in the person of Nick Carraway, Daisy's cousin (rather than uncle), while the liaison takes place during a period of heavy rain, and Gatsby's nervousness, and Nick's impatience with it, bear some resemblance to Pandarus's treatment of Troilus.[45]

Hoffman also discusses the comparability between the idealism of Troilus and Gatsby, where the sense in both cases is of a love that has enveloped its earthly object in a quest for the eternal. Nick talks of the "colossal vitality" of Gatsby's passion for Daisy as an "illusion . . . [that] had gone beyond her, beyond everything," and of how he had "forever wed his unutterable visions to her perishable breath."[46] Similarly, Troilus's love for Criseyde is represented throughout Chaucer's poem as the uncertain apprehension of a transcendental force, the "Love, that of erthe and se hath governaunce" (III.1744), which in Boethian terms is dimly refracted to Troilus through his lover but again goes far beyond her. But we must note the contrast between the conclusion of Chaucer's poem, where Troilus discovers (or at least approaches) the true source of "pleyn felicite" (V.1818) that had been the concealed end of his love all along, and the fact that *Gatsby* is ruthlessly shorn of any palinode. The close of the novel is a lament for those dreams of fulfillment that are ever illusory, ever recurring, a dissipation of the Chaucerian finale in terms of an unending modern absence: "So we beat on, boats against the current, borne back ceaselessly into the past" (188).[47]

The prime instance of the undoing of the Chaucerian ending, however, is arguably Margaret Atwood's *The Handmaid's Tale* of 1986, a novel that informs us that Chaucer's name will still be celebrated in the year 2195. "Celebrated" needs perhaps to be understood ironically; the "conference proceedings" from that year appended to the novel show how the unnamed woman's memoir has suffered an act of male academic appropriation and jokery even down to the motive behind the title it now carries:

> Strictly speaking, it was not a manuscript at all when first discovered, and bore no title. The superscription "The Handmaid's Tale" was appended to it by Professor Wade, partly in homage to the great Geoffrey Chaucer; but those of you who know Professor Wade informally, as I do, will understand when I say that I am sure all puns were intentional, particularly that having to do with the archaic vulgar signification of the word *tail;* that being, to some extent, the bone, as it were, of contention, in that phase of Gileadean society of which our saga treats. *(Laughter, applause.)*[48]

Of course, the punning as well as the title have been learned from Chaucer, who exploits this vulgar signification of the word "taille" in the "Shipman's Tale" (VII.416). That Atwood's novel itself is not exactly an act of homage to the "great" poet is seen in its resistance to the text it most obviously evokes, the "Clerk's Tale." Like Griselda, Atwood's heroine has been subjected to a system of ruthless male power and ownership, with her little daughter forcibly taken away; the system is upheld by neomedieval gender roles, drummed into its subjects at things like the "Women's Prayvaganzas":

> The Commander continues with the service . . .
>
> "Let the women learn in silence with *all* subjection." Here he looks us over. "All," he repeats.
>
> "But I suffer not a woman to teach, nor to usurp authority over the man, but to be in silence.
>
> "For Adam was first formed, then Eve . . ." (233)

Although Chaucer's tale can hardly be said to acquiesce in the justice of Walter's behavior toward Griselda, which is directly criticized by the Clerk as he narrates it, the tale itself ends with the reincorporation of the woman into a marriage that has fiercely victimized her, whereas Atwood's novel not only lets the heroine tell her own tale but ends with her eluding a tyrannical patriarchy. The nature of this elusion is admittedly unclear, and in this sense the novel offers no "happy" conclusion, Chaucerian or otherwise; indeed, its open-ended uncertainty is characteristic of many modern analogues, as we have seen. As Professor Pieixoto's concluding lecture states, she may have escaped, she may have been recaptured "or even executed" (324). But one thing she does escape is ultimate ownership by the male historical record: as Pieixoto ruefully admits, after outlining his success in identifying some of the men in the Handmaid's story, "when we turn to look at her we glimpse her only for a moment, before she slips from our grasp and flees" (324). Here her very anonymity preserves a private identity and the integrity of a voice free from academic capture.

Another recent novel that bears an interesting relation to the "Clerk's Tale" is Alice Walker's *The Color Purple* (1983). Here the correspondences have been traced in some detail by Deborah Ellis, who documents the common situation of the oppressed woman, deprived of her children by the father and then having to accommodate her husband's new partner in her home (Griselda's own daughter and Shug Avery, respectively).[49] Indeed, Ellis sees Celie as a "clinical case in Griseldian behaviour" (193); like the protagonist of Atwood's novel, however, she is endowed with her own voice and finally manages to surmount such behavior, though in a far more positive and unproblematic way. The tyranny of the male partner is overthrown with the assistance of Shug herself, especially in that part of the novel where Celie is installed in Shug's house in Memphis and achieves independence through the "Folkspants" business she sets up.[50] As Ellis says, domesticity "liberates Celie because she redefines it in woman's terms," whereas Griselda always "accepts it completely in man's terms."[51] In outlining this contrast, Ellis again shows a tendency to use the Chaucerian text, and Griselda's passivity within it, a little unthinkingly and solely as a foil to Celie's liberation, and she does not explore any of the suggestions of Griselda's empowerment that critics like Elaine Hansen have recently advanced.[52] She does, however, recognize that the reconciliation ending of *The Color Purple,* with even Mr. —— welcomed back into Celie's reformed domestic ethos ("just after I say Naw, I still don't like frogs, but let's us be friends"),[53] contrasts with the ongoing "marriage debate" in the *Tales.*[54] Even if individual tales may often end on a seeming note of reconciliation, the Canterbury links remain particularly the site of that "ultimate irreconcilability of . . . voices" that Strohm analyzes and that many modern writers and commentators, in positing a placid Chaucerian unity, overlook.[55]

The tale of Chaucer's for which criticism has claimed the greatest number of modern analogues is, however, a story concerned with men rather than women, the "Pardoner's Tale." Some of these can be quite straightforward retellings, as in Jack London's short story "Just Meat" (1911), where two thieves who make off with a hoard of jewelry after murdering a third man then poison each other in the lodging house where they hole up with their loot: one gets strychnine in his coffee, the other in his beefsteak in the meal they jointly prepare.[56] The title of the story comes from the bleak views on death one of the men advances: "Did you ever see a man two weeks dead? . . . Well I have. He was like this beefsteak you an' me is eatin'. It was once steer cavortin' over the landscape. But now it's just meat. That's all, just meat. An' that's what you an' me an' all people come to—meat."[57] Here the correspondence with Chaucer informs a tale of roughneck males with equally hard-bitten views on existence, and it is perhaps no coincidence that the "Pardoner's Tale" turns up again as a source for the feud between two rival lumber camps in Dave Godfrey's story of the Canadian outback, "River Two Blind Jacks" (1961), where the theme of mutual betrayal closely parallels the fate of Chaucer's "riotoures."[58]

The "Pardoner's Tale" itself, however, is far more than simply a story of male brawling, a kind of "Showdown at Death Tree." It is sited, for example, in a complicated narrative context in which the Pardoner uses the tale for fraudulent purposes, and a sustained religious symbolism underlies its action; thus the desire of the rioters to "sleen Deeth" and their request for "breed and wyn" to be brought from the town

(VI.699, 797) establish their actions as a travesty of the divine office and of the sacraments. Some of this more complex significance is understood in the best known of the modern analogues (and recognized as such shortly after its publication), Rudyard Kipling's story "The King's Ankus," from *The Second Jungle Book* (1895).[59] D. Maureen Thum's detailed article argues that the close of the story, with the three men lying dead around their meal of "unleavened bread," does, like the Chaucer tale, play off a postlapsarian "cult of matter" against "religious allusions which suggest quite a different view of reality."[60] Thum also argues that the "frame" of the "Pardoner's Tale," the performance of the Pardoner himself, which invites criticism of the "pervasive commodification of spirituality . . . found throughout the late medieval Church" (267), raises issues also addressed in Kipling's story, with its critique of socioreligious corruption from the standpoint of Mowgli's "unfallen" jungle world.[61]

The frame of the "Pardoner's Tale" is also the main focus in Wolfgang Rudat's use of Chaucer to explicate the final scene in Hemingway's novel *The Sun Also Rises* (1926). The narrator, Jake Barnes, has been sexually disabled through injury sustained in the First World War, and in the finale to the novel undergoes what Rudat terms a "catharsis" akin to that experienced by the "eunuch" Pardoner.[62] In each case the protagonist is brought to realize the full extent of his disablement through an adversarial encounter: in Chaucer with the Host and in the novel with Brett, who forces Barnes into a recognition that his disguised sexual foreplay with her, which it is impossible for him to fulfill, is thereby illicit. She thus "paves for Jake the way to a spiritual-psychological rehabilitation" (53). Once again, however, the effect of employing the parallel with Chaucer is to smooth over the voices of dissension in Chaucer's own text in reading it in terms of an amicable closure: "In his cathartic encounter with the Host, the Pardoner grasps the truth about himself. He comes to realize that he is both physically and spiritually isolated from humanity . . . the Pardoner has to have this catharsis first before he can be reintegrated into humanity." The sign of this reintegration is what Rudat calls the "redemptive kiss" bestowed on the Pardoner by the Host (51).

Rudat's confident categorization of the Pardoner's physical state as a "eunuch," only lacking that which otherwise would allow for a reconciliation with the (heterosexual) norm, flies in the face of several recent responses claiming the Pardoner for a homosexual politics, as in Allen Barnett's story "Philostorgy, Now Obscure," where a man suffering from

AIDS represents the Pardoner as forebear, "the first angry homosexual . . . the first camp sensibility in English literature."[63] I owe this reference to Steven Kruger, who indeed wishes to keep the Pardoner "unintegrated" as a figure constantly challenging, on behalf of gay men and women, the heterosexual norm represented by the Host's homophobic assault and the anxieties underlying it: "The very act of containing the Pardoner—the verbal violence that needs to be done to silence him—reveals the violent force needed to contain the queer; it simultaneously reveals the force, the effort needed to construct and maintain the dominance of what Harry Bailly represents."[64] For Kruger, the "Pardoner's Tale" itself is not about "real men," as Jack London might have seen it, with their drinking, swearing, and murdering, but offers in various ways the Pardoner's "parody of heterosexuality," the Host's violent reaction to which betrays the homophobic anxiety of both the poet and his culture (131).

What conclusions might we draw at this stage about the "presence" of Chaucer in the works of modern writers? I shall return to this question in my final chapter, where further examples will be discussed, but given that I have here referred to much though not all of the critical work that has attempted to establish that presence, one might conclude that the yield is fairly thin: after all, to take the case of Chaucer's "rival" Dante, entire books have been devoted to topics like Eliot and Dante, Pound and Dante, Joyce and Dante, and so forth.[65] We have seen criticism that ranges from a general paralleling of oeuvre and outlook to an examination of specific texts, sometimes in unconvincingly intricate detail, but in no case at a length beyond that of the self-contained article or chapter, and we are left perhaps with the sense that the modern impact of Chaucer is a scattered and somewhat random affair.[66] On the other hand, a recent article by Velma Richmond on Chaucer and Muriel Spark ends with a much higher bid for him than this:

> Similarities to Chaucer could also be noted in the fiction of Evelyn Waugh, Graham Greene, Flannery O'Connor, and other Catholic novelists. Each is distinctive, but all create a fictional world in which the grotesque, the absurd, the aberrant, are cast against belief in the divine, in a transcendent world that is not described in conventional religious lyricism with its outpouring of feeling but as a skeptical view of this world, a satiric showing

> of human failing. This is possible because of a deep religiosity, an ultimate perception, the nothing of contemplation that mystics describe. It is a perceiving that God is all that matters.[67]

Whether we can really apply this final sentence to Chaucer is a moot point, but the earlier part of Richmond's argument encourages the inference that any writing setting the mixed character of the human world against an apprehension of the next has its counterpart in Chaucer. The difficulties of making this position into more than a truism are nevertheless shown in the body of the article itself, where Chaucer and Muriel Spark can only be brought together on the most general of grounds. However, one could generalize further: as the "founder" of the modern novel, as critics from earlier chapters in this study like Kittredge and Chesterton would have it, and as the "inventor" of a whole range of things from English scientific prose to the iambic pentameter, as Pearsall declares,[68] an act of Chaucerian homage is implied practically every time any modern writer sits down to work. Even those texts like *The Handmaid's Tale* that might be seen as having an oppositional relationship to Chaucer are thus enabled by him.[69] In this sense Chaucer is, like the air we breathe, essential, diffuse, and taken for granted; omnipresent and often invisible.

7

Translated Chaucer

Translations of Chaucer constitute, of course, one of the main channels for the wider dissemination of his work outside the academy, though the fact that no major authors in the twentieth century have put their hand to translating that work arguably signals once more the rather limited engagement with Chaucer that characterizes modern literature. In earlier periods poets like Dryden, Pope, Wordsworth, and Elizabeth Barrett Browning all produced modernizations, whereas more recently Chaucer translation has been left in the hands of writers with negligible reputations as poets, like Nevill Coghill, Frank Ernest Hill, and David Wright. This lack of reputation has perhaps intensified the scorn (or outright neglect) that has often greeted such translations from within the academy and elsewhere, as in the notoriously acid *Listener* review of Coghill: "Where Dryden and Wordsworth trod, should he not venture? Why not? Always remembering that they are poets . . . and that Mr Coghill . . . emphatically is not."[1]

Indeed, the whole subject of Chaucer translation is a contentious one, raising among other issues the fraught relationship between the more "popular" Chaucer and the Chaucer of academic study that my final chapter in particular considers. Defenders of the practice will argue for the difficulty of Middle English and the fact that the resources needed to master it are unavailable to the many, even though a widespread pretense remains that modern readers can master Chaucer's language with only a "casual amount of study," in Hill's phrase: "convinced that Chaucer is too English to approach as a foreign poet," Hill continues, we collude in denying him the means of translation whereby he might escape remaining "but half-appreciated as a native one."[2] The introduction to Hill's translation, written in 1930, is entitled "The Unknown Poet" and argues for translation, however (inevitably) inadequate, as a means of redressing the modern neglect of Chaucer discussed at several points in this study. Hill is mercifully not disingenuous enough to claim his version as a mere stepping-stone back to the original Chaucerian text, as many translators are; his forthrightness in wanting his translation to be "first of all a modern English poem" (xviii) signals indeed some modest success in this endeavor, as we shall argue. Derek Pearsall has noted that "people who read translations of Chaucer very rarely move on to the original," and certainly translators should be honest about their intended audience: you cannot at the same time write for those unable to read Chaucer's original text while claiming to find fresh generations of readers for it.[3] The concluding remark in the introduction to David Wright's verse translation, that it is offered as "an introductory prolusion to the real thing," reads, after the time he spends detailing the difficulties of the "real thing," as the mere formula of appeasement.[4]

Pearsall has put the case very strongly against Chaucer translation *tout court* in his review of Wright:

> Translation does not act as a transition in the way that Wright suggests, and the better the translation the less likely it is to do so. . . . the difficulties of reading [Chaucer] should not be minimized (in fact, to be proper, they should be maximized), but a moderate amount of effort and concentration and sensible use of a good glossary reap immediate rewards. Every line read in the original contributes to an advance in understanding; every line read in translation seals off Chaucer and his English more finally. (200)

Not only is such translation unnecessary, it provides a substitute for Chaucer rather than a bridge to him, and effectively ousts him from the nest, thus setting the seal on Chaucer's neglect rather than remedying it, as Hill claimed.

Whether or not Chaucer translations are necessary, and whether they do lead (some) readers to Chaucer who would otherwise not make the journey, one thing is certain: like wars and taxes they are inevitable, and in the face of this, to quote Chaucer's Theseus, "whoso gruccheth ought, he dooth folye" (I.3045). A good translation of Chaucer or of anyone else is a matter for celebration, part, after all, of the endless textual adventure that constitutes literature, though Pearsall might take some comfort from the fact that the vast majority of modern Chaucer translations are decidedly disappointing. Any reader sufficiently satisfied with them to seek no further is no great loss to a genuine Chaucerian readership. There are, however, degrees of perniciousness: translations that offer themselves as no more than a crib to Chaucer, often in parallel text or some sort of interlinear arrangement, might be cumbersome to use and open to abuse by lazy students, but at least declare themselves explicitly to be no more than an access to the "real thing"; while genuine re-creations that achieve the status of "a modern English poem," in Hill's phrase, need no further justification, although in my opinion only Coghill's version can make such a claim. The danger lies with all those versions that lie between these poles, particularly in those cases where a failure of transmutation means that Chaucer remains stranded halfway between his own language and ours, to result in a ghastly mishmash of Middle and modern English. As the *TLS* reviewer of Hill remarked, "What in all poetry can be more dead than an antiquated modernization?"[5]

The fact is, of course, that translating Chaucer is an enormously difficult enterprise, and arguably presents greater challenges than those facing translators working from foreign languages. The fact that many lines from Chaucer will "go" into modern English with only slight modification, whereas others will not, inevitably leads to the treacherous ground of part translation, where root-and-branch renewal is often a more productive option. Moreover, those slight modifications can often be enormously telling; take for example Arcite's famous line on the solitude of the grave in his final lament, "Allone, withouten any compaignye" (I.2779). The need to substitute "withouten" while preserving the meter inevitably impairs the stark simplicity of Arcite's line, and Coghill, for example, can do no more than repeat Hill's "Alone, alone, with none for company!"—where the repetition (always a ready but dangerous device for translators trying to fill gaps left by Chaucer's inflections) threatens to dilute rather than enforce the melancholy.[6] Wright, in a bid to avoid this, has "Alone, and with no kind of company!" (70), a line harshly but not unjustly treated by Pearsall in his review (201). If we add to these difficulties the fact that translators of Chaucer will have a far greater number of silent observers looking over their shoulders as they work and claiming a competence in modern and Middle English, then the problems appear formidable indeed.

In earlier periods, when we can accept that there was far greater agreement that Chaucer was, in Dryden's words, a "rough diamond," who "must first be polish'd e'er he shines,"[7] translators could go in for the uninhibited modernization that became unacceptable during the course of the nineteenth century, a period synonymous with the painstaking retrieval of an original Chaucerian text rather than with offering modern substitutes. Once this process had been largely accomplished, however, modernization could start again in earnest, and the Edwardian period offers evidence of this in the work of Skeat, Percy Mackaye, and Arthur Burrell, as well as the special category of children's versions discussed in chapter 4. Skeat is a particularly interesting example of the type of diluted modernization that leaves Chaucer uneasily stranded between past and present; in 1904 he began a series of contributions to the King's Classics imprint with a three-volume selection of various tales, all announcing themselves as "done into modern English." In these versions, Skeat claims that "not only obsolete words but obsolete idioms and modes of expression have been excluded," yet the text itself hardly bears this out, as in the following passage from the opening of the "Nun's Priest's Tale":

> By husbandry of such as God her sent,
> She found herself, and eke her daughters twain.
> Three well-grown sows she had, and yet again
> Three cows, and eke a sheep whose name was Mall.
> Full sooty was her bower, and eke her hall,
> In which she ate full many a slender meal.
> Of pungent sauce she needed not a deal.[8]

Although there is some modernization of spelling and diction here, this hardly amounts to anything we can call a modern translation. The unmodern syntax of the first line simply reproducing the original; the occurrence of "eke," "twain," "bower," the "full sooty . . . full many" phrasing; and the construction of the last line (again simply aping Chaucer) all point to the evasion of the challenge to find equivalents for obsolete expressions. The meaning of the original has, of course, been clarified for the modern reader, but one might argue (charitably) that Skeat is simply too wedded to the original text to "do" it into modern English in the way he claims; a virtue in an editor but not in a translator.

One might argue (uncharitably) that he has simply been lazy; after all, one of the greatest challenges facing any translator in verse is not the conversion of more ornate passages but that of simple, repetitive, and stubborn monosyllables (indeed like "eke"), where to preserve the meter the entire arrangement of lines has sometimes to be recast. Throughout his versions, Skeat shies away from doing this, and the result is that Chaucer is half-naturalized to modern eyes, becoming (the translator's sin of sins) "quaint," with all the dire implications this word has for Chaucer's modern standing.

As Hill noted, Skeat's versions "failed to establish themselves."[9] Skeat kept to the more formal tales, where archaic diction and construction might be justified as more "suitable" (his "Knight's Tale" opens with the line "Whilom, as olden tales record for us,"[10] and never touches the fabliaux; he even edited other tales of possible improprieties [lines 3177–78 of the "Nun's Priest's Tale," where Chauntecleer "feathers" and "treads" Pertelote, are omitted in his version, as are the declamations of the "Pardoner's Tale" in lines 505–660]). The whole enterprise is marked with a caution that seems regrettable, perhaps, until one turns to versions that, while showing failings similar to Skeat's, throw caution to the wind.[11]

A signal and sorry example here is J. U. Nicolson's *Canterbury Tales: Rendered into Modern English,* first published in 1934. This is a "modern" English liberally sprinkled with terms like "wight," "pelf," "swive," and phrases like "by my crown," and it shows a particular difficulty in managing the rhyme scheme: thus the "little birds" of the opening of the "General Prologue" are pricked on by Nature to "ramp and rage" (to accommodate the rhyme with "pilgrimage"), and the Squire who "slept no more than does a nightingale" does so while "night told her tale."[12] In the portrait of the Friar we have the couplet "Therefore, instead of weeping and of prayer, / Men should give silver to poor friars all bare" (8), the last two words being a characteristic instance of desperate padding to save the rhyme. The version shows in general an erratic oscillation between unwarranted additions to the original and a slavish mirroring of its word order; thus in the "Reeve's Tale" we have thoroughly "unmodern" lines like "There durst no man to call her aught but dame," "Was purposeful to make of her his heir," and, of the miller's past "restraint," "For theretofore he stole but cautiously" (110–11), the latter instance making one appreciate Coghill's brilliant "For up till then he'd only robbed politely" (110), which, apart from its contemporaneity and freshness, also makes better sense of Chaucer's adverb "curteisly." The highlight of the translation's incompetence is arguably the miller's outraged line in the same tale on being told by Aleyn that he has "swived" his daughter—"'You scoundrel,' cried the miller, 'you trespassed?'"—where the final word has an astounding rhythmical and dramatic inappropriateness (118). There is no attempt at a modern version of Chaucer's northern dialect in this tale, which is perhaps just as well. All in all, one has to sympathize with the *Spectator* reviewer of Nicolson, who was unable to get over his dismay at the very first couplet: "When April with his showers sweet with fruit / The drought of March has pierced unto the root" (1).[13]

Nicolson's version is prefaced by an appropriately entitled "Apologia," where he talks of his work as a "diluted drink" that may lead some readers to "an enduring thirst for the older and more potent liquor" of Chaucer himself (xii). It is difficult to believe that such self-abasement, though warranted, justifies what follows, or that such a "thirst" will be prompted in readers other than through desperation. Although I have singled out particular infelicities above, I am not so much concerned in this chapter with individual blemishes (which no translation will be free from and, as one reviewer of Coghill remarked, are often pounced upon by the knowledgeable in a spirit of gratified vanity)[14] as with the skill with which rhythm, rhyme, diction, and idiom are handled in general, and the defects of the Nicolson version are pervasive and ingrained. One is surprised to see it reprinted as recently as 1988 (London: Michael O'Mara), with no indication on the title page that its so-called modern English was by then fifty years out-of-date (nor even modern in 1934).

In "The Unknown Poet" Hill noted that the only translation able to establish itself as "widely and actively in use" (xiii) in the first part of the present century was the *Modern Reader's Chaucer* of Tatlock and Mackaye, a prose version of *The Complete Poetical Works* first published in 1912 and frequently reissued. Prose versions of Chaucer comprise a special category (some might say a peculiarly abysmal one), and the whole exercise is riddled with contradictions that do not seem to occur to the authors in the present instance. There may be a case for such versions where they present themselves as no more than a "crib," and preferably where they are tied to the original in parallel text so that even the most incurious reader can hardly be unaware of how much is being lost (for example, Chaucer's variation in stanza form, which is of course obliterated in prose).[15] The translators themselves talk about Chaucer as a "many-sided poet" in their preface, but the admission is embedded in a statement that suggests how they regard their version as not simply a help to Chaucer but as a work with its own independent validity: "Hitherto a more nearly adequate idea of a marvelously individual and many-sided poet could be obtained only through his original text."[16] Although a routine admission is then made that reading Chaucer in the original is preferable, the translators show a mounting confidence in the powers of the prose medium to reproduce that original:

> The editors have striven always to paraphrase as little and to be as faithful to the original as they could; certainly never to misrepresent it. They have departed from it only to save their version from one or another of four possible stumbling-blocks: rhyme and excessive rhythm, obscurity, extreme verbosity, and excessive coarseness. . . . the editors have tried to keep as much of Chaucer's raciness and archaic savor as is consistent with the reader's ease. . . . they have tried to let him feel that he is reading Chaucer, and nothing else, so far as Chaucer can ever be found in modern prose. (vii–viii)

The final clause notwithstanding, the idea that *anything* can remain of a "many-sided" poet put into a uniform prose from which the above "stumbling-blocks" have been removed is decidedly problematic.[17]

For example, the whole point of the pilgrim Chaucer's "Sir Thopas" is lost in prose, even though the Host is made to continue with his injunction "you shall rhyme no longer," which sounds absurd in the circumstances (109). Not only does the prose have a dreary, homogenizing effect across the works as a whole, but within individual elements a lack of variation in syntax and rhythm makes the act of reading one of drudgery from the outset. For example, in the portraits of Knight and Squire from the "General Prologue," Chaucer is careful to vary the itemization incurred by the repetition of the phrase "he was" by deploying it at different points in the pentameter, whereas Tatlock and Mackaye have a cumulative chain of main clauses beginning with "he was" or "he had been," which reduces each portrait to little more than a curriculum vitae. Some variation is admittedly achieved by reproducing a few short passages from the *Works* in verse form, such as the "Envoy de Chaucer" at the end of the "Clerk's Tale" (217–18) or the man in black's lay (lines

475–86) from the *Book of the Duchess* (322–23), but there is little consistency in this regard, and whereas the "Canticus Troili" from book I of *Troilus* is given in verse, that from the end of book III is not (384, 455). In this particular poem the prose severely mitigates Chaucer's lyricism, an effect emphasized by the complete omission (without any indication in the text) of lines like III.1247–50 describing the beauty of Criseyde's body.

It is hard to believe that these lines are an example of the "excessive coarseness" that the translators note they are concerned to omit, but certainly the fabliaux are heavily censored, not only of the grosser passages but even of individual details like Alison's being described in the "Miller's Tale" as fit "for any lord to leggen in his bed" (I.3269), which becomes "to be any lord's sweetheart" (54). A line like the Pardoner's comment on the belly, "At either ende of thee foul is the soun" (VI.536), is simply omitted, with no indication that this is so (149). The "Merchant's Tale" has the following tepid climax: "Ladies, I pray you be not wroth; I cannot gloss, I am a rough man. And forthwith this Damian received her" (236), a euphemism practically indecipherable, and not illuminated by the tasteful illustration to the scene by Warwick Goble in which May is shrouded in so much oriental finery that any sudden gratification would be impossible. One further omission the translators draw attention to above, that of the effects of "rhyme and eccessive rhythm," leads in practice to the simple truncation of Chaucer's couplets, resulting in a peculiar flatness, as in lines from the portrait of the Monk: "He gave not a plucked hen for the text that hunters are not holy," and "How shall the world be served? Let St. Austin have his work to himself" (4). Although they thereby avoid the intrusion of poor rhymes that verse modernizers often fall foul of, the result is hardly preferable. In short, the Tatlock and Mackaye version is characterized by its techniques of omission, and its unimaginative prose has few virtues of its own with which to compensate. The so-called modern English does not renew Chaucer's language but is, rather, parasitic upon it, such that, to take the final paragraph of the "Miller's Prologue," terms like "churl," "methinks," "wight," "deem," "whoso," "eke," and "bethink" are simply passed down. At least the other well-known prose translation of the *Tales,* that by David Wright, attempts a genuine modernization. One would hope finally that the translators were not spared some embarrassment in translating the poet's aspiration from book V of *Troilus and Criseyde* (lines 1795–96): "Pray also to God that none copy thee wrong nor mar thy metre through defect of his tongue" (514).

Another early-twentieth-century version noted above, the Everyman edition by Arthur Burrell, first published in 1908 and frequently reprinted, has an eccentric approach to the original that can justly be labeled one of "antiquated modernization." Although there is some updating of diction and spelling, much is left almost entirely as it stands in the original ("And bathed every veyn in suche licour," "And palmers for to seeken strange strandes," I.3, 13), and where Burrell does "modernize" he frequently "remedievalizes" the spelling: thus in the comparative passages from the "Knight's Tale" describing the Temple of Mars quoted in his introduction, "brenning" is replaced by "burnyng," "mordring" by "murtheryng," "bibledde" by "y-bled," and "chirking" by "shriekyng" (I.2000–4).[18] Burrell is concerned to modernize the text "just enough to leave its quaintness," the latter word here used as a term of approbation (viii), but the result comes dangerously close to pastiche. And the more licentious tales are not modernized at all; here Burrell adopts the familiar strategy in such cases of leaving "unpalatable" matter in the original language, for these are "so broad, so plain-spoken, that no amount of editing or alteration will make them suitable for the twentieth century" (vii–viii).

It is American translators of the 1930s like Nicolson and Hill who finally confront the fabliaux, the latter justifying Chaucer's bawdiness as a sourcebook for the "facts of life," as we noted in chapter 2, and arguing that it is presented "not only as something inoffensive, but also justly and humorously a part of human experience."[19] Hill's sumptuous 1934 two-volume limited edition of the *Tales* was reprinted with corrections (and minus the introduction) throughout the 1930s in a series of cheaper editions, and like his 1930 selection from Chaucer's poetry referred to at the outset of this chapter was generally well received.[20] Such a welcome was merited insofar as his translation was the first remotely to substantiate the claim to present the *Canterbury Tales* in *modern* English, especially compared with its exact contemporary the Nicolson version. Thus if we take the various cumbersome lines from the latter's rendering of the "Reeve's Tale" quoted above, we find that the equivalents in Hill are brisk and clear: "None dared to call her anything but 'dame'"; "Had it in mind that she should be his heir"; and "for then he took his toll discreetly, / But now the fellow was a thief completely" (100–101). Where Nicolson will reproduce a line like that on the Yeoman in the "General Prologue," "wel koude he dresse his takel yemanly"

(I.106), with a minimum of invention ("Well could he keep his tackle yeomanly,"4), Hill nicely recasts it: "He kept his gear the way a yeoman should" (3). There are a fair number of awkward rhymes in his work but equally occasional felicities, as in the miller's sarcasm in the "Reeve's Tale" at the clerks' learning (particularly in the genuine re-creation of "Lat se now if this place may suffise, / Or make it rowm with speche, as is youre gise" (I.4125–26) in the final couplet below):

> The miller answered: "Yea, if there be any,
> Such as it is, that will I share with you.
> My house is small; but ye are schooled, ye two,
> And by your arguments can make a place
> A mile in breadth from twenty feet of space!
> Let us see now if this will hold us all,
> Or talk it larger, if it be too small!"
>
> (104–5)

One would not wish to overstate the case for Hill; he is more often sensible than inspired, but one should also add that his is one of the few modern versions to include the "Melibee" and the "Parson's Tale"; it is ironic that the prose versions referred to above give us none of Chaucer's prose tales except in brief summary. We often find him close to Coghill, as in lines 2773–79 of the "Knight's Tale," but any extended comparison with Coghill serves to show how much more pedestrian Hill generally is. Take, for example, the following passage from the "Nun's Priest's Tale" (preceded by Chaucer's text itself):

> This Chauntecleer stood hye upon his toos,
> Strecchynge his nekke, and heeld his eyen cloos,
> And gan to crowe loude for the nones.
> And daun Russell the fox stirte up atones,
> And by the gargat hente Chauntecleer,
> And on his bak toward the wode hym beer,
> For yet ne was ther no man that hym sewed.
> O destinee, that mayst nat been eschewed!
> Allas, that Chauntecleer fleigh fro the bemes!
> Allas, his wyf ne roghte nat of dremes!
> And on a Friday fil al this meschaunce.

O Venus, that art goddesse of plesaunce,
Syn that thy servant was this Chauntecleer,
And in thy servyce dide al his poweer,
Moore for delit than world to multiplye,
Why woldestow suffre hym on thy day to dye?
O Gaufred, deere maister soverayn,
That whan thy worthy kyng Richard was slayn
With shot, compleynedest his deeth so soore,
Why ne hadde I now thy sentence and thy loore,
The Friday for to chide, as diden ye?
For on a Friday, soothly, slayn was he.

(VII.3331–52)

This Chanticleer stood high upon his toes,
He stretched his neck, he made his eyes to close,
And thus began to make a mighty cry.
Sir Russell Fox up-bounded instantly
And by the throat he seized this Chanticleer,
And flung him on his back, and sped from there
Off toward the wood, and no man saw him run.
O Destiny, that none of us may shun!
Alas! That Chanticleer flew from the beams!
Alas! That Pertelote recked not of dreams!
And on a Friday fell all this mischance!
O Venus, that art goddess of pleasance,
Since Chanticleer was servant unto thee
And spent himself to serve thee faithfully,
More for delight than the world to multiply,
Why wouldst thou suffer him on thy day to die?
O Geoffrey, master dear, supreme, and skilled,
That when King Richard was with arrow killed
Made for thy noble lord complaint so sore,
Why do I lack thy meaning and thy lore,
Friday to chide with singing, as did ye?
(For truly, on a Friday slain was he.)

(256)

Rather than being a translation into modern English verse, this passage cannot claim much greater status than that of being a modernized spelling version of the Chaucer, with much of the Middle English diction and sentence structure retained.[21] The point can be enforced by a comparison with some lines from the same passage by Coghill:

> Sir Russell Fox leapt in to the attack,
> Grabbing his gorge he flung him o'er his back
> And off he bore him to the woods, the brute,
> And for the moment there was no pursuit.
> . . . .
> And on a Friday too to risk their necks!
> O Venus, goddess of the joys of sex,
> Since Chanticleer thy mysteries professed
> And in thy service always did his best,
> And more for pleasure than to multiply
> His kind, on thine own day, is he to die?
> O Geoffrey . . .
> Would that I had thy skill, thy gracious breath,
> To chide a Friday half so well as you!
> (For he was killed upon a Friday too.)
>
> (228)

Here we have a fluent modern idiom played off against the rhetorical apostrophe of the original that captures the vigor and humor of Chaucer's writing, particularly in lines 4 and 8 of the above passage, and in the final couplet. There are admittedly blemishes, particularly the unwarranted rhyme-words "brute" and "breath," and some will balk at the modernizing bravado of the "necks"/"sex" couplet, but the challenges of actual translation have not been shirked, as is the case with Hill's simple repetition of terms like "mischance" and "pleasance."

Before proceeding to discuss Coghill in the context of other versions from the last few decades, we might note the rather bizarre method of making Chaucer available to "present-day readers" followed in Hitchins's selection from the *Tales,* first published in 1946 (and perhaps owing something to Burrell). Thus the opening lines:

When that Aprillė with his showrės soote
The drought of March hath piercėd to the root,
And bathėd every vein in such liquor
Of which virtue engendered is the flower;
When Zephyrus eke with his sweetė breath
Inspirėd hath in every holt and heath
The tender croppės, and the youngė sun
Hath in the Ram his halfė course y-run . . .[22]

This is obviously neither translation nor modernization, though in his preface entitled "Where Angels Fear to Tread" Hitchins attempts to justify his text as in fact more accessible to modern readers: some obsolete Middle English terms have been substituted by modern expressions, and modern spelling has been largely adopted, coupled, however, with medieval terminations to preserve the meter: as Hitchins instances, "smalle fowles" for "smale foweles." On the other hand, commonly used Middle English words ("atones," "wight") have not been substituted but are translated in a prefatory glossary, and to complete the eclectic apparatus a running glossary is provided for others. Hitchins admits to producing "a conglomerate of Middle and Modern English" that some will find "horrid" (viii), but one really has to question the serviceability of the entire enterprise: the opening lines quoted above show that the "present-day reader" has still been left with a fair amount of work to do, and as we go through the "General Prologue" terms like "corages" (line 11), "wenden" (line 21), "dalliance" (line 211), "purchaser" (line 318), "gat-toothed" (line 468), and many more are neither translated nor explained. Why any reader would not for the cost of a little more labor go directly to Chaucer is a mystery, especially when Hitchins blithely notes in his preface that "both in the stories and the discourses I have often omitted whole blocks of lines that are not important to the matter in hand" (viii).

When Nevill Coghill's translation of the *Tales* first appeared in printed form in 1951 (extracts from it having previously been heard on several occasions on BBC radio, producing in broadcasting terms "one of the most successful experiments of the post-war years"),[23] it sparked a heated debate that has never in fact gone away; the acrimonious *Listener* review referred to earlier and the correspondence for and against the translation it prompted has been mirrored recently in a debate on the Internet among the Chaucer Discussion Group, which included absurd (and alarming) calls to ban Coghill from the shelves.[24] Such a furor is a measure, of course, of Coghill's success, since no one would trouble thus to indict versions that have passed into oblivion, like many of those we've discussed. To judge from the outcry on the Internet, the *Speculum* reviewer of 1952, who suggested that the attack in the *Listener* was "not directed at the present translation as a translation, but at the fact that an Oxford don has 'sold the fort,' that learning has come down into the dust and heat of the day," but who felt that such outrage might be occasioned in Britain but not America, could be accused of showing a premature optimism (538–39). However, more recent criticism of Coghill has confused the issue of the translation with Coghill's later ventures into areas like *Canterbury Tales—the Musical* (discussed in chapter 8), where the sin of popularization is felt to be even grosser.[25]

Coghill's main competitor in England in recent years has been David Wright's verse translation of the *Tales*, published in 1985. Wright had previously brought out a prose version in 1964 that, whatever the defects attaching to such versions, as outlined above, did at least live up to the "modern" language claims of its subtitle (while having the good sense to switch into verse for pieces like "Sir Thopas"). Thus, for example, the Shipman of the "General Prologue" is renamed "Sea-Captain," and we hear that "he was certainly a bit of a lad, for he had lifted any amount of wine from Bordeaux while the merchants were napping," while we are told of the Wife of Bath that "in company she laughed and rattled away" ("In felaweshipe wel koude she laughe and carpe," I.474) and of the Host that he was "a bit of a wag" ("right a myrie man," I.757).[26] This procedure is less happy in the "Knight's Tale," where the challenge of providing a modernization that will yet retain something of the formality of the original is a weighty one. Wright produces a rather chatty discourse ("Now I'll give Palamon a rest, and leave him to stay in his prison while I tell you more about Arcite," 34) that makes repeated use of conversational phrases for the Knight like "I suppose," "I dare say," "I may as well go on to describe" (42–43), "and that's enough about Mars and Venus" (50), and so on. Theseus intervenes at the end of the tournament to say, "Stop! No more! It's all over!" ("Hoo! namoore, for it is doon!," I.2656), and the various knights take their farewell with "'Goodbye! Good luck!' and it was all over" ("Ther was namoore but 'Fare wel, have good day!'" I.2740). Although one might argue that these latter examples are reasonable modern equivalents, the overall tone produced by featuring them in prose rather than verse is far more casual and unresonant than in the original. This is even the case with the fabliaux, as when Nicholas urges Alison, "For God's sake, sweetheart, let's make love this minute, or I'll die" (64; compare "Lemman, love me al atones, / Or I wol dyen, also God me save!" I.3280–81).

Wright himself presumably felt some dissatisfaction with this attempt, leading him to approach Chaucer once more, this time in verse, although many turns of phrase are common to both versions. He and Coghill take radically different approaches to the particular problems of verse translation, and it makes sense to consider the two together. Wright's major departure from tradition is in the part abandonment of Chaucer's rhyme; we have already seen some problems that rhyme caused for Coghill (and its complete flooring of Nicolson), and Wright suggests in his introduction that the "real poetry" of Chaucer is made up of "immediacy, directness, and plain speech," qualities that the maneuverability gained by the sacrifice of rhyme can bring out, though he is still concerned to "suggest" that rhyme through devices like half rhyme and assonance (xx). Reviewers were quick to pick up on the results in comparison with Coghill and consider how far the gains outweighed the losses.[27]

In my view, Wright's part adoption of rhyme makes for a good deal of confusion and distraction, and it is impossible to discover any rationale behind its periodic occurrence and disappearance. Take the following two-verse-paragraph passage from the "Wife of Bath's Prologue":

> I grant all this; I've no hard feelings if
> Maidenhood be set above remarriage.
> Purity in body and in heart
> May please some—as for me, I make no boast.
> For, as you know, no master of a household
> Has all of his utensils made of gold;
> Some are of wood, and yet they are of use.
> The Lord calls folk to Him in many ways,
> And each has his peculiar gift from God,
> Some this, some that, even as He thinks good.
> Virginity is a great excellence,
> And so is dedicated continence,
> But Christ, of perfection the spring and well,
> Did not bid everyone to go and sell

All that he had, and give it to the poor,
And thus to follow in His tracks; be sure
He spoke to those who would live perfectly;
And, sirs, if you don't mind, that's not for me.
I mean to give the best years of my life
To the acts and satisfactions of a wife.

(221–22)

The success of the second paragraph here, particularly in the last couplet, makes one wonder why rhyme has been eschewed in the previous lines, where a characteristic rhythmical flatness is the result, especially in the first four lines of the extract. Wright's version is full of these dormant passages, as in the same "Prologue":

No fear, you know as well as I do, that
The Apostle, where he speaks of maidenhood,
Says he has got no firm precept for it.
You may advise a woman not to wed,
But by no means is advice a command.

(220)

Often a passage will begin with well-controlled couplets that build up narrative flow and momentum, only to hit a patch of choppy water where the "stay" of rhyme, for no good reason, is suddenly taken away; examples are the portrait of the Monk in the "General Prologue" (the change occurring with the line "You can keep your labour, Augustine!" 5) and the opening of the "Knight's Tale," where the lines from "And of the feast they held for the wedding" to "Let every fellow tell his tale in turn" (23) deviate into eye rhymes like "now"/"furrow" and "plough"/"enough" (23). Wright has a particular habit of suddenly (and bathetically) omitting the rhyme at the end of a verse paragraph, where one is expecting a clinching couplet, as in "To rise at dawn next day to take the road / For the journey I am telling you about," and in the portrait of the Merchant: "He was a really estimable man, / But the fact is I never learnt his name" ("General Prologue" 1–2, 8). Where he does follow through Chaucer's rhyme in these positions, the effect is one of great relief for the reader and the sense of how much less satisfying Wright's alternative procedure is, as in the Clerk: "Moral virtue was reflected in his speech, / And gladly would he learn and gladly teach" ("General Prologue," 9). On the other hand, the willful destruction of some of Chaucer's most memorable couplets is common, again often in passages otherwise rhymed, as with the Man of Law: "And nowhere would you find a busier man; / And yet he seemed much busier than he was" ("General Prologue," 9). In Chaucer's stanzaic narratives, too, such as the Man of Law's and Prioress's tales, rhyme is frequently forsaken, nor is it kept to wholly in "Sir Thopas," where it is necessary to the jog-trot effect.

One might argue that Wright's earlier experience of translating the *Tales* into prose has not altogether been shaken off in the new verse translation, or more generously that there is here a sophisticated postmodern deconstruction of Chaucer taking place, an undoing of the canonical status of the rhyming iambic pentameter allied to various intensifications of the scurrility of the original that amount to acts of vandalism against the master text; thus the ending of the "Cook's Tale" is especially vicious ("Whose wife kept, as a respectable front, / A shop; but earned a living with her cunt," 112; compare Chaucer's "and swyved for hir sustenance," I.4422). The Host's words to the pilgrim Chaucer on interrupting Sir Thopas are "Your shithouse [for "drasty"] rhyming isn't worth a turd!" (172), and the "Reeve's Tale" throughout employs an extravagant northern dialect form for the two students that is rather more demotic than in the original; thus Aleyn's "mistake" in groping his way back to bed after "stuffing" the daughter: "'By Christ,' / Thought he, 'Aah's gyen aa' wrang; Aah's up shit creek'" (108) (for "'By God,' thoughte he, 'al wrang I have mysgon,'" I.4252).[28]

Some readers will welcome what is in some respects the most uncompromising modernization of Chaucer that we have, but the present writer agrees with the strictures expressed by Pearsall in his review of Wright, especially in his complaint that the effect of the part adoption of rhyme "is one of bewilderment, for it is neither one thing nor the other"; as Pearsall adds, "the occasions when [Wright] does use full rhyme make one long for more of this Coghill-like kind of snappiness" (202). The result is a version that shows a curious kind of struggle with its source text, an uneasy oscillation between subservience and rebellion. Coghill by comparison shows a far greater sense of relaxation and ease in the face of the original, partly because he is more uninhibitedly committed to a process of fundamental renewal.

Turning then to his version, we can indeed find faults aplenty, but I would argue that these are usually localized ones; that is, where the choice of individual word or phrase, often with the accommodation of rhyme in mind, can be questioned. But with regard to the more important question of continuity, Coghill succeeds very well in areas that have troubled other translators and that I have called attention to above: there is skill and consistency throughout in his employment of rhyme and an overall commitment to modernization that can still retain a measure of formality where appropriate and avoid vulgarization. Moreover, at the level of the individual couplet he is frequently extremely inventive; his translation is not without its pains, but there are very few pleasures to be found in those surveyed above. Take, for example, the Wife of Bath's lines on keeping her options open in her "Prologue":

> I holde a mouses herte nat worth a leek
> That hath but oon hole for to sterte to,
> And if that faille, thanne is al ydo.
>
> (III.572–74)

Compare this with Coghill:

> I never think a mouse is up to much
> That only has one hole in all the house;
> If that should fail, well, it's good-bye the mouse.
>
> (273)

In the "Reeve's Tale" the miller's sarcasm in lines 4125–26, which we saw rather well handled by Hill above, is even better in Coghill, where the French phrase captures just the right note of philistine dismissiveness: "Take a look round and see if it will do, / Or make it bigger with your parley voo" (113). And there is possibly Coghill's best-known couplet in the description of Alisoun in the "Miller's Tale": "High shoes she wore, and laced them to the top. / She was a daisy, O a lollypop" (90).

I could quote many further examples, but I should like to turn to Coghill's major strength in comparison with other versions; that is, a sense of discursive ease and clarity across extended passages. It should be remembered that, as I remarked earlier, his translation originated in a radio commission (in 1946), and in spite of the many revisions it has gone through, the sense of a fluent voice speaking to listeners has remained constant, contrasting with the cumbersome stiffness often apparent in other versions. Coghill indeed argued that Chaucer was "peculiarly well-suited to broadcasting" because he himself wrote "to be read aloud to a small circle of listeners." The sensitivities of a Third Programme audience also played a part in ensuring that some of the bawdier lines in the original were handled with comparative discretion, which, given some attempts to ape Chaucer's vulgarisms, quoted above, is perhaps just as well.[29]

The sense of fluency and the notion of addressing a circle of listeners are both apparent in a passage like the portrait of the Manciple from the "General Prologue"; this is a rather complex piece in Chaucer because of the switching of the subject from the Manciple himself to his masters, and then to their masters the peers, but it is rendered here with great ease and with little compromising on accuracy:

> The *Manciple* came from the Inner Temple;
> All caterers might follow his example
> In buying victuals; he was never rash
> Whether he bought on credit or paid cash.
> He used to watch the market most precisely
> And got in first, and so he did quite nicely.
> Now isn't it a marvel of God's grace
> That an illiterate fellow can outpace
> The wisdom of a heap of learned men?
> His masters—he had more than thirty then—
> All versed in the abstrusest legal knowledge,
> Could have produced a dozen from their College
> Fit to be stewards in land and rents and game
> To any Peer in England you could name,
> And show him how to live on what he had
> Debt-free (unless of course the Peer were mad)
> Or be as frugal as he might desire,
> And make them fit to help about the Shire
> In any legal case there was to try;
> And yet this Manciple could wipe their eye.
>
> (18–19)

A further example might be the penultimate paragraph of the "General Prologue," a simple act of reportage that Coghill renders neatly and expeditiously:

Of course we all agreed, in fact we swore it
Delightedly, and made entreaty too
That he should act as he proposed to do,
Become our Governor in short, and be
Judge of our tales and general referee,
And set the supper at a certain price.
We promised to be ruled by his advice
Come high, come low; unanimously thus
We set him up in judgement over us.
More wine was fetched, the business being done;
We drank it off and up went everyone
To bed without a moment of delay.

(25)

Wright's version of the same passage, though adequate, is stiffer and far less rhythmically convincing:

To this we all agreed, and gladly swore
To keep our promises; and furthermore
We asked him if he would consent to do
As he had said, and come and be our leader,
And judge our tales, and act as arbiter,
Set up our dinner too, at a fixed price;
And we'd obey whatever he might decide
In everything. And so, with one consent,
We bound ourselves to bow to his judgement.
And thereupon wine was at once brought in.
We drank; and not long after, everyone
Went off to bed, and that without delay.

(21)

The only version contemporary with Coghill's that comes remotely near it in terms of fluency and in control of the couplet is, in my opinion, Theodore Morrison's (first published 1949), although Morrison presents an abridged Chaucer in which the tales written in stanzaic form (with the exception of the "Prioress's Tale" and "Sir Thopas") are omitted. Presumably a discomfort with rhyme royal in particular led Morrison to the bizarre decision to translate *Troilus and Criseyde* into blank verse; he has also compressed this last poem into half its original length, in a literal quest for the "portability" that is the imprint of the series his translation figures in.[30] No doubt to counteract the currency of the Morrison version in the States, where his rendering of the *Tales* features in several anthologies of literature used by students,[31] Ronald Ecker and Eugene Crook have recently brought out a complete translation of the *Tales,* prose included, that offers itself in the preface to just such students on survey courses of "British and world literature" who "may now gain a more balanced view" of Chaucer's varied genius.[32] Comprehensiveness is indeed the major virtue the translation can lay claim to, since a gauche handling of rhyme in particular is apparent from the opening: "When April's gentle rains have pierced the drought / Of March right to the root, and bathed each sprout" (1). A recurrence of labored and unnatural language to save the rhyme is constantly distracting the reader: "No ointment that could cleanse, to keep it simple, / And rid his face of even one white pimple"; "he had no beard and never would, / So smooth his face you'd think he'd shaved it good"; "He'd make more money in one day alone / Than would the parson two months come and gone" (17–19).[33]

In 1971 Coghill published his verse translation of *Troilus and Criseyde,* a version that has aroused far less controversy than his *Tales* translation, in part because the work is a little "safer" in keeping to some of the properties of Chaucer's Middle English, in particular its formal syntax and elevated diction. It is indeed rather less modernizing than the version produced in 1965 by Margaret Stanley-Wrench; compare, for example, the following passages from book 1 of the poem, where Troilus sees Criseyde in the temple, first in her version, then in Coghill's (I.260–75):

> Now to my special point, to Troilus,
> The prince I spoke about, King Priam's son.
> I mean to tell his life without more fuss,
> He is my hero, so no more digression,
> His joys, his cares, here, in this single session
> I mean to tell, so back to my beginning,
> The thread thus twisted I must go on spinning.
>
> Inside that temple, gay and light of heart,
> Pleasing himself by glancing to and fro
> At this and that girl, musing from what part

She came, from suburb, east, or west end, so
It happened that in staring high and low
His gliding glances came to rest at last
On Criseyde, and there they were held fast.

He was quite overcome, thrown back, astounded,
And unobtrusively tried hard to see
Her better . . .[34]

But to proceed with what I have to say,
And more especially of this king's son,
Leaving collateral matters by the way,
It is of him I mean to speak or none,
Both in his joy, and his cold cares begun,
And all he did, as touching this affair;
Having begun, let me return to where

This Troilus and his knights were gallivanting
About the temple, quizzing and pointing out
This or that lady, all the while descanting
On where she lived, within town or without,
And it so fell that, looking through the rout,
His eye pierced deeply and at last it struck
Criseyde where she was standing, and there stuck.

And suddenly he felt himself astounded,
Gazing more keenly at her in surprise . . .[35]

Both in his retention of more of Chaucer's vocabulary ("collateral," "cold cares," "rout") and in his reproduction of the original phrasing, for example "as touching," Coghill retains a stateliness that Stanley Wrench frequently sacrifices in the interests of conversational immediacy, rapidity, and a procedure that tends to deelevate the courtly original. She prefers a simpler, main-clause style in comparison with Coghill, and also uses punctuation and enjambment to make Chaucer's stanza structure looser. Coghill in fact can be seen as occupying a middle ground between Stanley Wrench and the other modern verse version of *Troilus* by George Krapp (first published 1932), which makes plentiful use of inversions of word order and archaisms.[36]

I noted at the outset of this chapter a common academic reluctance to see any merit whatsoever in modern Chaucer translations, together with a desire to overlook their existence (except when recalcitrant students bring them into class), and suggested that this was symptomatic of a wider gulf between the academy and the various popularizing treatments of Chaucer we are looking at in this study. Surprisingly, there has been hardly any comparative discussion of such translations by Chaucer scholars, and although the present chapter can make no claim to be an in-depth study of the versions treated, it is one of the few examples of such discussion; where Chaucer scholars have condescended to look at translations, the result has often been unrelieved disdain.[37] But really there is little point in academics berating all modernizers by fastening on individual words and phrases of questionable "accuracy" and ignoring the wider mechanics of translation as a practice, and although in the space available to me here I have had to curtail the number of textual samples used, I have attempted to talk about *characteristic* defects and successes.[38] In a discussion in the *Chaucer Review* of some of the issues involved, Peter G. Beidler has made an attempt to face up to the fact of translation, although he retreats from a measure of openness into a final scholarly defensiveness that affirms, "However much care they take, and however much skill they show, [translators] can never make their translations as good as the original."[39] But such an observation in its banality is at the very most the starting point for discussion, not its final word. Beidler does at least recognize, however, that instead of turning in horror from Chaucer translation, we academics might integrate it into our procedures and even put it before our students to highlight by contrast, in Beidler's words, "the finer delights of the Chaucerian originals" (299). But we can do more with it than this: instead of using it as a mere dummy to play opposite Chaucer, we might encourage our students to make discriminations between the translations, and not to dismiss them all out of hand, for although there are several that I too would happily see disparaged (especially those in prose), there are others where there are many good things, even in Wright's case, though I regard his approach as fundamentally mistaken. In other words, we could encourage our students to distinguish between the differences in poetic rhythm, diction, and syntax that this particular branch of translation practice offers us, and rather than seal Chaucer off from such questions, we might find that the exercise in discrimination ultimately serves his cause, too.

8

Performance Chaucer

Although the translators whose work we looked at in the previous chapter are obviously bidding for a wider audience for Chaucer, it is via modern media like radio and television that such an audience is most instantly reached. As we have seen, Coghill's translation originated in a BBC radio commission in 1946, and it was Coghill who led the way in the genre of performance with his work on the musical of the *Canterbury Tales* (1968), cowritten with Martin Starkie, and, with the same collaborator, his television adaptation of 1969, a major BBC investment that harnessed the efforts of "one producer, three directors, and 100 actors . . . to put the earliest English classic on the box," as the *Radio Times* put it.[1] Although this chapter will look at the various television, radio, film, and stage versions of Chaucer created in the postwar period, it has to be said that Chaucer has not really taken hold of the public in any sustained manner; the same *Radio Times* feature noted the television version's ambition to meet the "obvious challenge to the BBC's reputation for successfully recreating the big books of English literature in television terms," but whereas other "big books" and authors (like Austen, Dickens, Hardy, and so on) come around again and again for television treatment, the *Canterbury Tales* experiment has not been repeated, unless it be in the recent animated version discussed below.[2] The difficulties in performing the *Tales* in anything like a manner that remains faithful to the original are indeed formidable, and most modern versions involve a complete distortion of that original.

In this sense, the television version of 1969 does deserve credit for attempting to give an overview of the *Tales* and for not reducing it to only the more "accessible," fabliau-type elements, as many performances do. Beginning with the "Knight's Tale" and concluding with at least a gesture toward the "Parson's Tale" (in the form of a short sermon) and Chaucer's "Retraction," it even attempted to take in en route such things as "Sir Thopas," "Melibee," the "Monk's Tale," and that of the Canon's Yeoman, although with seven fifty-minute episodes at its disposal the scope for coverage was much greater than that afforded by the single film or stage-version format.[3] Even with this balance of "sentence" and "solaas," however, the series was largely sold to the public under the headline of "Chaucer's bawdy pantomime" (see the *Radio Times* feature), and the cover of the same *Radio Times* issue showed photographs of various pilgrims above the caption "They met in a pub. Got very very merry. They started telling tales. Lechery, treachery, that sort of thing. Free nosh for the best story." This emphasis on hilarity and inebriation was picked up in the opening episode, which, while introducing us to Coghill's translation as the basic script for the series, included additions (common also to the musical) that promoted the pub-outing atmosphere of the whole affair, with the Host advising the pilgrims to take the journey at a leisurely and self-indulgent pace: "Where but in England can you find a pub?" As the Miller echoed, in the rhyming couplet employed throughout, "Take your time, / And take your mug of English ale, it's prime." The pilgrims are frequently seen eating and drinking along the way, with the Host providing relevant encouragement, as at the end of the "Reeve's Tale": "Look, there is a pub nearby I think / I judge it's time we went to have a drink." Such insertions also consolidate the necessary linking format over the seven episodes, whereby the actual Chaucerian links are fleshed out with frequent scenes of the pilgrims on horseback, at table, or at various stopping-off points, where some of the tales are told, with the final episode culminating in the arrival at Canterbury Cathedral and the shrine of Saint Thomas (to Chaucer's own voice-over reciting his "Retraction"). These frequent stops also answer the objections of the realistically minded to the unlikely idea of the tales actually being told in horseback procession.

This foregrounding of the linking activity of the narrators outside their various tales is often sacrificed in other modes of performance; it plays very little part in the Pasolini film of 1972, for example, as we shall see. Beyond its use as a structuring device, it also indicates how far the television version picks up some traditions discussed in chapter 2, so that the "earliest English classic" is filtered through the "merrie England" theme. England is not only the land of pubs, however, as the Knight reminds the company before they leave the Tabard in episode 1: "Well, let us take things easily and ride / Through England and her pleasant countryside." The frequent outside location shots of the procession crossing downs and woodland, or threading various half-timbered village streets, do contribute to a sense of national picturesqueness, an effect emphasized by the contrasting settings of the tales themselves, which were mostly prerecorded in austerely stylized studio landscapes. In the opening episode's "Knight's Tale" there were recurrent cuttings from the studio location to the pilgrims' wandering in England's "pleasant countryside," a contrast minimized in later episodes, where the shorter length of the tales meant that the framework recurred at its appointed times at beginning and end. At such times what one might call the "fracas device," common to many performances of Chaucer, also came into play, whereby Chaucer's indications of dissension between the pilgrims was extended to become a more general hue and cry. Thus the Miller's "Prologue" in the television series featured a comic-violent altercation in which all the pilgrims get caught up, and episode 1 ended with the Miller in chase after the Reeve; later in the series the Friar and Summoner have to be physically restrained from a fight, and so forth. Such scenes obviously contribute to the air of farcical riot.

Even so, the extent of such drunken revelry does not really match what the *Radio Times*'s publicity seems to promise, nor is it easy to regard the adaptation in terms of "bawdy pantomime," to repeat the feature headline, especially when compared with some genuine pantomime versions (considered below). The feature centers on an interview with the actress who played the "sexy" Wife of Bath, but the Wife has no particular prominence in the pilgrim party (compared with other versions where she remains from first to last the focus of attention, as in the Haydn Evans radio version of 1991, where she is raucously interventionist throughout). It is possible that an original intention was indeed to highlight her role, given that the scripts show some saucy horseplay between the Wife and an ostler as the pilgrims arrive at the Tabard that was not carried through to the transmitted version.[4] But the fact that the first episode was largely taken up with the decorous "Knight's Tale" seems to have disappointed a fair proportion of viewers, misled, perhaps, by the advance publicity; according to the BBC's own "Audience Research Report," these found the tale "rather lacking in . . . the famed 'salt' of Chaucer."[5] Although the televised "Knight's Tale" hardly encompassed the more philosophical themes treated in the original, such as the human quest for order and significance in the face of the random brutalities of existence, and the political and ideological uses of such a will to order as embodied in Theseus (the pagan gods did not appear, nor was there any amphitheater with its three temples), the tale did conclude with a generous extract from Theseus's "faire cheyne of love" speech (I.2987–3074), a speech that is often a complete casualty even in those performance versions that do feature the "Knight's Tale." The generous allocation of time to nonfabliaux tales like the Clerk's, Franklin's, Canon's Yeoman's, and Manciple's, together with the unexpectedly discreet treatment of the fabliaux themselves, perhaps justify producer Ron Travers's description of the adaptation as a "purist version" of Chaucer, even while he remains insistent that "Chaucer's notorious bawdiness is still all there."[6]

As in some of the children's versions of Chaucer we looked at in chapter 4, the "General Prologue" is not given in one necessarily static "chunk" at the outset of the tales but is introduced piecemeal throughout the journey, with Chaucer's description of the teller prefacing the individual tales. Sometimes, to vary the situation of the Chaucer figure speaking these descriptions direct to camera, the "General Prologue" is converted into dialogue, so that the portrait of the Prioress, for example, is split between Chaucer and the Nun's Priest, and that of the Squire emerges from conversation between Chaucer and the Franklin. Such measures obviously reflect the desire to incorporate both the pilgrimage context, with its attention to teller as well as tale, and the interaction between parts that the dramatization requires. Other performances, as we shall see, negotiate the difficulties in staging the relation between tales and pilgrimage framework by discounting, or reducing, the latter. Henry Raynor, reviewing the opening episode in the *Times*, noted "the unsatisfactory compromise between drama and narration" that emerged, but felt that given the inevitable difficulties, the BBC production had made a "tolerable" job of handling them.[7]

Pier Paolo Pasolini's film *I racconti di Canterbury (The Canterbury Tales)*, made in 1972 and released in both Italian and English versions, reproduces and indeed amplifies "Chaucer's notorious bawdiness" in a manner that highlights just how "respectable" the television version in fact was.[8] Pasolini includes only the Merchant's, Friar's, Cook's, Miller's, Reeve's, Pardoner's, and Summoner's tales (in that order), with a dramatization of the "Wife of Bath's Prologue" (but not her tale) inserted between the Miller's and Reeve's tales, and with the sequence ending on the "Summoner's Prologue" and a spectacular staging of the dwelling place of the "nest of freres" in Satan's "ers" (III.1690–91). Although the "General Prologue" is represented insofar as the pilgrims are shown gathering together (the party here indeed being dominated by the Wife of Bath, who cries out in words from her prologue her justifications of sexuality), once the Host has proposed the tale-telling competition we see almost nothing of the pilgrims again. Thus all the ensuing tales are staged without any reference to a narrator, and at the conclusion of one we often pass straight to the next without any intervening links. Given what seems the totally arbitrary ordering of the tales, of course, any such linkages would have had to be devised anew and could have made little use of the existing Chaucerian material, while their absence at least solves the problem of the "unsatisfactory compromise between drama and narration" noted above.

The major, if intermittent, linkage is in the concentration on the artist figure, Chaucer himself. Unlike the television version, where Chaucer takes his place as one more of the pilgrim-narrators (and a duly unsatisfactory one, as the Host's interruption of "Sir Thopas" shows), here Chaucer is explicitly a *writer,* frequently seen with pen and ink in hand. At the conclusion to the "Friar's Tale," we briefly return to the pilgrims settling down for a night's sleep, while the Chaucer figure, gazing at them vigilantly, is seen writing the title of the "Racconto del cuoco" ("Cook's Tale") under a heading "Appunti per un libro sui racconti dei pellegrini verso Canterbury" ("Notes for a book on the tales of the Canterbury pilgrims"). Here the emphasis is very much on the artist's powers of invention, just as later in the film Chaucer is seen on two occasions musing in his study before getting down to work on the "Miller's Tale" and the "Pardoner's Tale." In this latter case the script notes, "Chaucer, allo scrittoio, sbadiglia. Non ha piu idee. Sembra perduto dietro vani pensieri. Poi, improvvisamente, l'ispirazione. Intinge la penna nel calamaio e scrive di fretta" ("Chaucer is yawning at his desk. He has no more ideas. He seems lost in fruitless thought. Then, suddenly, inspiration. He dips his pen in the ink and writes hurriedly").[9] At the end of the film a brief scene of the pilgrims at Canterbury Cathedral is sandwiched between two more shots of Chaucer smiling to himself in his study, where he pens the words "Qui finisco i *Racconti di Canterbury* raccontati per il solo piacere di raccontare" ("Here end the *Canterbury Tales* told solely for the pleasure of their telling").

Where the television version, as we saw, promoted the values of fellowship, conviviality, and the Englishness of location, grounding the *Tales* and their author in an empirical and social context where he functions as an attentive witness rather than a writer touched by "ispirazione," Pasolini's *Tales* are presented as the product of the artist's whimsical fantasy, unconstrained by time, place, and moral responsibility, both of the pilgrimage and outside it, and largely self-reliant. The "Cook's Tale," where we first see Chaucer in the act of writing, is a celebration of this sense of artistic freedom, given that Pasolini (who himself plays the Chaucer figure in the film) here makes his lengthiest interpolation into the original: out of Chaucer's short fragment Pasolini constructs a series of exploits for Perkyn Revelour, dressed out as a Charlie Chaplin figure, complete with Keystone Cops–type chases and other tributes to the silent-film era. At the end of the "Cook's Tale" we move to Chaucer in his study reading and laughing over a copy of the *Decameron;* less, one would suggest, an incidental piece of nationalistic promotion on Pasolini's part than another instance of his emphasis on the artist's keeping the company only of other artists, or of the self alone, in a manifestly self-conscious promotion of the artistic vocation.

In an essay of 1975, in which Pasolini "abjured" the three films—*Decameron* (1971), *Canterbury Tales* (1972), and *The Flower of the Thousand and One Nights* (1974)—that make up the so-called *Trilogia della vita* (Trilogy of life), he noted how the conspicuous attention to nudity and to the sexual elements of the *Tales* was part of "quella lotta per la democratizzazione del 'diritto a esprimersi' e per la liberalizzazione sessuale, che erano due momenti fondamentali della tensione progressista degli anni Cinquanta e Sessanta."[10] Pasolini's abjuration of the *Trilogy* (although he notes he does not repent of having made it) is occasioned by what he sees, in the mid-1970s, as the harnessing of this sexual liberation to a widespread and corrupting consumerism, so that the "innocence" of the body has now become irretrievably degraded.[11] If Pasolini was drawn to Chaucer because of what D. H. Lawrence called his "lovely" and "fearless" acceptance of sexuality (see chapter 6, note 38), his film of the *Tales* not only exhibits the joyful sexual couplings of the fabliaux but supplements these with various scenes of uninhibited display; for example, the first thing John and Aleyn see on approaching the mill in the "Reeve's Tale" is the miller's wife's and daughter's naked buttocks stuck out side by side over a windowsill above the cesspit. In the opening "Merchant's Tale" Pluto and the "ravysshed" Proserpine, rather than affording a parallel to January and his bride, are both young, naked, and smiling as they stroll about the garden, affording a kind of tableau of a sexual golden age; later in the film the scenes of homosexual activity that preface the "Friar's Tale," denounced to the Summoner by one of his spies, explain the Summoner's own fate in being carried off to Hell as the punishment for agents of sexual repression, among their other crimes.

There are less "liberated" inserted scenes, however, that might be read as anticipating Pasolini's attack in the "Abjuration" on the corruptions of sexual license.[12] At the beginning of the "Pardoner's Tale" the rioters are actually shown in one of the "stywes," or brothels, that Chaucer refers to in passing, purchasing various sexual services including flagellation and fellatio; one of them then urinates from a balcony over the company in the hostelry below. By comparison, the television version's equivalent scene of "riot"—men rolling over the tavern floor with fully dressed serving wenches—seems pretty regulation stuff. The manifest uncouthness of Pasolini's protagonists in this tale, together with the painful deaths they experience, suggest, however, a judgment upon them and the degradation they embody. The emphasis, therefore, on "la liberalizzazione sessuale" and on the artist's freedom to be constrained by nothing other than the "pleasure" of telling seems to coexist with the moral stance spelled out later in the "Abjuration" in which the commercialization of sex is attacked. Pasolini himself regarded Chaucer as a more "knowing" writer than Boccaccio, and one whose work "foresees all the victories and triumphs of the bourgeoisie, but . . . also foresees its rottenness." Whereas the more innocent sexual freedoms of the *Decameron* and of its filmic version represent the newly born bourgeoisie in its first flush of youthful energy, the *Tales* belong to a historical moment when this has already passed, and Chaucer's moralizing prescience of corruption—what Pasolini calls his "unhappy conscience"—accounts for the darker sexuality on display in the film.[13] Many critics have, however, felt that Pasolini is deeply implicated in the developments he deplores, and that his *Canterbury Tales* "suffers not so much from being bawdy—so is Chaucer—but from crudeness, vulgarity and blatant commercialism"; according to Dilys Powell writing in the *Sunday Times*, Pasolini has reduced the *Tales* "to a series of bums and farts."[14] Other details in the film, like the conspicuous erections characters like Damyan and Nicholas carry around with them in their lust for the young wives, lend some support to these assessments.

We have already noted one writer (Gillian Evans; see chapter 7, note 25) who regarded the Pasolini film, together with the musical version of the *Tales*, which opened in London's West End on 21 March 1968 and ran successfully for five years, as evidence of a vulgarizing malaise overtaking Chaucer, though the musical version does not promote nudity: "Even in our own dear Whitehall farce / We never see a Chaucerian naked arse."[15] The decisions facing Coghill and Starkie in creating the musical version were different from those required a year later in adapting Chaucer for television; as we have seen, with much more time at its disposal the latter series was able to thread a variety of tales, in a more or less recognizable order, onto the unifying pilgrimage framework, whereas the musical, like all theatrical adaptations, is forced at once into compression and selection. Even so, the pilgrimage theme remains important in the musical, and the selection actually allows for a narrative shaping that is intended to impart an idea of spiritual progression to parallel the arrival in Canterbury, where the show ends. By contrast, the seemingly random order of the Pasolini selection indeed promotes the idea of a sequence "told solely for the pleasure of . . . telling."

Even though the emphasis in the musical was on the fabliaux, so that theater bills could announce it as "the raciest, bawdiest, most good-hearted and good-humoured show in London," the final tale, told by the Wife of Bath, was meant to exemplify a harmonious love between partners that countered the bawdiness of the previous tales (Miller's, Nun's Priest's, Reeve's, and Merchant's, in that order).[16] After the Wife's tale we get the Prioress's "April Song," picking up the theme of seasonal renewal from the opening of the "General Prologue," followed by a short sermon on the seven deadly sins from the Parson to mark the arrival in Canterbury, followed by the Prioress (and company) once again with a song entitled "Love Will Conquer All."[17] Chaucer then spoke the opening two sentences of his "Retraction," using Coghill's translation (as the musical does throughout), before a grand musical finale brought the whole cast together. What we have, therefore, is a conflation of natural and spiritual desire under the umbrella term "Love," although this might be regarded as a synthesis that Chaucer's poetry does precisely *not* achieve, given that the opposition between sexual love and religious prohibition is staged repeatedly through his work; an ideal of liberal compromise is, however, a particular feature of several performance versions, as we shall see. The "good-hearted" and "good-humored" emphasis and the way the selection is arranged mean the elision of those vocal dissensions that the *Tales* embodies; thus there is no "Knight's Tale" for the Miller's to "quite," and the Wife of Bath becomes the voice of concord rather than gender polemic (a situation abetted by her prologue being uncoupled from her tale, as also happened in the television version, and being inserted piecemeal throughout the musical as a linking device). Thus a tone of inebriated amity governs throughout, encouraged by insertions like the Reeve's drinking song ("Fill your glass") and the Miller's song in praise of beer.

If at about the same time the Beatles were recording songs with titles like "All You Need Is Love," we should reiterate the point made in chapter 2 that the similar sentiments of *Canterbury Tales—the Musical* are already developed in Coghill's writing on Chaucer from the 1940s and 1950s, with its insistence on a Chaucerian "joy" that "expresses itself in harmonies, forgivenesses, bounties, and tolerances," and which "makes a happiness, which is an image of that final joy, an affirmation and a laughter, because all shall be well."[18] In the musical, as Julia Fitzsimmons has argued, the compressed project of reconciliation owes something structurally to Kittredge's focus on a separate "marriage-group" within the *Tales,* ending in the harmonious "Franklin's Tale."[19] Coghill saluted this tale as showing "that wise equability and kindliness that is so great an attribute of Chaucer's mind" in his *Geoffrey Chaucer* of 1956,[20] though presumably the "Wife of Bath's Tale" was thought to be a more efficient coda for the musical, given the utilization of the Wife throughout and the need to restrict the number of tales used. Over the thirty years of its existence, however (in which it has played worldwide), the format of the musical has varied in some details. Thus the most recent run (at the Haymarket Theatre, Basingstoke, 11 December 1998–9 January 1999) has the "Wife of Bath's Tale" preceding the Merchant's, with the Host then putting the question whether man or woman should have the dominance in marriage and being answered by the Knight, who argues for a Franklin-type equality. The program for the production summarizes the plot of the musical as "follow[ing] the eternal argument between men and women about who should be the boss," with the answer lying in joint obedience and a "loving regard for each other's mutual needs."

Although the performances we have looked at thus far can be said to modernize Chaucer in different ways, none of them has this as an explicit aim, and indeed we may infer that Coghill and Pasolini regarded their versions as authentically "Chaucerian." "Chaucer Made Modern" is, however, the subtitle of the Phil Woods and Michael Bogdanov stage adaptation of the *Tales* of 1974, in which, as the preface notes, "we do not for one moment pretend that we are in medieval England."[21] Here, versions of the Knight's, Reeve's, Cook's, Wife of Bath's, Franklin's, Nun's Priest's, Pardoner's, Merchant's, and Miller's Tales are performed, in that order, with the language, if not the plotting, departing widely from Chaucer's text; instead of the Host of the "General Prologue" we have a Master of Ceremonies explaining to the audience that the company has assembled for the annual "Geoffrey Chaucer Canterbury Tale-telling competition" and that the audience is to judge which of the above figures tells the best tale (7). In the complete absence of any pilgrimage framework, linkage between the tales is provided by the boisterous Miller, who has initially been outlawed from the competition and spends the evening in an auditorium seat intervening between some of the tales with his "mucky" jokes, until the exasperated MC lets him tell his own piece at the end.

If in *Canterbury Tales—the Musical* we began with the Miller, here we end with him, an arrangement that emphasizes the entertainment as one of stand-up comedy of a rather broad kind. Occasionally the narrators are introduced with lines from Chaucer's text itself, in translation, but once the action is under way the authors' own couplets take over. Thus John's words of regret in the "Reeve's Tale" that Aleyn and not he is getting some satisfaction for the fraud, "A joke's a joke, but this is ridiculous. / I feel a right fool, while they're both knickerless" (25–26), or January's expression of marital delight, "O goody, goody, breakfast in bed. / One of the joys of being wed" (55, where the "joke" is January's inability to consummate the marriage and May's consequent frustration). The execrable poetry and the insertion of crudities throughout, often in song form like Molly's "I'll sing you a song about a young farmer Dick" from the "Reeve's Tale" (23–24), are in a deliberate and well-recognized tradition of seaside-postcard humor, and even the MC's claim at the end to have in his hand a piece of Chaucer's own handwritten text in "Old

English" (63) can be interpreted as willful cultural oafishness rather than mere ignorance.

Perhaps we should indeed see the Woods-Bogdanov version as an act of would-be cultural vandalism of a "carnivalesque" kind, which takes, in the words of the book's blurb, "a deliberately unacademic approach to Chaucer's classical work"; the reprocessing of Chaucer in terms of crude comedy accosts not only the academic proprietorship of Chaucer but the original "classical" text itself. By contrast, the carnivalesque elements that feature in Chaucer's own work are conducted with a good deal of poetic finesse and narrative sophistication; one need only compare the original "Miller's Tale" with its Woods-Bogdanov counterpart, the latter translated into pantomime doggerel and "deliberate" vulgarization:

> ALISON:
> I'm so fed up it's disconcerting,
> To think that I could be out flirting.
> I don't enjoy these household chores,
> Washing stairs and scrubbing floors.
> My John's too old to be my lover,
> All I am's his full time scrubber.
>
> NICHOLAS: *(Creeps up behind her)*
> Oh what a face! what a figure!
> Part of me is getting bigger.
> I'll creep up on her from behind,
> I bet she likes the other kind.
>
> (64)

The involvement of the audience in Woods-Bogdanov (as judges and drawers of lots to decide the order of the tales), together with the fact that it is invited on stage to take refreshment between the tales ("beer, mulled wine, coffee, mince pies, sandwiches, etc.") and the fact that the cast are encouraged to chat and ad lib to it freely, emphasizes the ambitions toward an all-embracing carnivalesque festivity. As the stage directions put it for the interval at the end of act 1, "Refreshments, songs, and general merriment" (29).

What therefore survives of "Chaucer" at all in this *Canterbury Tales: Chaucer Made Modern?* The show plays on expectations of Chaucer's work (and perhaps the "medieval" more generally) as guarantee of ribaldry and bawdiness, while at the same time supplementing its shortcomings in this respect, to produce a self-confessed travesty of Chaucer that yet wants the imprimatur of Chaucer's name, or, as the blurb puts it once again, that retains "the original's sense of fun, chivalry, and satire." It is this parasitic status that makes some readers quail; as a comic "assault" on the original, the Woods-Bogdanov version has its own rationale, but it is difficult not to agree with B. A. Young's review of the 1978 Young Vic production: "If the Young Vic . . . is to be turned into a working men's club, well and good. . . . [the audience] may snigger happily at the smut, as many of them did when I was there, but they will come away with the idea that Chaucer was someone very different from the man he was."[22] The printed play is, after all, not above quoting from reviews that suggest the version is an authentification of Chaucer, rather than a contribution to a wearying mythology about his work; thus the *Western Mail* excerpt on its back cover: "Anyone labouring under the misapprehension that medieval English literature is dry and academic should catch up with this splendid dramatised version of Chaucer's *Canterbury Tales.*" Nothing drives out misapprehension as effectively as new misapprehension.

There are certain similarities between Woods-Bogdanov and the "contemporary" American stage adaptation of the *Tales* by Arnold Wengrow, first performed in 1979. In particular, the rock music references in the former's treatment of the "Nun's Priest's Tale," where Pertelote is a "Rhode Island redhead" and Chauntecleer performs an Elvis Presley song (42, 44), are much extended in the later work. Thus in the "Merchant's Tale" Proserpine enters as "a finger-snapping rock singer" at a disco, Absolon ("Miller's Tale") is played like "Mick Jagger prancing at a concert," and again in the "Nun's Priest's Tale" the finger-snapping hens jive around the central couple: "When they strutted together, it was outta sight!"[23] In spite of the recurrent insertion of modern idiom, however, leading to the trivialization of some of Chaucer's darker or more disturbing episodes (as in the "Pardoner's Tale," or the "you naughty man" giggling of the maiden supposedly raped in the "Wife of Bath's Tale," 11), the Wengrow version is less of a crudely comedic assault on its source text than Woods-Bogdanov. It keeps closer to the original, insofar as it uses for the most part (without acknowledgment) Coghill's translation, and although its selection of tales is by now familiar (Wife of Bath's, Merchant's, Miller's, Reeve's, Pardoner's, Nun's Priest's), its ending with this last tale permits the narrator's final words ("Saint Paul says that all that's written well / Is written down some useful truth to tell") to become a concluding moralization of sorts:

> HOST:
> Then take the wheat and let the chaff lie still.
> And now, good God, if it be Thy will,
> As says Lord Christ, so make us all good men . . .
>
> COMPANY: *(In unison)*
> And bring us into His high bliss. Amen!
> *(They bow as the music builds and the lights fade)*
>
> (97)

This finale excludes any linking use of the "Canterbury" theme, in that we never see the pilgrims actually arriving anywhere, as we do in most of the other performance versions. We do, however, return to the pilgrims between the tales miming the idea of journey, "cantering on imaginary horses" (23) or enacting the "pantomime of a picnic" (7), but there is little individualization of the pilgrim party; this party rather forms a "pool" of players out of which the tales themselves are enacted, and since a balance of men and women is needed for the tales there can be no marrying of their respective number with Chaucer's own pilgrim framework. It is indeed in the relation between the tales and the links between them that Wengrow's version is most innovative, addressing the problem of how a narrator "tells" an enacted tale by having each tale's protagonists using third-person narration to describe their own actions; thus it is the carpenter in the "Miller's Tale" who says, "Now this carpenter had lately wed a wife . . . ," and so on (48). The most striking elision of the narrator relates, however, to "Chaucer" himself, who has no role in the version, and these elisions confirm its lack of interest in several of the subjects discussed thus far: the figure of the artist, the cult of boisterous (English) personality, and ideals of bawdy and convivial fellowship.

For Wengrow the *Canterbury Tales* is rather seen as a set of purely theatrical problems and challenges, with the emphasis on mime and balletic formation and on the quick transformation of the company from pilgrim role to tale role, with the surplus cast at any time even forming the props: tables, chairs, and notably beds (see the elaborate description of how "six actors/actresses" form the bed for the "Wife of Bath's Tale,"

18). When in the "Miller's Tale" we are told that even the blade Absolon thrusts at Nicholas is to be played by a "small actress," we perhaps feel that the theatrical kinetics have gone too far (it is interesting to speculate how Elaine Tuttle Hansen would have incorporated this detail into her discussion of the blade episode as representing Absolon's phallic self-assertion; see chapter 10).The absence of any developed linking context tends to leave each tale curiously isolated, and the whole without any particular narrative rationale; I have already noted the sudden and rather arbitrary conclusion, whereas individual tales like the Pardoner's are forced into a melodramatic climax addressed to the audience in lieu of the Pardoner's designs on his fellow travelers:

> Now, good men, God forgive you each trespass,
> And keep you from the sin of avarice.
> *(He hisses out the final word)*
> *(The spotlight slowly fades out)*
>
> (89)

The final performance to be looked at in any detail is the BBC radio version of the *Canterbury Tales* created by Colin Haydn Evans and broadcast in 1991. This consisted of four episodes, each running for just over forty-five minutes, featuring the Pardoner's, Wife of Bath's, Miller's, and Franklin's tales, in that order, and linked by a prominent Canterbury pilgrimage theme.[24] Although there was no real "General Prologue," other than Chaucer narrating in general terms the assembling at the Tabard, followed by the Host's explanation of the tale-telling competition, portrait details from the "Prologue" are often converted into dialogue and interspersed among the tales themselves, in a manner reminiscent of the television version. Thus the Wife of Bath says of the Pardoner as he is about to tell his tale, "He looks more mare than stallion," and so forth. The tales are separately enacted with the narrators' voices coming back in at intervals for descriptive passages within individual tales; there are also more general interruptions where the pilgrims themselves offer midtale comment and reaction, a feature answering the need to keep the whole cast of the work in play for the listener.

In many ways this radio version is a conflation of several of the performance elements we have considered thus far. The comedy is cruder than in the original, the tales being recited to a constant backdrop of knee-slapping, guffawing, and inebriated laughter from the pilgrims, but they also use throughout a prose that eschews modern idiom in favor of a "medievalesque" raciness, felt to be appropriate to, though nowhere found in, Chaucer. Thus Alison's exasperated words to Absolon, "You are a greater problem than extra shite in a full midden" (she has already told him to "piss off"), or the Wife of Bath commenting on the Miller, "He talks like a slow fart some days." In the "Miller's Tale," Alison and Nicholas (usually pronounced Nicholarse) make love at the outset and during the course of the tale (there is double entendre on the word "banging" while John is constructing the barrels), and the weary old "Pollux" joke arising from Nicholas's star-gazing (misheard as "ballocks") gets another undeserved outing after its use in the Woods-Bogdanov version (65). Crudification is also present in the much-truncated "Wife of Bath's Prologue," which is a series of simple diatribes: a husband is "a sorrowful necessity," men "are blind to all that matters in life," "man is catastrophe in disguise," and so on.

At the same time, there is a pervasive sentimentalization of Chaucer—the pilgrims are frequently reduced to tears by the tales—reminiscent of *Canterbury Tales—the Musical,* where all is fundamentally "good-hearted." With only four tales, some of the more embittered dissension on the pilgrimage is simply removed (the Friar-Summoner feud, for example, or that between the Miller and Reeve), and the Pardoner-Host confrontation is sparked by the Host having fallen asleep during the tale rather than by any threat to him that the tale might carry, such as we discussed at the close of chapter 6. In the tales themselves there is a similar calming of Chaucerian troubled waters. Thus the "Wife of Bath's Tale" is rewritten to suggest that what women "moost desiren" is not "maistrie" over their men but self-fulfillment through an equal and mutual love, the gist of the knight's answer to the queen: "In the end it is only giving that is the true return, one to the other." The knight's sensitive enlightenment actually leads him to make love to the old hag, having understood her inner worth: "I have found who you are, and I will not wish it otherwise"; the hag's subsequent transformation reflects the knight's ability to "see" with this moral eye: "My new beauty is your awakening," she tells him.

The elision here of problematic questions relating to power and gender continues in the astounding rewriting of the concluding "Franklin's Tale," where Dorigen of her own accord visits Aurelius and, in return for his repentant release of her from her pledge, bestows a single night of love on him: "We shall burn together and be done in a single time." She then announces what she has done to Arveragus, who approves her generosity, and all go off happily, though perhaps in a different spirit of accord from that at the end of the "Franklin's Tale" itself. "Everyone a winner," as they say, and the concluding tale in Kittredge's "marriage-group" is offered as the note of harmony and "mutual forgiveness" on which the pilgrimage ends, with the Host indeed deciding that he cannot choose between the tales and that they should all win. The final scene takes place in a sunlit field overlooking the cathedral, with Chaucer noting his fondness for the pilgrimage party relaxing about him and for the spirit of amity they have arrived at among them, a spirit extending to the radio audience itself, addressed here by Chaucer as "good friends—lesser would have been the journey without your company." This universal embrace of the "true and smiling face of God's creation"—we are all part of "God's Plenty"—is offered by a Chaucer who has been prescient all along of futurity "tuning in" to the tales, and who at the outset had told a baffled Host of "others . . . join[ing] us on our way . . . more than we perhaps originally envisaged." As mediator between the pilgrims and their radio public, and among the pilgrims themselves, who often turn to "master Chaucer" to resolve their disagreements, Chaucer's status as the voice of humane concord, between individuals and down the ages, is endorsed.

Before concluding we should briefly note Kenneth Pickering's *Some Canterbury Tales* of 1988 (music by Derek Hyde), Jim Sperinck's pantomime based on the *Tales* of 1993, and the recently televised animated version of the *Tales*. Although Pickering's subtitle notes that his play is "freely adapted" from Chaucer, far fewer "liberties" are taken with the tales he includes than in many of the versions above: his own translation, in couplets, avoids extraneous material, and in the sequence he chooses ("General Prologue," Knight's, Wife of Bath's, Pardoner's, Franklin's or Nun's Priest's, and Miller's tales), the changes arise from excision and compression rather than outright rewriting. His major innovation, however, is in his handling of the pilgrimage framework. Here the Miller is first on stage telling the audience, "This is the old road to Canterbury and when I last passed this way Master Chaucer himself was with me"; the tale-telling that unfolds is then to be seen, presumably, as the Miller's memory, in flashback, of that journey, although "Master Chaucer" himself makes no appearance.[25] The Miller also wraps things up with an epilogue, again fondly recalling the journey and the goings-on that took place in Canterbury on arrival, recommending the audience to "read Master Chaucer's book" for the full story of these (47; although of course such things are precisely what we won't find there, but rather derive from the "Tale of Beryn"—see chapter 4).

Pickering's desire for fidelity and supplementation at once leads to a very odd compromise. For example, he keeps the Host's words from the "General Prologue" (lines 790–801) about each pilgrim telling four tales on the journey and about the prize supper taking place back at the Tabard (5); by the end this has been forgotten, apparently, as the pilgrims reach Canterbury and the supper is awarded there (the winner chosen on the basis of audience applause). The "Prologue" introduces two serving girls, Kit and Moll, who also make the journey; when lots are drawn later to decide whether the "Franklin's Tale" or "Nun's Priest's Tale" is to be told, we are informed that the narrator of either tale has been "lost upon the way," and the tale is told by Kit (or "Another"). Such features add to the confusion as to whether what we are seeing is indeed the "original" Canterbury pilgrimage, via the Miller's memory, or a later journey undertaken by the Miller et al. that incidentally refers to the first. But they indicate above all the need (and the danger) of finding some new angle, or gimmick, to use in staging the familiar scenario of Tabard, pilgrims, tales, Canterbury—a need already betrayed (if rather halfheartedly) in Pickering's title, "*Some* Canterbury Tales" (my emphasis).

There is certainly no doubting the originality of Sperinck's *The Canterbury Tales Panto*.[26] Here Chaucer's tales have been whisked around in a blender to produce a soufflé entertainment of a customary seasonal kind, with King Harry of Tabardinia sending the suitors for his daughter's (Princess Alisoun's) hand off to Canterbury in search of a magic story. Squire Aurelius outwits the dastardly Franklin to find this and win his bride; other competitors include the Wife of Bath (the traditional Dame), who finds husband number six in the shape of Arveragus, who has opened his stately home in Canterbury to the public as a "medieval holiday camp" (35). Other characters include Percy Pardon, Cyril Summons, Chanter, Perty, Reeve ("the choleric estate manager," p. v), and many more. The whole text is a kind of treasure hunt of references to Chaucer that, as Sperinck says in an appendix, "I am sure devotees will pick up" (53).

Pantomimes that draw on Chaucer are not in fact a recent idea, nor are performance replottings of the *Tales* that arguably border on the absurd.[27] Of the dramatizations listed by Olena S. Bunn in 1949, several of which have been noted in these pages, the "most interesting and professional" (and certainly the most substantial) was in her opinion Percy Mackaye's *The Canterbury Pilgrims* of 1903.[28] Subtitled "A Comedy," the play features a plot of intrigue and disguise whereby on the road to Canterbury the Wife of Bath is hoping to capture Chaucer himself as her next husband, while he shows an amorous interest in the Prioress. The latter has arranged to meet on the road her long-lost brother, whom Chaucer realizes is actually the Knight before the Prioress herself does; the Wife, however, refusing to believe the story of a family connection, wagers with Chaucer that the Knight and the Prioress are lovers; if Chaucer loses he has to accept the Wife in marriage.[29] The Wife then, with the help of other pilgrims, binds and gags the Knight, dresses in his clothes, and proceeds to woo the Prioress in order to fool Chaucer (91, 105, 172), though all is eventually righted and forgiven.

If such a performance indicates, like several more modern versions, that the *Canterbury Tales* is little more than a repository of colorful dramatis personae to be redeployed at will, Mackaye's work also shows a fervent response to the figure of Chaucer himself that has no parallel in versions looked at previously in this chapter. Not only does he have a central role in the fiction, but also his "great name" as "Dan Chaucer—laureate of chivalry" is well established among the pilgrims themselves, who refer to him in awe (93). Moreover, he himself voices a tribute to "Merry England"—

> Which nature cirqued with its green wall of seas
> To be her home and hearth-stone; where no slave,
> Though e'er he crept in her lap, was nursed of her . . .
> (113)

—and to its eternal return in his work:

> they who drink the vintage I will brew
> Shall wake, and see a vision, in their wine,
> Of Canterbury and our pilgrimage:
> These very faces, with the blood in them,
> These moving limbs, this rout, this majesty!

For by that resurrection of the Muse,
Shall you, sweet friends, re-met in timeless Spring,
Pace on through time upon eternal lines
And ride with Chaucer in his pilgrimage.

(207)

It is significant that Chaucer's "resurrection" is here staged through a pseudo-Shakespearean comedy of errors, endorsed, moreover, in passages of blank verse heavily influenced by John of Gaunt's famous "sceptred isle" tribute to England in the speech from *Richard II* (2.1.31–68). The first text we shall look at in the following chapter, a text contemporary with Mackaye's play, can also only approach Chaucer as hero through a Shakespearean filter. But by the second half of the century, as we have seen, performance versions have little interest in promoting the nationalistic status of either the author or his text, even if the pilgrims still on occasion do "ride with Chaucer" through an attenuated Merrie England.

The final performance offering of the twentieth century, the animated *Canterbury Tales* directed by Jonathan Myerson (1998–2000), certainly gives little sense of a Chaucer concerned with weighty matters like upholding the national heritage; indeed, a cartoon format by definition might seem the acme of a postwar concern with entertainment pure and simple, though this particular project has been partly funded by BBC Education, reflecting the desire to address both an adult audience and one of schoolchildren. The powerful animations certainly do more than offer a picture of the Middle Ages as one of innocent diversion, given the reminders of death and disease the pilgrims encounter on their journey, from the shot of the limbless beggar who begins proceedings to the deformed bodies and plague-carrying rats that frame the "Pardoner's Tale," where the tale's animated puppets share the same world as the pilgrims themselves.[30] In this emphasis the animated version is akin to another 1990s creation, the gruesome Chaucerian world of P. C. Doherty, discussed at the close of chapter 9. Other sinister features include the looming power of the gods in the "Knight's Tale," who occupy a far greater proportion of the narrative than in Chaucer's original, and the illusory nature of the old hag's transformation in the "Wife of Bath's Tale," where the knight is only duped into thinking that his nightmare partner has become young again.

These dark and disturbing undertones offset the tradition of inebriated merriment, which also remains, yet overall the ambition of the animated *Tales* is to offer the viewer, whether child or adult, an easily assimilable Chaucer. With three tales fitted into each half-hour format, much of the original is excluded or miniaturized, and the emphatically modern prose translation pares the text down to a series of blunt formulations: "We've both been cretins," says Chauntecleer to the fox, after escaping from him into the tree (for "I shrewe us bothe two," VII.3426), and the elaborately rhetorical disowning of rhetoric from the Franklin (V.716–27) becomes simply "I'm an uneducated sort of chap, lords and ladies, so excuse my sort of lingo." Chaucer's "Retraction" is boiled down to the inappropriate plea, "But whatever you do, don't take me too literally"; the moral of the "Nun's Priest's Tale" becomes "there's something to learn in everything, you just have to know what"; and the emphasis throughout is to make everything directly obvious. This mania for accessibility necessarily carries through into the parallel version that uses Chaucer's own text, often filleted into single lines that have to stand for an entire passage, and sometimes placed into the mouth of a pilgrim speaker different from that in the original poem. A sound bite is still a sound bite, even if in Middle English.

In an interview Myerson gave to the Radio 4 program *Start the Week,* he answered the interviewer's charge that in the modern version he had "just murdered Chaucer's rhythm and rhyme" with enthusiastic agreement: "Absolutely, that was one of my serious goals."[31] Developing the position that the iambic pentameter in particular simply gets in the way of the modern appreciation of Chaucer, Myerson went on to suggest that Chaucer's literary importance lies in the psychological portrayal of the tellers through their tales and in the rather more topical, "postmodernist" intrusion of the author into his own fiction. The interviewer, Jeremy Paxman, himself a graduate in English, noted that he was a "fan" of Chaucer though he hadn't "picked him up" since university, while Myerson went on to remark of the *Canterbury Tales,* "Everyone feels in England a sort of sense of ownership about it but they haven't read it." This last observation could indeed stand as a motto for this present book, which is concerned to document Chaucer's repeated presence in our culture as well as our fundamental neglect of him, but whether the "Chaucer made easy" of the animated format and the carefree "murder" of Chaucer's poetry is a worthwhile way to address that neglect is a question best left to our concluding chapter.

9

Novel Chaucer

The historical novel that centers on Chaucer's life or times is arguably a more ephemeral and obscure discourse than any considered hitherto in this book, and the fact that such works are rarely if ever reprinted perhaps testifies to the difficulty of writing Chaucer as the standard novelistic hero, as we shall see. On the other hand, novels in which Chaucer is a more marginal figure and the "romance" of fourteenth-century life is able to dominate proceedings have sometimes enjoyed great vogue, as in Anya Seton's much reprinted *Katherine* (1954), which details the titanic love of Katherine Swynford and John of Gaunt. Such a genre is worth examining because the depiction of Chaucer, whether a primary or secondary concern, clearly confirms the changing emphases that, in the passage from the Victorian to the contemporary, have been traced in preceding chapters. Before offering a conclusion to this study in the following chapter, therefore, I should like here to provide a recapitulation of some of the concerns of the present century by looking at this particular brand of Chauceriana.

Emily Richings's *In Chaucer's Maytime* of 1902 shows an infatuation with what I described as the flower-and-leaf Chaucer discussed at the outset of this work in the context of Morris and Burne-Jones, together with quaintly medievalizing modes of speech of the "forsooth we wot not as yet" variety.[1] The novel concerns itself with Chaucer's courtship of his wife Philippa, the couple first meeting outside "a secluded convent buried in haunted Arden" where Philippa is sent on her mother's death:

> Valemere Abbey looked a veritable "haunt of ancient peace," steeped in the bloom and verdure of that ideal Maytime, which transforms "woody Warwickshire" into fairyland.

> "Verily the heart of England is rich in beauty" mused Chaucer, gazing down a long vista, where a sea of bluebells, etherealised by a veil of azure haze, like the visible incense of the languid perfume, melted away in sapphire light. (8, 28)

How Chaucer has come to stray into Shakespeare territory is not very clear, but throughout the novel his wooing is framed by the flowers and fairies of "haunted Arden," whether transposed to Woodstock (171ff.) or underwriting the "Midsummer Night's Dream" and "Midsummer Idyl" sequence described in chapters 33 and 34 (184ff.). Such a setting requires a romantic, ardent hero, and Chaucer in his "Maytime" is indeed presented as the complete suitor, handsome, endowed with a "rich tenor voice" (22) and even "tall" (46), as if proceeding out of the Kelmscott Chaucer illustrations rather than from the more common images of the "elvyssh" or portly figure. Moreover, although young, this Chaucer of the 1360s seems to be at the height of his career, "rich in personal charm and high in royal favour" (120), famous as a poet throughout the land and holder of many noble female hearts "in thrall" (45–46). Chronology is blithely disregarded to grant him already the office of Clerk of the Works (127) and to bring the date of composition of some of his poems forward by two decades: thus the opening lines of the *Parliament of Fowls* are quoted to instance the patience he needs to win Philippa (168), and at one point Hugh Swynford dilates on Chaucer's suit in a similar vein:

> Aye, and two lines of a poem writ by Dan Chaucer, the which our head minstrel did sing to the twanging of his lute yesternight, can best explain such constancy! . . .
>
> "The godde of Love! Ah Benedicite!
> How mightie and how greate a lord is hee!" (198)

Apart from this reference to the "Knight's Tale," however, the novel is notable for its complete lack of interest in Chaucer's major compositions, like the *Tales* or *Troilus and Criseyde*, the action ending with Philippa's death and the period of domestic harmony preceding this that the Chaucers achieve with their three children, Thomas, Lewis, and Elizabeth. An epilogue set in September 1496 (the novel skipping over the period intervening since Philippa's death when much of the *Tales* must have been written) restores Chaucer to the bosom of nature in the form of John of Gaunt's gift to him of Donnington Castle, complete with the celebrated "Chaucer oak" (401–8), a fanciful tableau mercilessly derided by Lounsbury a decade before Richings's novel was published (see chapter 2, note 30).

Chaucer can be seen, as Alfred Pollard noted in 1893, as an "exceptionally late" developer in poetic terms—what would he have achieved had he died at forty? Pollard asks.[2] The concentration on his "Maytime" has to forgo what is arguably most significant about him, however much certain dates in his biography are reinvented, and the gap is filled here with lush descriptions of nature and the general sensitivities of his poetic temperament, to produce someone akin to figures like Lysander or Orlando, roaming the "enchanted ground" of Arden (37). "Maytime" stands as a poetic refuge from the public sphere, and in spite of Richings's dutiful inclusion of episodes like the Peasants' Revolt (chapter 53, 364–78), her Chaucer is as out-of-the-world as even Burne-Jones might wish. The attempt to fictionalize this youthful romancer has not been repeated, unless it be in the Regina Kelly volume discussed in chapter 4, a work that also contrived to suggest, as we saw, that Chaucer had accomplished everything of note while scarcely out of adolescence. The other fictionalizations we shall consider below accept in various ways a more mature if inevitably less "romantic" protagonist.

The contrast is at its greatest with Anya Seton's *Katherine* of 1954, as I have already hinted. Here the emphasis is not on Chaucer and Philippa de Roet but on the latter's sister, the novel's eponymous heroine, and on her affair with John of Gaunt that concluded in their marriage in 1396.[3] Chaucer and his wife are featured only sporadically in the novel, but act as an important foil to the beautiful and passionate couple who dominate the action and whose tempestuous relationship is fully caught up in the warfare, political intrigues, and social turbulence of the times. On the contrary, Philippa is no beauty like her sister but small and "plump," while Chaucer is introduced as "by no means [a] romantic figure . . . short, not much taller than Philippa herself and though . . . only twenty-six, already inclined towards stoutness."[4] Nor are the two particularly in love with each other, in contrast to the poetic fervor that informs *In Chaucer's Maytime;* the passions of the "sensible" and good-humored Chaucer are in fact reserved for the Duchess Blanche, though "his practical future lay with Philippa, who suited him well enough" (42, 45). Eventually the two settle for a life of separation:

"Though Philippa sometimes . . . visited her husband in his lodgings over Aldgate, where she cleaned and clucked and harried him out of his easy-going bachelor habits, these visits sprang largely from a sense of obligation, and the Chaucers were both more contented apart" (291).

Chaucer here, then, provides a vein of antiromance throughout the novel, and Seton shows herself comfortably versed in the affable, corpulent, and unimpassioning figure that the twentieth century has taken to its heart; by the time Chaucer has become "fat and forty" she even labels him "staid" (381). Not that he is treated unsympathetically on the whole; thus his keen, observant intelligence is remarked on throughout, and Seton shows some interest in his work as a poet, though largely insofar as this reflects the interest he himself is supposed to take in the hypnotic figure of his sister-in-law and her affair with Gaunt. Thus in the "Author's Note" prefacing the novel, Seton suggests that Katherine Swynford may have inspired in part Chaucer's portrayal of Criseyde (11), an idea incorporated at several points into the narrative itself, though Katherine "never suspect[ed] in how many tender ways she had been Criseyde's model" (472). Moreover, her own confession to Chaucer, at one point, of her sense of sin in living as Gaunt's mistress and the "agony of penitence" she goes through shame Chaucer into realizing how far "he had himself been drifting into light-minded worldliness"; the result is that not only is she responsible for the portrayal of Criseyde, but also for the palinode that concludes Chaucer's poem (471–72). In short, Chaucer and his work are seen as the mere reflex of the mighty lives around him, while the *Canterbury Tales* are only referred to at one or two points as offering a harmless merriment incapable of touching the protagonists in their deeper moments of crisis, as when the neglected Katherine declares "'twould take more than the tales of junketing to Canterbury to cheer me today" (545), as if the *Tales* had nowhere anything to say about things like contrition, endurance, or self-examination.

One might say that in *Katherine* Chaucer pays the price for a complacency that his work and biography have often been held to exhibit, the lack of a sufficient involvement in the issues of the day. One lengthy section of the novel (413–59) describes the dangers Katherine is caught up in during the Peasants' Revolt and the attack on the Savoy, where she is in residence; during the same period Chaucer is "snugly ensconced in his rooms over Aldgate . . . and there he had stayed unmolested, reading and writing during the three days of the violence" (468). His marginal status in this historical novel that is certainly the most meticulously researched of the works considered here (see the "Author's Note" for a list of the "standard histories," sourcebooks, and Chronicles consulted) follows on inevitably from well-established traditions of Chaucer's indifference to his historical moment, so to speak, and an implied critique of that position runs through Seton's book, not offset by any compensating praise for Chaucer as a universal or "timeless" classic. The problems indeed of finding meaningful lines of communication between important events and personages of the fourteenth century (like the Peasants' Revolt, Gaunt, Richard II) and the Chaucer who is always present yet curiously distant surface in all the novels under consideration, a difficulty not merely for the novelist, but for historians and biographers also (see chapter 2). If Richings, for example, responds to this by omitting the history, others like Seton are well prepared to curtail the Chaucer.

A novel that in fact attempts to hold the two in balance is Wallace B. Nichols's *Deputy for Youth* of 1935. Chaucer here occupies center stage, though the novel again accepts that he cannot do this in terms of the conventional hero: "Poet and famous though he might be, he made hardly a romantic figure, for he was a little too portly and rather too humorous to be authentically thrilling as a lover."[5] Chaucer is, however, returned to the realm of youthful passion by agreeing to the request of his ward, Edmund Staplegate, that he should intervene to rescue Staplegate's beloved, Cecilia Chaumpaigne, from a marriage arranged for her by her parents.[6] Chaucer's participation in this exploit on behalf of true love, as Edmund's deputy, authenticates the youthful poet who produced such things as the *Romance of the Rose,* while Philippa's nagging him for his stupidity in intervening (80) does full justice to the comic domestication that is often seen as Chaucer's fate in middle age (largely, it would seem, on the basis of lines 560–66 of the *House of Fame*).

Fiction is here, of course, put to the service of clearing Chaucer's name, for ever since the discovery in the late nineteenth century of the deed of release to Chaucer from Cecilia Chaumpaigne from any legal action concerning her *raptus,* questions have been raised as to the extent of Chaucer's culpability in the case; whether he was guilty of rape or merely of abduction of Cecilia on someone else's behalf, whether she was bought off, and even whether Chaucer could have been "framed," as Ezra Pound asked.[7] *Deputy for Youth* provides an answer to this enigma, staging an abduction in which Cecilia is entirely compliant and an abductor who is in keeping with the kindly, avuncular Chaucer portrayed throughout. Not that the *raptus* episode is other than the starting point for a novel that is a curious farrago of history, romance, and literary biography: once Chaucer's deputizing is completed, he largely disappears from the lengthy drama of the Peasants' Revolt and march on London (occupying the last third of the novel), in which, however, Edmund and Cecilia are excitingly caught up, the former proving his valorous swordsmanship in an episode centering on the Tabard Inn, where Harry Bailly has been forced to admit some of the rebels (279–80). Chaucer may be absent from the scene here, but the scene is obviously filtered through his writing. Chaucer's poetry is indeed featured frequently, even if it stands outside the novel's picaresque action; at one point, entitled "Interlude," Chaucer and Gower discuss *Troilus and Criseyde* over a supper of roast swan in the former's Aldgate lodgings (165–81), and in the "Epilogue" that concludes the novel after the collapse of the Peasants' Revolt, attention returns to Chaucer as the plan of the *Canterbury Tales* begins to take shape in his mind (313–19). These headings—"Interlude," "Epilogue"—bear witness to the fact that the novel's literary and historical concerns are seen as disjunct rather than co-involved. Although the novel ends (as we might reasonably expect of any novel featuring Chaucer) on the *Canterbury Tales,* we find their author musing on the work at the price of not seeing a parade of Richard II passing before his eyes and being upbraided by Philippa for this once more:

> "Was it not a gay sight?" said Philippa, suddenly appearing at his elbow.
> "Sight? Gay sight? What sight?" he asked.
> "Why, the riding through of the King and an escort of knights," she answered. "Did you not see it?"
> "No," he said, blinking. "But I was in thought, wife."
> "You are always looking on the ground and seeing nothing," she replied tartly. "You never see anything!"
> "No, my dear, no; no, poppet," said Chaucer, and began to laugh inwardly. (319)

These final words indicate that although historical events may be the stuff of the action of the novel, their significance is ephemeral compared with the enduring legacy of a Chaucerian inner vision that is at odds with them.

Nichols's book is not the first that attempts to intervene on Chaucer's behalf in the Chaumpaigne affair; it is anticipated by the even more curious novel of 1905 by C. E. D. Phelps, *The Accolade*. Whereas *Deputy for Youth* largely accepted the *Tales* as a fiction conjured by Chaucer from the resources of his inner vision, this novel, like that by Richings, reports the Canterbury pilgrimage as an event in Chaucer's life that, we are to surmise, he subsequently writes up (though neither novel shows more than a marginal interest in that writing). This means that the pilgrims themselves are free to enter the action alongside Chaucer, and fact, fiction, and fantasy blend together to produce the situation whereby Cecilia herself participates in the pilgrim party, dressed as the nun accompanying Madame Eglentine.

The novel opens in 1372 when the Franklin of the future pilgrimage, his son Gervas, and their yeoman Jenkin come across Chaucer (already "near fifty years of age") and rescue him from an attack by robbers on the outskirts of London.[8] The three are returning to their home in Dorset, where Gervas is paying suit to Cecilia, who is their neighbor; her uncle, however, puts a stop to this by having Gervas and Jenkin abducted and carried off to Bordeaux by a shipman whose vessel is called the "Magdelayne" (56). In France the two escape and after several dramatic exploits run into Chaucer again, journeying toward Genoa on the mission of 1372–73 (122ff.); henceforth they accompany him to Italy in his service. Here the action becomes somewhat murky; Gervas meets Niccolo Rucellai, the father of Cecilia's uncle (who, in fact, disguised as a friar, had already helped him in France) and decides to stay in Italy to work with Niccolo in quest of the philosopher's stone. When this enterprise fails, Gervas journeys back to France, teams up with Jenkin once again, and, after many more adventures, falls in with a monk bound on a pilgrimage to Canterbury. From him he learns that "among many notables" this same pilgrimage will be joined by "Master Chaucer, the king's envoy" and by "Mistress Cecilia Chamberlayne, a west-country heiress [who] will then make her profession. She hath abode single many years . . . waiting for a faithless lover, but is now minded to espouse the church" (315).

At this, Gervas (disguised in canon's costume) and his yeoman hasten to intercept the pilgrimage, and thus constitute, as it were, the episode described by Chaucer in the latter part of fragment VIII of the *Tales*. Dressed as a canon, Gervas is able to approach the clerics of the party in a way that "could cause no surprise" and surreptitiously make himself known to Cecilia; he then enlists Chaucer in his cause, racing off ahead to Canterbury to arrange the abduction, Jenkin allaying suspicion over his flight by telling the pilgrims his "brain is turned" with seeking the stone, before embarking on a "rough-hewn, long-winded tale" that draws on Gervas's alchemical experiences in Italy (336–41). Chaucer assists in the abduction in Canterbury as promised, and the very last paragraph in the novel describes the day more than a year later when Chaucer receives a document that he reads out: "Galfridus Laureatus—de meo raptu—Cecilia Chamberlayne. All is well,—the lady pardoneth me for her rape. So mote it be. Here's for thee, good lad. And now, Adam Scrivener, bring us the 'Wife of Bath's Tale'"(352).

Although Chaucer is allowed a more exotic role in this novel than that of hen-pecked husband, as for example in his sojourn in Italy where he acts as royal negotiator as well as meeting Petrarch (153–84), the main focus of adventure remains with Gervas and his yeoman. However, the strange combination of the *raptus* case and the *Canterbury Tales* pilgrimage does provide the terminus of these adventures, the novel showing itself as much interested in fictionalizing Chaucer's fiction, as his biography. As we saw in chapter 8, this type of refictionalization of the *Tales* is found in other work contemporary with *The Accolade,* namely Mackaye's *Canterbury Pilgrims,* and might be seen as in some ways a more fertile enterprise than biographical reconstruction, given that far more is known, for example, about the Wife of Bath than about Philippa Chaucer. If fictionalizations/dramatizations of Chaucer's life do indeed become more scarce in the second half of the twentieth century, the pilgrimage itself continues to be rewritten by dramatists and librettists, as we have seen, and by novelists. Thus Vera Chapman's *The Wife of Bath* (1978) is largely a reinvention of Chaucer's famous "Prologue": here the Wife tells her story not to the pilgrims as a whole, but solely to Chaucer, by the fireside after the first day when the other pilgrims have gone to bed. We are thus given a great deal of extra information: the names of her husbands, the fact that she had five children, details of many sexual adventures inside and outside marriage, and, most important, the knowledge that the battling virago Chaucer portrays misrepresents the affectionate and supportive woman she was to most of her partners. The final chapter of the novel, "Miracle at Canterbury," shows the powerful physical attraction she still holds for figures as diverse as the Knight, the

Squire, and the Summoner, but after slipping on the floor of the cathedral and banging her head (an accident that cures her deafness), it is the Franklin's arms she comes round in. They recognize each other as erstwhile youthful lovers, and he becomes her sixth husband without delay.[9] If Chaucer comes across in conventional terms in the novel as pleasant, affable, wise, but not charismatic ("queer little fellow, whom [the Wife] liked almost as much as any she had met—but somehow, not as a sweetheart," 128), he is also seen as more intent on his poetic falsifications of her life story than on reproducing the account she gives (19). Here Alison puts the record straight, however, in a novel that might be seen as a fictional counterpart to some of the feminist critical support of her that dates from the later 1970s and the 1980s, though the final act of marriage answers the need for a romantic closure that is practically a tradition in modern rewritings of Chaucer: the Wife has, after all, claimed in marriage at different times several of the males on the pilgrimage party.[10]

The most extended use of the Canterbury pilgrimage in modern fiction lies in the series of "medieval mysteries" that P. C. Doherty has been publishing since 1994, a series that adopts Chaucer's pilgrims and their journey but gives them wholly new tales to tell. After their assembly at the Tabard, in the first novel of the series, Harry Bailly rehearses the tale-telling competition but with a new twist: each of them

> "should tell at least two tales. One will be for the day, but what about the nights? . . . when we move out tomorrow to St Thomas's watering hole, let us tell a merry tale to instruct or amuse. But, at night," his voice fell, "let it be different." He stared around the now quiet company. "Let us tell a tale of mystery that will chill the blood, halt the heart and curl the locks upon our heads."[11]

The Knight insists on telling the first of these tales, about "horrors sprung from the very pit of Hell" (6), and begins it that very evening before the pilgrims' departure, finishing it the next day on the first night's stopover. In three further novels Doherty gives us the "night tales" of the Man of Law, Franklin, and Priest (Chaucer's Parson), tales of murder, horror, Satanic cults, the supernatural.

This blackly "Gothic" Chaucer follows the fashion set by Umberto Eco's *The Name of the Rose* and the medieval whodunits of Ellis Peters in seeing the Middle Ages as an appropriate locus of sinister crime, a veritable "dark age" affording an absolute contrast with the surfeit of picturesque beauty with which we start the century in Richings's novel and the Burne-Jones legacy.[12] Doherty's "Knight's Tale," for example, concerns a series of brutal murders committed in Oxford by vampires, or "Strigoi," originating in Wallachia; the "Priest's Tale" recounts the curse that falls on a Kentish village, leading to murder, premature death, and ghostly possession, after the participation of its menfolk in the massacre of a party of Knights Templar. The novels are particularly keen on setting events in gruesomely realized urban contexts ("Southwark was a veritable hell-hole") that are a congeries of "filthy alleyway[s]," "open sewers," diseased beggars, and desperate criminals, often with a gibbet on the street corner where the latest moldering corpse swings.[13] Nor does any nostalgic idea of the beautiful English countryside obtain beyond the town: rather than Morris's "rose-hung lanes of woody Kent," the Kent through which the pilgrims travel is "wild" and brigand-infested, and frequently has them seeking refuge.[14] Even the sweet weather of April that heralds Chaucer's pilgrimage is interrupted by "grey and sullen" rain and the boiling up of "the devil's fog."[15] In short, the novels wholly rewrite the hilarity and jovial comfort that the tales are traditionally seen as providing.

Obviously there are problems in making these "night" tales congruent with the scheme of Chaucer's journey, given that the one-pilgrim-per-night arrangement would prolong that journey inordinately. However, the heavy rain mentioned above detains the pilgrims in their lodgings during the day and occasions the "Man of Law's Tale," while the aforementioned fog makes them lose their way and creates a delay filled by the "Priest's Tale." Although the topographical details are rather sketchy, there is certainly the sense that after four novels and four tales we are nowhere near Canterbury, and the "Priest's Tale" is by no means seen as a "knitting up" of proceedings, as its equivalent is in Chaucer (X.28). This sense of an open-ended sequence is enforced at the level of the individual tales themselves, which are all autobiographical; thus the Knight telling of the Strigoi is himself the figure charged with tracking them down in his story (as we gradually learn), and his hunt for them is a lifelong mission; indeed, the Monk of the party, with eyes that, "half-hidden in a hooded cowl, glittered maliciously" and "lips curled in a grin like that of a hunting dog," is described thus as one of their number as the tale ends. Similarly the Franklin tells a tale that leaves as its epilogue an unfinished bloody feud with the Summoner, as the story again gradually reveals—"He hunts me and I hunt him"; in fact, most of the pilgrims play a part in each other's accounts.[16]

Of all the novels we have looked at that draw on Chaucer, whether his life or his text, the Doherty series represents the most nominal and least engaged use of him; even Vera Chapman's tale, which largely resists the Chaucerian account, draws on Chaucer for some of its substance, as in the description of the fifth marriage with Jankyn and the lecturing that led to the book-burning episode (103–7). With Doherty, however, references to the *Tales* are completely incidental, largely a matter of providing continuity across the series through recurrent details of the Cook scratching his ulcer, the Prioress fussing over her dogs, or the Miller farting. The figure of Chaucer himself is unaccountably missing from the first novel and the assembling at the Tabard, and only turns up as one of the party in *A Tapestry,* and there is the merest reference to the tales told during the day; that is, to those of the original poem. This opportunistic and even parasitic use of Chaucer, who provides a ready-made framework and a historical context that, as we noted above, has become a fashionable locus for thriller writers in the 1980s and 1990s, has the effect of rendering its source text innocently harmless and jejune compared with this other, nocturnal world that now emerges sensationally from it, even if there are organizational difficulties, as we saw, in making the two worlds tally. Perhaps the major difference, however, is the complete suspension of any fiction of orality that occurs in the Doherty novels; whereas Chaucer's tales are animated by the ongoing sense of interaction in the course of their telling between speaker and pilgrim-audience, the Doherty pilgrims speak in a seamless prose that evokes not tale-telling but precisely the written novel itself, addressed to practiced readers of the horror/thriller genre rather than to a set of present listeners. Although the pilgrims do comment during the course of the stories, they do so in self-contained "Words between the pilgrims" before the writer takes pen again to begin another "chapter." The conspicuousness of generic features appropriate to the modern thriller is hardly appeased by the awkwardly grafted Chaucerian element, and the formulaic horror elements themselves add up to a collection of ghouls, ghosts, and corpses far less horrific (to this reader) than the action of, say, the "Prioress's Tale" or the Pardoner's. Of course, if the series is still incomplete, the possibility remains that it has yet to say something significant "about" Chaucer himself, whose pilgrim-embodiment, like the others, has his "secrets" and is occasionally seen to smile enigmatically (*Tapestry of Murders,* 4), and who at some stage may be required to tell his tale. Given that the sequence follows the modern fashion of telling tales that are to a greater or less degree autobiographical or biographical confessions (see chapters 6 and 10), we may find ourselves once more in or near Cecilia Chaumpaigne territory.

Apart from the works discussed here, the character of Chaucer sometimes appears incidentally in historical novels centering on other fourteenth-century figures, as in Florence Converse's *Long Will* of 1903, based on the life of Langland, or Harold Begbie's *Rising Dawn* (1912), set in John of Gaunt's household (other examples are given in Bunn's bibliography).[17] And yet our trawl of modern novels that feature Chaucer is not a large one, which, given the picturesque possibilities of the life he lived, is at first sight a surprise. Derek Pearsall has commented on the irresistible attraction such a life provides to the biographer, given among other things Chaucer's closeness to the centers of power: "He lived and worked in London; was a courtier, soldier, and civil servant; travelled in France, Spain, and Italy; served various of the great men of his time; was in Parliament and in and out of favor; and lived to a good age."[18] If the biographer has to resist the snare of talking more about the court and about the various "great men" of the time than of Chaucer himself, the novelist, freer to invent, is able to supplement the Chaucer life records and retain more easily an appropriate focus. And yet we have seen very little that wishes to pursue the theme of Chaucer as soldier, for example, or as parliamentarian, and I have been concerned to offer some reasons why Chaucer-as-hero is a rare novelistic event. Of the works considered in this chapter it would be true to say that only Richings's *In Chaucer's Maytime* even retains Chaucer as principal character throughout: indeed, to be pushed to the margins in one's own fictionalized life story is not the least telling instance of the modern demotion of Chaucer "beyond the academy" that this present study has drawn attention to.

10

Concluding Chaucer

In Hugh Holman's murder mystery *Up This Crooked Way* (1946), its title taken from the "Pardoner's Tale" (VI.761), the "big, quiet, uncouth . . . almost illiterate" detective on the case, Sheriff Macready, startles a college class on Chaucer that he participates in during the course of his investigations by suddenly declaiming in Middle English the description of the Summoner from the "General Prologue."[1] Thus established as a self-declared but unlikely "lover of Chaucer" (132), Macready proceeds through the rest of the book without mentioning Chaucer again, nor does his enthusiasm figure in any of the other books by Holman I have been able to consult that constitute the Sheriff Macready Detective Story series, as in *Another Man's Poison* of 1950.[2]

I cite this as a kind of epigraph to my concluding chapter, a small but symptomatic instance of the difficulty Chaucer has had in establishing himself in common parlance, where even using his work as a gimmick has had a halfhearted, unfulfilled quality about it. More generally, we can say that despite Chaucer's foundational status, not simply as "Father" of English poetry but, as Chesterton would have it, "the Father of his Country,"[3] and despite his crucial bequests to poets, novelists, and even writers of scientific prose (see chapter 6), this book has perforce returned to the relative obscuring of Chaucer in our culture at large. Reasons for this—the difficulties of Middle English, Chaucer's appropriation by academics, the counterattraction of Dante, the absence of patriotism, a patronizing attitude toward him from later writers, and an inability to function as novelistic "hero" (what one undergraduate put to me rather deftly as Chaucer's "image problem")—have all been treated, and latterly writers like Margaret Atwood and Vera Chapman have indicated how Chaucer's incrimination within masculinist traditions might also inhibit contemporary appeal. However, this book is also evidence, necessarily, of a general Chaucerian diffusion into many fields of endeavor in the modern period, however difficult it is to find specific texts or writers that have exercised a deep and lasting influence on Chaucer's behalf. Outside the academy, one might say, it is not easy to see where Chaucer centers himself: in a sense he is everywhere and nowhere, a paradox that suggested an atmospheric metaphor for this presence at the end of chapter 6. Chesterton's comparison of Chaucer to an "emblematic giant" traced on the landscape, and only uncertainly visible from a great height (see chapter 5), is perhaps a better way of stating this situation.

Perhaps Chaucer is most obviously visible in the modern period in the stimulation his work gives for handy titles and headings for fiction and journalism of a confessional bent. I quote as a representative example *The Barmaid's Tale: The Remarkable Story of the Woman Who Put Ronnie Kray behind Bars,* by Mrs. X.[4] Many fictional works of a similar titular type, like Arnold Bennett's *The Old Wives' Tale* (1908), John Wain's *The Pardoner's Tale* (1978), R. K. Narayan's *The Grandmother's Tale* (1993), and Nora Naish's *The Magistrate's Tale* (1995), represent at once, however, acknowledgment and departure. As I noted in chapter 6, such "tales" are likely to be those of the eponymous protagonists' lives, rather than tales told by the protagonists out of a collective and impersonal tradition of story, and the interest of such lives often lies in the isolation from community they represent, or at least in the exploration of a singular privacy that often amounts to solipsism. Thus part 2 of Naish's novel, entitled "The Priest's Tale," internalizes the system of sin, punishment, and contrition recounted by Chaucer's Parson in his tale: we accordingly have the monologue of a guilt-ridden homosexual priest, confined to an asylum after a breakdown occasioned by the murder of a child in his care by his own housekeeper: "I'm just a failed clergyman—failed man, in fact. Somebody—was it Sartre?—said Hell is other people; but he was wrong. Hell is myself."[5]

These neo-Chaucerian titles therefore often signal a modern distance from Chaucer, suggesting at once the lack of an erstwhile communal identity but also, more significantly, the opening up of the realm of interiority, so that we moderns have, as Woolf put it, "things of greater interest to say."[6] In Vance Bourjaily's 1976 novel *Now Playing at Canterbury* the storytelling takes the form of significant episodes from the protagonists' life histories; the title of the work suggests that it is "enabled" by Chaucer, but its final emphasis, in accord with what we have noted above, is one of individual atomism rather than of communal and collective direction.[7] Although the opera company the novel centers on comes together for a successful summer production, its director Billy Hoffman ultimately rejects a permanent position with it, and like a peripatetic Harry Bailly commits himself to the endless supply of new stories coming his way "on the road" as the novel closes:

> Hoffman on a bus, traveling again. . . . Ready to be filled with stories, again. . . . Old Billy Bigears, with an empty seat beside him: Take it. There's a story you could tell to pass the time as the lovely, polluted California seascape passes. So could we all, every man his own Homer, blind, caught in the endless wonder of the words, of the cries, of the shouts, of the laughter, of the tears of the things of the stories of our lives. There we go.[8]

Here there is an unusually exhilarating sense of the plenitude and wonder of "the stories of our lives," even if there is little guarantee that they cement interpersonal ties in any other than a transient manner. A rather less optimistic angle on such stories is provided in Graham Swift's novel *Last Orders* (1996), which again evokes Chaucer in its plot of the ritualistic journey undertaken by a band of friends from their pub in Bermondsey out along the Canterbury route to Margate, where they are to scatter the ashes of one of their number.[9] Along the way they recount to the reader in a series of monologues significant but furtive events in their past that lie hidden from each other. Here, as in many modern works, the replication of Chaucer's tale-telling might be regarded as bearing out Marlow's famous dictum from the beginning of our century, in *Heart of Darkness*, that "[w]e live, as we dream—alone."[10]

Although what we might call traces of Chaucer are then plentiful, to survey the material presented in this book from our viewpoint at the end of the century is to conclude that Chaucer's absence from our general literary culture is as significant as his presence, and also that such an absence may even have increased as the century progressed. Thus types of discourse like children's versions of Chaucer and popularizing accounts of his work seem to have reached a peak of frequency before and during the First World War, as I noted in earlier chapters; nor is there much sign, in more recent times, of a nonspecialist writer offering a study of

Chaucer to a nonspecialist audience, along the lines of Chesterton's work or that by Marchette Chute. Some academics have, it is true, written accounts that continue the Kittredge-Lowes tradition of offering an accessible Chaucer speaking directly of common human concerns and obviating "the need for interpretation," in Patterson's phrase. I am thinking here of works like Helen Corsa's *Chaucer: Poet of Mirth and Morality* (1964) and Ruth Ames's *God's Plenty* of 1984.[11] There are also novelized biographies like John Gardner's *The Life and Times of Chaucer* (1977), a self-confessed telling of that life as novel rather than "history," featuring dramatic evocations of such things as Chaucer's perilous journeys over the Alps ("He would look down tentatively past his furs and the flanks of his wary horse and make out, far below him, dazzling icy rocks . . . and he would close his eyes for a moment and whisper 'A Goddes half!'") and the extraordinary deathbed scene where he scratches out his "Retraction" in the nick of time before "falling violently toward Christ."[12]

Other attempts to break out of the walls of the academy include Jay Breckenridge's 1984 dissertation "A Visit with Geoffrey Chaucer," which consists of a "ninety-minute playscript in modern English, dramatizing [Chaucer] speaking to an audience of students" and "a video-taped reading of the script in which I act the role of Chaucer."[13] The fiction is that Chaucer, like a modern performance poet, has taken it upon himself to make the weighty journey to the University of St. Andrews shortly before his death to read from his work (4). Although the show is aimed at facilitating the teaching of Chaucer at "high school and college level," Breckenridge also hopes to make Chaucer more approachable by these means to "the general population" (2–3). In the process of this dissemination, however, the Chaucer figure brings very little of the medieval text with him: he may come onstage reading the opening of the "General Prologue" in Middle English, but then he introduces the rest of the pilgrims in a modern English account that incorporates digressions on Chaucer's life and times, including information on medieval pilgrimages, religious orders, medicine, and agriculture. A flavor of this is given in a shortened account of the scheme Breckenridge published in an article of 1990; thus after describing the Clerk of the "General Prologue" "Chaucer" continues: "I must admit to a fondness for books myself. I now own some sixty or so. A substantial library. Larger, in fact, than the collection at Oxford, but nothing like the great collection of seven hundred at Christ Church in Canterbury, which contain some three thousand separate writings."[14] By the end of this one-person show the audience has "met" Chaucer, learned something about the Middle Ages, and heard a version of the "General Prologue" and of two tales in shortened prose format (the Nun's Priest's and the Pardoner's). It has also been introduced to Chaucer's talents as a juggler—in an interlude during which the performer "will juggle three (and perhaps four) velvet-covered bean bags" in order to "break the potential tedium of hearing one voice (albeit that of a great poet, sometimes disguised) for over an hour"—and as an instrumentalist.[15] The title of Breckenridge's article, "At Last, Geoffrey Chaucer in Person," shows a similar confidence in the authenticity of the scheme and of its long-awaited desirability, but the "Chaucer" who emerges, elderly, genial, rambling, continues in an entirely familiar tradition of popular modernization, even if he takes coziness and chattiness to extremes.

The main interest of Breckenridge's scheme is precisely its desire and indeed the sense of responsibility it displays to communicate outside the academy, but similar motives are rarely apparent in the tide of detailed historicized and theorized scholarship that has been built up by professional medievalists over the last twenty years. If Chaucer flourishes anywhere today it is precisely as an academic subject: the bibliography of the 1997 *Studies in the Age of Chaucer* volume amounts to 323 items for that single year, many of which contextualize Chaucer within complex fields of gender, narratology, and postmodernist debate. If in 1941 Percy Shelly could complain that nonspecialists have been unable to retrieve Chaucer from an academic possession that makes them feel "overborne and awed by learning" (see chapter 2), there is little likelihood that the situation is not, in Shelly's terms, more alarming today.[16] Indeed, when the celebrated International Congress of Medieval Studies held at Kalamazoo can announce a session in its 1999 program on "constructing a social history of the fart in medieval culture," the reverse situation, whereby academic discourse is appropriating ever more numerous areas of what one might call "popular" expression, is marked. Shelly at least was able to point to some commentary on Chaucer by writers like Woolf, Huxley, Masefield, and so forth; a list of names, however scanty, that one would have difficulty matching from the second half of the century.[17]

On the other hand, the undoubted success of Nevill Coghill's translation of the *Tales,* which has been revised and reprinted many times, must indicate a numerous readership for Chaucer in this same period, in however adulterated a version; many of these readers, it is true, will be students at school taking a temporary interest in aids to Chaucer as a means of passing exams. It is Coghill's collaborator Martin Starkie who probably represents in the 1980s and 1990s the most earnest attempt to bring Chaucer to a wider public, and if, to revert to the beginning of this chapter, we are looking for a nonacademic "center" to Chaucer today, it is perhaps to Canterbury itself we should turn. Thus Starkie has been responsible for setting up the Chaucer Heritage Trust, housed in the Chaucer Heritage Centre in Canterbury, and for establishing in 1985 an annual Chaucer Festival, with events throughout the year. Since 1987 the Trust has also promoted an April "Canterbury Tales Pilgrimage" along the Southwark-Canterbury route. The festival offers a program in both London and Canterbury, consisting of exhibitions, readings, shows, commemorative church services, and processions, related not only to Chaucer but to figures associated with him, like Caxton and William Morris, while the Heritage Centre promotes a Chaucer interest alongside activities of a more general medievalizing kind, such as calligraphy, weaving, and archery. A permanent exhibition at the center opens with Starkie's broadside aimed at the general Chaucerian neglect:

> Geoffrey Chaucer should be enjoyed by a much wider audience than a few hundred academics. It is a wonder that so little is known about the man and that so little of his work is read, even in translation outside school and universities. The scant sum of knowledge about Shakespeare's life has never prevented people from writing libraries about the man but, when it comes to Chaucer, there is a vast and puzzling silence. Particularly as there is a wealth of documentation about his life. . . . why, most mystifying of all, is he now only remembered for a few lines of ancient language learned at school and then so quickly discarded?

Whatever the validity of this last question, the ways Starkie offers to redress the situation are decidedly problematic. The standing exhibition at the Chaucer Heritage Centre focuses not on Chaucer's text but on a Chaucer already modernized in the form of *Canterbury Tales—the Musical,* discussed in chapter 8, a show that is often at the center of the Chaucer

Festival as well. Thus most of the exhibits and displays relate to the staging and costume history of the piece, with much wall space being given over to reviews, programs, cast photographs, and so forth. There is also a continuously running video prominently featuring extracts from the show. Moreover, the other activities the center runs—using Chaucer as a springboard for courses that include crafts, "medieval gardens, herbs and flowers," music, food, and drink—again suggest the eclipsing of Chaucer by a recreational panoply of Chauceriana that can only doubtfully claim to contest that "vast and puzzling silence" which Starkie refers to. In this general "heritage" hullabaloo Chaucer himself seems to have slipped out unnoticed.

The results are evident in the report of festival happenings in the *Kentish Gazette* of 24 April 1992, which begins with the inspiriting news that "the memory of Geoffrey Chaucer is alive and well and living in Canterbury":

> And to prove it a dazzling troop of costumed pilgrims marched through the city centre in celebration of his name on Easter Monday.
>
> The cavalcade . . . included strolling minstrels, jugglers, jesters and knights in armour.
>
> The pilgrimage, part of the one-day Chaucer Festival, was welcomed by the Lord Mayor, Cllr John Purchese, who praised the works of Chaucer.
>
> He told the assembled crowd that the name of Chaucer was forever linked with the city through the *Canterbury Tales*.
>
> "All of you here have taken part in a cavalcade which has arrived on April 20," he said.
>
> "That date is important, for it was on April 20, 1387, that Chaucer's pilgrims—as we are told in the book—arrived in the city to go to the Cathedral to ask favours at the tomb of the martyr, Thomas Becket."
>
> He added: "The book is not merely a work of genius, but the embodiment of an epoch."
>
> The day's events included juggling, dancing, and storytelling [at the Chaucer Centre], medieval combat displays and a banquet at St. Augustine's Refectory.[18]

Whatever book the Lord Mayor has been reading (for his information about the original "arrival" and its date), it is certainly not, of course, the *Canterbury Tales,* though this hardly seems to have stopped the celebration of civic pride and self-marketing. That Canterbury has caught on (rather belatedly) to the value of having a major poet "forever linked" with it is shown by the opening of another Chaucerian venue in the 1980s, the Canterbury Tales Visitor Attraction (and Gift Shop). This offers something slightly more resembling the *Tales* itself than *Canterbury Tales—the Musical,* in the form of life-size figures composed in tableaux who, through various lighting and sound effects, enact several of the tales and their pilgrimage context to a voice-over recounting the narrative. The framing vocal commentary is offered by the pilgrim-Chaucer himself, inviting the visitor in friendly tones to join the pilgrimage in a manner reminiscent of the 1991 radio version discussed in chapter 8, and the journey, as we would expect from a Canterbury attraction, climaxes once again in an opulently "breathtaking" reconstruction of Becket's shrine in the cathedral, a rather bizarre doubling of an original monument that is only a few hundred yards away. The "tales" themselves are much truncated (we do the pilgrimage in forty minutes) and are offered in modern prose. Afterward we can buy, among other things, a bottle from the "'Geoffrey Chaucer' range of Fine Medieval Alcoholic Beverages" in the shop. This, to adapt a term from Terence Hawkes, is Danbiz.[19]

This marketing of Chaucer is of recent growth, and before the 1980s there seems little evidence of any municipal association between Chaucer and Canterbury; the Local History Department of Canterbury Reference Library has no holdings relating to any previous "Chaucer Festivals," and, to return to the quincentenary celebrations mentioned in chapter 2, there is a complete silence in the issues of the *Kentish Gazette* and *Canterbury Press* for October 1900 regarding any commemoration. Whereas events like the Edgbaston Chaucer Pageant of 1924 (see chapter 2) are on more authentic topographical ground in adopting as venue the Tabard Inn and concluding with the pilgrims proceeding "on their way," the recent vogue for Canterbury answers to that need for completion and closure that we have seen modern performance versions in particular, and some children's versions, cater to. In *Canterbury Tales—the Musical* we noted how the arrival in Canterbury paralleled a thematic "arrival" emphasizing good-humored conciliation under the banner of "Love" conquering all, and it is clear that the whole idea of an arriving cavalcade of jugglers (with whom popular Chaucer seems forever fated to be linked), jesters, knights in armor, and so forth, is using Chaucer's name as a shorthand for nostalgic ideals of picturesque social unity and a secure sense (actually and metaphorically) of direction. Again and again in this study we have seen versions of Chaucer with a more "popular" affiliation that present his work as smoothing over dissension and presenting a lost amity or, as in the case of Yeats, creating a set of false coherences, ideas that scarcely survive (again as Yeats found out) a little reading in Chaucer's text. The relocation of Chaucer in Canterbury represents, however, the persistence of a Chaucer who thus "concludes."

While performance versions that bring the *Tales* to such a conclusion have been a notable feature of the past few decades, the emphasis of much academic criticism over the same period that considers the *Tales* as a whole has been in a reverse direction: away from Canterbury, so to speak. The *Tales* does not need "finishing" because it stands in its present state as "an artistically unified whole," its so-called incompletion part of a deliberate design; this understanding of the *Tales* has been "one of the most remarkable features of Chaucerian criticism in the last three decades," according to the Riverside editors (797). In this reading, there may be good reasons for *not* reaching Canterbury, particularly as the Parson, asked by the Host to complete the lack of the one tale that shall "knytte up wel a greet mateere" (X.16–28), suggests a rerouting of the journey's conclusion from the physical realm to the spiritual:

> . . . Jhesu, for his grace, wit me sende
> To shewe yow the wey, in this viage,
> Of thilke parfit glorious pilgrymage
> That highte Jerusalem celestial.
>
> (X.48–51)

As E. T. Donaldson put it, "the pilgrimage seems no longer to have Canterbury as its destination, but rather, I suspect, the Celestial City of which the Parson speaks."[20] To be sure, this position can itself lead to an overly "concluded" Chaucer in the work of critics who give undue prominence to the "Parson's Tale" as Chaucer's orthodox "last word," a moralizing gloss on the other tales and their tellers in which their main value is to illustrate the various categories of sinfulness that the Parson finally and definitively rehearses. Thus, although there may be excellent reasons for not reaching Canterbury, the dangers of this alternative route to the celestial Jerusalem are just as "worrisome," in Charles Muscatine's phrase, if it seeks to establish a stabilizing moral stranglehold over a text whose unfinished and unfinishable plurality of voices is, in the eyes of many readers, its most notable feature.[21] Nevertheless, the relentless desire for arrival in Canterbury and for ceremonies and performances that bespeak that desire is one of the constants of recent popularizing versions, and many of these further proclaim a secular emphasis in not featuring, or alternatively not foregrounding, Becket's shrine. On the other hand, the most recent transference of Chaucer into popular prose idiom, the Doherty thrillers we considered at the end of chapter 9, in which the set of benighted pilgrims shows little likelihood of ever reaching Canterbury, hardly redresses the balance. Received opinion about "Canterbury Chaucer" and all it stands for is hardly more fanciful than the grisly founderings that, by a simple antithesis, Doherty presents.

An accessible Chaucer who represents unproblematic completion and empirical (even epistemological) security is also the inference we often take in cases where canonical modern writers have drawn on him, as we indicated in chapter 6. Modern novels and stories that might be regarded as analogues of individual tales or of other works like *Troilus* will offer themselves as what I called "unraveled" versions of their originals (see chapter 6), with the implication that Chaucer's work and his world are neatly intact in ways that cannot be applied to modernity; such a view is endorsed, as we saw in the same chapter, in critical pronouncements by writers like Eliot and by scholars of modern literature promoting Chaucer as a source. The sense that Chaucer's modern fate, whether in the hands of serious writers or popular appropriators, is essentially to be condescended to as representing naive coherence seems inescapable.

How then might this situation be addressed? Is it, indeed, a matter of justifiable concern? While I have no wish to diminish Canterbury's tourist revenues, further questions that present themselves to me at the conclusion of this study are first, can Chaucer's presence at various levels of nonacademic culture be bolstered and increased, and second, can this be done without perpetuating simplifications and trivializations of his work, so that a hearing might be gained both for its range (for example, work beyond the *Tales*) and for its complexity? Of course, the fact that Chaucer wrote in Middle English, and indeed the fact that he wrote *poetry*, will always act as a brake on any very great following or understanding, and one might also ask whether his qualities are less recognized "at large" today than those of any number of past figures: Milton, for example, or Wordsworth. Whose loss will it be if fifty years from now Chaucer remains known outside the academy only as the mouthpiece of an uncomplicated bawdy affability? To revert to the comment of Kipling's imaginary newspaper editor that forms my epigraph, "Our . . . Dan lies closer to the national heart than we wot of": perhaps we will still need to content ourselves with such a response, simultaneously a recognition and a put-down. Nevertheless, it is worth reformulating some of the above questions to ask how far the issues that animate contemporary academic discussion of Chaucer can be carried over into a wider domain; if the academy is truly the modern "powerhouse" of Chaucer, then surely we should look to it as a source of energy and information that can counter that obscuring of Chaucer we have been discussing? These questions are given added point by the fact that the year 2000, and the sexcentenary of Chaucer's death, are upon us: if, to revert to chapter 2 of this book, there were complaints that the quincentenary was a rather tepid affair, the likelihood of any greater public recognition in the midst of a host of millennial excitements must be held to be remote.

One could launch at this point a series of simple brickbats: accusations that the general public, as well as poets, novelists, and impresarios, have taken too little and the wrong sort of interest in Chaucer, and that academics in latter times who might combat this situation have taken too little interest in communicating their ideas outside the academy. But I have no real commitment to these recriminations: I have spent several years studying popular expressions of Chaucer, have found the whole experience rarely less than engrossing, and would not wish to suppress or outlaw a single instance. What I would like to see, however, is this popular and often predictable Chaucerism having a somewhat harder fight on its hands, rather than commanding a general acquiescence; that is, having to contend with other and fresher ideas about Chaucer entering the public sphere. For instance, the hilarious bum-out-of-the-window scenario, which spoke so much to Coghill (see chapter 2) and which often features in the Coghill aftermath (posters for recent stagings of *Canterbury Tales—the Musical* make it a central comic icon,[22] and it is emblazoned across a T-shirt on sale at the Chaucer Centre), might be offset by a pondering of Elaine Hansen's interpretation of this episode: here

Absolon's encounter with Alison's nether parts and his would-be revenge with the hot blade represent, among other things, male fears of castration and the need to punish women for provoking that fear through an act of renewed phallic aggression.[23] In reading this episode as an account of male sadism and sexual insecurity, Hansen sees nothing to laugh about.

The point is not that Hansen's interpretation of Chaucer is "better" or more tenable than Coghill's, and there are many in the academic world who would themselves regard it as an extremist reading. But it is fertile and interesting and recasts familiar ideas of fun and frolic, and the general recognition of Chaucer might be galvanized by having to consider it. The problem remains one of effecting such consideration, a problem that relates of course not only to Hansen's work but to other weighty and complex academic treatments of Chaucer that have appeared recently and that do indeed make claims for Chaucer's contemporary social relevance. Foremost among these are possibly Patterson's *Chaucer and the Subject of History* and Strohm's *Social Chaucer,* the former in particular seeing Chaucer as offering an urgent message to the 1990s about our present need to "think socially" and not retreat into Thatcherite or post-Thatcherite self-aggrandizement, while at the same time retaining a belief in ideas of the importance and uniqueness of the individual in an increasingly standardized and homogenized consumer society. Chaucer's work holds the strenuous balance between the individual and the collective that we need to keep before us today.[24] Strohm's message is in many ways similar; his book ends on the assertion that Chaucer's work offers "readers in posterity a continuing opportunity to refresh their own belief in social possibility," by which Strohm endorses a social, multivoiced pluralism that again strives for coexistence without, however, effacement of difference.[25] Both books in some ways prolong a customary belief in Chaucer offering us a lost or threatened social model, but instead of the easy, inebriated amity of a static Merrie England we have a dynamic picture of a society that has to admit, and negotiate, constant tensions. Such works offer a kind of unity-in-disunity theme, steering a middle course in the argument discussed earlier in this chapter between those who see a resolved and completed *Tales* and those who reject any possibility of "wholeness."

How are such corrective views about Chaucer, however, enshrined in the pages of demanding, densely argued books published by university presses, to be disseminated? The question takes us on, of course, to the whole issue of Chaucer's place in the education system. "Hell, no! I had all the Chaucer I wanted at school," says a book-borrowing lieutenant in James Hall's memoir of running a library for prisoners of war, and a large number of students will doubtless remain impervious to Chaucer's interest, however he is presented.[26] But it may be that in the past fifteen or twenty years a growing emphasis in higher education on not sundering the study of medieval literature from the concerns that drive other areas of literary and cultural studies—gender issues, the historical situatedness of our own reading practices, attacks on institutions like the canon, the sacrosanct status of authorial intention, and the idea of characterization as valid only in terms of mimesis—will send more students out into the world with a range of ideas about Chaucer that do not require him to be seen as situated essentially on the far side of a premodern barrier where one must fall down or else o'erleap. That the discipline of "Medieval Studies" has at certain times of its history ring-fenced itself intellectually is incontestable, and the persistence of reductive ideas about Chaucer is hardly to be dissociated from the difficulty of access to the means of enlightenment. This is not to be construed as an attack on "traditional" historical, archival, and manuscript study, which must of course continue to be promoted, but surely alongside these new concerns. My own dismay in chapter 7 about the routine and reflex dismissal of Chaucer translation by many teachers of medieval literature was occasioned by the sense that this instances the survival of pedagogic insularity. Of course, one doesn't want students reading Coghill instead of Chaucer, but translations are themselves part of the nexus of commentary and exegesis on a source text (as Rita Copeland has encouraged us to see with regard to medieval translations of classical texts) that might press for a place alongside academic commentary in our teaching.[27] This book itself represents the attempt to add to our understanding of Chaucer by considering him in the context of a multifarious offspring that, however peculiar at times, can still bear fruit. And as this study might also indicate, there are arguably far "worse" modern versions of Chaucer, for those still disposed to think in terms of betrayal and corruption, than the productions of translators.

So perhaps, as far as the dissemination of new ideas is concerned, we can afford to be optimistic. A present generation of students, many of whom will be teachers, will be the bearers of a more modern outlook, one that will percolate down through the school system and its sometimes rather conservative examining approach to Chaucer and so out into the wider sphere.[28] Some of these students will doubtless be future novelists and poets, too, whose work will indicate that Chaucer is something more than a solid and simple stooge to be played off against complex modern supplementation and that he has his own formidable complexity also. Perhaps a recognition of what all writers in English owe to Chaucer, as remarked on at the end of chapter 6, will gather apace. And perhaps the movement in higher education toward "lifelong learning," and thus toward the establishing of a more continuous interface between the academy and our culture "at large," will reap dividends, in tribute to a Chaucer who himself encompassed the world of work and the world of books (*House of Fame,* lines 652–57).

Notes

1. Kelmscott Chaucer

1. Derek Brewer, ed., introduction to *Chaucer: The Critical Heritage,* vol. 2, 1837–1933 (London: Routledge and Kegan Paul, 1978), 21.

2. William S. Peterson, *The Kelmscott Press: A History of William Morris's Typographical Adventure* (Oxford: Clarendon, 1991), 232. For a discussion of the medieval depictions of Chaucer and of more modern images deriving from them, see Derek Pearsall, *The Life of Geoffrey Chaucer: A Critical Biography* (Oxford: Blackwell, 1992), appendix 1, "The Chaucer Portraits," 285–305.

3. Geoffrey Chaucer, *Works,* ed. F. S. Ellis (London: Kelmscott, 1896), 1. A facsimile of the Kelmscott volume, introduction by John T. Winterich, was published in 1958 (Cleveland: World Publishing). All page references in the text are to the 1958 edition. On Burne-Jones's interest in the *Parliament of Fowls,* see Malcolm Bell, *Sir Edward Burne-Jones: A Record and Review,* 4th ed. (1898), 27, 104.

4. The 1859 and 1871 essays (the latter by Stopford A. Brooke) are quoted in Brewer, *Critical Heritage,* 121, 157; the comment from 1886 is in George Dawson, "Chaucer," in *Biographical Lectures,* ed. George St. Clair (1886), 209–10, quoted in *Rare Early Essays on Geoffrey Chaucer,* ed. Carmen Joseph Dello Buono (Darby, Pa.: Norwood, 1981), 39–40.

5. Robert Bell, ed., *Poetical Works of Geoffrey Chaucer,* 8 vols. (1854–56); rev. ed., introduction by W. W. Skeat, 4 vols. (1878). See Skeat's introduction, 9.

6. For an account of the establishing of this canon, see F. J. Furnivall, *Trial-Forewords to My "Parallel-Text Edition of Chaucer's Minor Poems,"* Chaucer Society second series, 6 (1871), 5–7, and Furnivall, "Recent Work at Chaucer," *Macmillan's Magazine* 27 (1872–73): 383–88. By the end of the century Skeat could give his definitive judgment in *The Chaucer Canon: With a Discussion of the Works Associated with the Name of Geoffrey Chaucer* (Oxford: Clarendon, 1900).

7. Algernon Charles Swinburne, *William Blake: A Critical Essay,* new ed. (London: Chatto and Windus, 1906), 97; Malcolm Bell, *Burne-Jones,* 105. For Furnivall's attack on Swinburne's ascription of the "Court of Love" to Chaucer, see William Benzie, *Dr F. J. Furnivall, Victorian Scholar Adventurer* (Norman, Okla.: Pilgrim Books, 1983), 199. The status of the "Flower and the Leaf" is enshrined in the Chaucer window in Westminster Abbey (installed 1868), where scenes from it are depicted in the lancet heads; see the description of the window in F. J. Furnivall, *A Temporary Preface to the Six-Text Edition of Chaucer's "Canterbury Tales,"* pt. 1, Chaucer Society second series, 3 (1868), appendix 3, 133–36.

8. Malcolm Bell, *Burne-Jones,* 104.

9. For the divided state of present Chaucer criticism on the authenticity of the *Rose* translation, see Larry D. Benson's headnote to the poem in *The Riverside Chaucer,* ed. Larry D. Benson et al., 3rd ed. (Oxford: Oxford University Press, 1988), 686. All quotations of Chaucer's work are from this edition.

10. Burne-Jones, quoted in Peterson, *Kelmscott Press,* 250.

11. However, in Skeat's six-volume edition of *The Complete Works of Geoffrey Chaucer* (Oxford, 1894), the text of which Morris followed for the Kelmscott edition, the *Rose* is the first work to be printed (1:93–259), even though Skeat makes it clear on the contents page that "the chief part" of the *Rose* "is not Chaucer's." Burne-Jones must have been aware, of course, that the *Rose* was originally a French poem, given his knowledge of medieval manuscripts of the original in the British Museum: see Julian Treuherz, "The Pre-Raphaelites and Mediaeval Illuminated Manuscripts," in *Pre-Raphaelite Papers,* ed. Leslie Parris (London: Tate Gallery/Allen Lane, 1984), 167–68.

12. See Peterson, *Kelmscott Press,* 238.

13. Duncan Robinson, *William Morris, Edward Burne-Jones, and the Kelmscott Chaucer* (London: Gordon Fraser, 1982), 24.

14. Malcolm Bell, *Burne-Jones,* 106–8.

15. For a description of (and challenge to) the tradition that Chaucer was bored with writing the *Legend,* see Robert Worth Frank Jr., "The Legend of Chaucer's Boredom," in his *Chaucer and the "Legend of Good Women"* (Cambridge, Mass.: Harvard University Press, 1972), 189–210.

16. Uncertainty still exists over the precise content of the Red House scheme. According to Banham and Harris, the *Legend of Good Women* provided the inspiration for the scheme, though the actual figures depicted "do not correspond to those listed in Chaucer's poem." See Joanna Banham and Jennifer Harris, eds., *William Morris and the Middle Ages* (Manchester: Manchester University Press, 1984), 114; and Emmeline Leary, "The Red House Figure Embroideries," *Apollo* 113 (1981): 255–58. However, Linda Parry suggests that some of the figures do correspond, including a surviving hanging depicting Phyllis; Linda Parry, ed., *William Morris* (London: Philip Wilson/Victoria and Albert Museum, 1996), 237. The window cartoons were later reused for a series of windows in the Combination Room at Peterhouse, Cambridge, and are now in the City Museum and Art Gallery, Birmingham; see Duncan Robinson and Stephen Wildman, *Morris and Company in Cambridge* (Cambridge: Cambridge University Press, 1980), 45–46. On the Ruskin embroideries, see Martin Harrison and Bill Waters, *Burne-Jones* (London: Barrie and Jenkins, 1973), 60; and Banham and Harris, *Morris,* 198–204. Harrison and Waters also include illustrations of some tiles based on the *Legend* in the Ashmolean Museum, Oxford (69); see also Parry, *Morris,* 186. For various embroideries and tapestries designed by Morris and Burne-Jones and based on the *Romance of the Rose,* see Banham and Harris, *Morris,* 208–9; Harrison and Waters, *Burne-Jones,* 117; and Parry, *Morris,* 240–41.

17. The Victoria and Albert Museum possesses a stained-glass panel of the *Figure of Chaucer* (illustrated in Parry, *Morris,* 129). Banham and Harris speculate interestingly (*Morris,* 204) on the effect Chaucer's lines on the daisy had for "the importance of the daisy in Morris's early decorative work," pointing to the "Daisy" embroidered hangings for the main bedroom at Red House and the later "Daisy" wallpaper and tiles.

18. See Peter Faulkner, *Against the Age: An Introduction to William Morris* (London: Allen and Unwin, 1980), 39.

19. William Morris, *The Life and Death of Jason,* in *The Collected Works of William Morris,* introduction by May Morris, 24 vols. (London: Longmans, 1910–15), 2:259–60. All references to Morris's writing are to this edition.

20. Quoted in Faulkner, *Against the Age,* 39.

21. May Morris, introduction to *Works,* 2:xvi.

22. On the cartoon of *The Two Wives of Jason: Hypsipyle and Medea* produced for the Ruskin embroideries, Ruskin himself praised Burne-Jones for "seeing the good, and disdaining the evil" in his depiction of Medea, where "a common painter would have discerned only a cruel and enraged sorceress." Ruskin is, however, strangely silent on the stimulus for this treatment that the *Legend* itself provides in enrolling Medea among its "good" women. See John Ruskin, "On the Present State of Modern Art . . ." (1867), in *The Works of John Ruskin,* ed. E. T. Cook and Alexander Wedderburn, vol. 19 (London: George Allen, 1905), 208; quoted in Banham and Harris, *Morris,* 202.

23. Banham and Harris, *Morris,* 194, 197–98. Malcolm Bell reports on various independent watercolors, entitled *Chaucer's Dream,* produced by Burne-Jones and, from Bell's descriptions, clearly illustrative of the "Prologue" to the *Legend,* rather than of the poem "Chaucer's Dream," which was relegated to the apocryphal works during the course of the nineteenth century and is now known as the (anonymous) *Isle of Ladies.* See Bell, *Burne-Jones,* 34, 43. See also John Christian and Richard Dorment, "'Theseus and Ariadne': A Newly-Discovered Burne-Jones," *Burlington Magazine* 117 (July–December 1975): 596.

24. See Virginia Surtees, *The Paintings and Drawings of Dante Gabriel Rossetti (1828–1882): A Catalogue Raisonné,* 2 vols. (Oxford: Clarendon, 1971), 1:70–73, 2: plate 179; also Parry, *William Morris,* 104–5.

25. Henry Wadsworth Longfellow, *Poetical Works* (London: Oxford University Press, 1904), 344.

26. Longfellow, "Chaucer," in *Poetical Works,* 711; quoted in Caroline F. E. Spurgeon, *Five Hundred Years of Chaucer Criticism and Allusion, 1357–1900,* 3 vols. (Cambridge: Cambridge University Press, 1925), 2(3):120. To regard Chaucer's work as a refuge from modern (industrial) urbanization was a stock Victorian response; see also Aubrey De Vere's poem "Chaucer," which begins "Escaped from the city, its smoke, its glare . . . ," in his *Poetical Works,* vol. 3: *Alexander the Great . . . and Other Poems* (1884), 347–48.

27. Paul Strohm's *Social Chaucer* (Cambridge, Mass.: Harvard University Press, 1989) sees Chaucer's work as a site of "unresolved contention, of a struggle between hegemony and counter-hegemony, . . . crowded with many voices representing many centers of social authority" (xiii). For W. B. Yeats, Morris's "monotonous" lyricism in *The Earthly Paradise* missed precisely "what seems to me essential in Chaucer's art": his "variety" and "delight in the height and depth." See chapter 3 in this volume.

28. Delbert R. Gardner has noted how the comparison between Morris and Chaucer became a stock-in-trade of Victorian reviews of the former's poetry after 1867, with reviewers equally divided between those arguing for congruence between the two poets and those differentiating them on grounds of "characterization, dramatic power, antiquarianism, and tone." See "The Victorian Chaucer," chapter 3 of Gardner's *An "Idle Singer" and His Audience: A Study of William Morris's Poetic Reputation in England, 1858–1900* (The Hague: Mouton, 1975), 35–58. Occasionally, the two poets were even presented as the complete antithesis to each other; see "Geoffrey Chaucer and William Morris," *New Monthly Magazine* 149 (1871): 280–86.

29. Diana C. Archibald, "Beauty, Unity, and the Ideal: Wholeness and Heterogeneity in the Kelmscott *Chaucer,*" in *Studies in Medievalism,* vol. 7 (1995), ed. Leslie J. Workman and Kathleen Verduin (Cambridge: D. S. Brewer, 1996), 169.

30. Harrison and Waters, *Burne-Jones,* 165.

31. Archibald, "Beauty, Unity, and the Ideal," 178.

32. Peterson, *Kelmscott Press,* 236, 247.

33. William Morris, "Feudal England," in *Signs of Change, Works,* 23: 51–52.

34. Strohm, *Social Chaucer,* xiii, 157.

35. Ibid., 172–74. On the *Canterbury Tales* as a kind of counternarrative to the Peasants' Revolt, representing a "containment" or "warding off" of political insurrection, see Steven Justice, *Writing and Rebellion: England in 1381* (Berkeley: University of California Press, 1994), 207–31. Pearsall's discussion of Chaucer and the Revolt posits Chaucer's "view of the common people" as one of "routine contempt" (*Life,* 147); elsewhere Pearsall talks of Chaucer's "despising" the peasantry and of his aristocratic "snobbery" (69–70).

36. William Morris, *A Dream of John Ball, Works,* 16:227. The Chaucerian reference here is also noted by Mabel Wilhelmina Downer, "Chaucer among the Victorians" (Ph.D. diss., City University of New York, 1982), 69–70.

37. J. W. Mackail, *The Life of William Morris,* 2 vols. (1899; reprint, London: Longmans, 1922), 1:220. Chaucer seems to have resembled a good many people in the nineteenth century, including D. G. Rossetti (who posed for Chaucer in Madox Brown's famous painting *Chaucer at the Court of Edward III*) and R. W. Dixon. See Spurgeon, *Five Hundred Years,* 2(2):259, 2(3):21, and Banham and Harris, *Morris,* 197.

38. See the letter from Mary Howitt to Mrs. Alfred Watts, quoted in Faulkner, *Against the Age,* 55.

39. Dawson, "Chaucer," 207; quoted in Dello Buono, *Rare Early Essays,* 37.

40. See, for example, William Morris, "Art under Plutocracy" (1883), in *Lectures on Socialism, Works,* 23:175.

41. William Morris, "The Aims of Art" (1886), in *Signs of Change, Works,* 23:89.

42. William Morris, "The Art of the People" (1879), in *Hopes and Fears for Art, Works,* 22:40.

43. William Morris, *News from Nowhere* (1890), *Works,* 16:7–9; see also Morris, "The Lesser Arts" (1877), in *Hopes and Fears for Art, Works,* 22:11.

44. Mackail, *Life of William Morris,* 1:220.

45. The correspondence is quoted in Mackail, *Life of William Morris,* 1:203–4.

46. Alfred Noyes, "Chaucer," pt. 1, *Bookman* 76 (April–September 1929): 194. The article was reprinted under the title "The Eye of Day" in Noyes's book of essays *The Opalescent Parrot* (London: Sheed and Ward, 1929), 222–34.

2. Popular Chaucer

1. Furnivall, "Recent Work at Chaucer," 383, 389.

2. The comments are by Leigh Hunt and R. H. Horne, respectively, quoted in Spurgeon, *Five Hundred Years,* 2(2):89, 235.

3. Furnivall, *Trial-Forewords,* 42.

4. On Furnivall, see *Frederick James Furnivall: A Volume of Personal Record* (London: Oxford University Press, 1911); Benzie, *Dr F. J. Furnivall* (see chapter 1, n. 7); Peter

Faulkner, "'The Paths of Virtue and Early English': F. J. Furnivall and Victorian Medievalism," in *From Medieval to Medievalism,* ed. John Simons (Basingstoke: Macmillan, 1992), 144–58; Donald C. Baker, "Frederick James Furnivall," in *Editing Chaucer: The Great Tradition,* ed. Paul G. Ruggiers (Norman, Okla.: Pilgrim, 1984), 157–69.

5. Thomas R. Lounsbury, *Studies in Chaucer: His Life and Writings,* 3 vols. (New York, 1891; London, 1892), 1:xi–xii.

6. George Lyman Kittredge, *Chaucer and His Poetry* (Cambridge, Mass.: Harvard University Press, 1915), 108.

7. The bust of Chaucer, by George Frampton, was completed in 1903, and is at present on display in the Guildhall Library.

8. Neither Furnivall's nor Yeats's speech at the Whitefriars dinner seems to have survived. Furnivall's was entitled "The Modern Spirit in the *Canterbury Tales*" (as reported in *Literature,* 27 October 1900, 313); Yeats's, to judge from the report in the *Westminster Gazette* of 24 November, seems to have taken a contrary view: "[Yeats] denied the existence of the modern spirit in the *Canterbury Tales,* and in a dirge . . . lamented 'the depredation which we call Progress.'" The RSL lectures were published as *Chaucer Memorial Lectures, 1900,* ed. Percy W. Ames (London: Asher, 1900).

9. See "Notes and News," the editorial on p. 2 of the *Daily Mail:* "Today is not only noteworthy as the anniversary of Balaclava with the famous Charge and Agincourt, it is also the cobblers' holiday. In other words, this is St Crispin's Day."

10. E. A. S., "The Chaucer Celebration," *Speaker,* 24 November 1900, 202.

11. Noyes, "Chaucer," 191.

12. Percy Van Dyke Shelly, *The Living Chaucer* (Philadelphia: University of Pennsylvania Press, 1940), 1.

13. G. K. Chesterton, *Chaucer* (London: Faber, 1932), 9.

14. John Richard Green, *A Short History of the English People,* rev. Alice Stopford Green (London: Macmillan, 1916), 222.

15. Percy W. Ames, introduction and "The Life and Characteristics of Chaucer," in *Chaucer Memorial Lectures,* xii, 168.

16. Lounsbury, *Studies,* 1:126.

17. Spurgeon includes a whole host of nineteenth-century tributes to Chaucer's manliness, from Coleridge's "[Chaucer's] manly cheerfulness is especially delicious to me in my old age" (*Table Talk,* 15 March 1834) to Swinburne's upholding him as the "standing type and sovereign example of noble and manly happiness" ("Short Notes on English Poets," 1880); see Spurgeon, *Five Hundred Years,* 2(2):190, 2(3):132.

18. Henry Dwight Sedgwick, *Dan Chaucer: An Introduction to the Poet, His Poetry and His Times* (New York: Bobbs-Merrill, 1934), ix, xi.

19. Frank Ernest Hill, trans., *The Canterbury Tales . . . Rendered into Modern English Verse,* 2 vols. (London: Limited Editions Club, 1934), 1:xix. For the healthiness of Chaucer as an aid to longevity, see James B. Herrick, M.D., in his after-dinner address to the meeting of the Association of American Physicians, 5 May 1931: "No hideous nightmare spoils the sleep after reading [Chaucer], the blood pressure does not rise nor the arteries grow tense over his pages, no melancholy hangs heavy over one as one lays down his volume." Herrick, "Why I Read Chaucer at Seventy," *Annals of Medical History,* new series, 5 (1933): 72.

20. "Chaucer," *Literature,* 20 October 1900, 297.

21. Noyes, "Chaucer," 193; Hill, *Canterbury Tales,* 1:xxii.

22. "Chaucer," 294; Burton Rascoe, *Titans of Literature: From Homer to the Present* (London: Routledge, 1933), 292.

23. Tudor Jenks, *In the Days of Chaucer,* introduction by Hamilton Wright Mabie (London: Authors' Syndicate; New York: Barnes, 1904), xii–xiii.

24. Chaucer's father was a prosperous wine merchant rather than an innkeeper and at one time held "the important position of deputy in the port of Southampton to the king's chief butler (the man who looked after the royal wine-cellar)." See Pearsall, *Life,* 14. For discussion of what he calls "the tavern myth," see John Matthews Manly, *Some New Light on Chaucer: Lectures Delivered at the Lowell Institute* (London: Bell, 1926), 19–20. Manly attributes the origin of the myth to Furnivall, presumably to his *Life-Records of Chaucer,* pt. 2, Chaucer Society second series (1876), vii: "We have him as a boy at his father's wine-shop or tavern in narrow Thames St, chatting, no doubt, with English and foreign seamen, with citizens who came for their wine, helping to fill their pots, perhaps—a natty, handy lad, but full of quiet fun—messing, I dare say, in Wal-brook, that bounded his father's place; fishing in the Thames, I should think . . ." (there is a good deal more in this suppositious vein).

25. Jenks, *Days of Chaucer,* 26.

26. Margaret Willy, *Life Was Their Cry* (London: Evan Bros., 1950), 54.

27. See Noyes, "Chaucer," 191: "Critics, searching for his sources, have laid too much stress on the foreign element in him, and on his debt to foreign authors." Chaucer's taste for (English) "life" can occasionally be to his discredit, as in Sedgwick's condemnation of (and blindness to the literary sophistication of) the "Miller's Tale": "The stuff that furnished forth the yarns that Chaucer heard at tavern and ale-house when he journeyed through the city, is tedious and distasteful enough. It would take many a mug of good pale ale to wash it down now. . . . The Miller's tale . . . is, in spite of its wit, as muddy as ditch water, and very like ditch water in its odoriferousness" (Sedgwick, *Dan Chaucer,* 280).

28. Hill, *Canterbury Tales,* 1:xx.

29. Marchette Chute, *Geoffrey Chaucer of England* (1946; reprint, London: Robert Hale, 1951), 78, 162, 164.

30. W. H. Thompson, *Chaucer and His Times,* introduction by W. L. Andrews (London: A. Brown, 1936), 20 (the modern illustration facing 20, based on the Hoccleve portrait, clearly accentuates the "merriment"). The process is similar to the canvassing as late as the nineteenth century of Woodstock as "a more becoming birthplace [for Chaucer] than the roar and smoke of London for one who loved the forest and sketched so well the wild wood with its song of birds"; see Lounsbury, *Studies,* 1:161. Lounsbury's discussion of the "Chaucer Legend" (1:129–224) also amusingly considers such things as the so-called Chaucer oak in the grounds of Donnington castle, Berkshire (179).

31. See E. A. S., "The Chaucer Celebration," 202; Ames, introduction to *Chaucer Memorial Lectures,* ix.

32. Shelly, *Living Chaucer,* 19.

33. Ibid., 19–20. Shelly is referring to Masefield's 1931 Leslie Stephen Lecture, *Chaucer* (Cambridge: Cambridge University Press, 1931).

34. Lee Patterson, *Negotiating the Past: The Historical Understanding of Medieval Literature* (Madison: University of Wisconsin Press, 1987), 17.

35. Kittredge, *Chaucer and His Poetry,* 1–2.

36. Brewer, *Critical Heritage,* 2:1–2.

37. Nevill Coghill, *Geoffrey Chaucer* (London: Longmans, 1956), 45–48. Dryden's famous judgment on the dramatis personae of the "General Prologue," "here is God's Plenty," and his labeling Chaucer "the Father of English Poetry" are in the preface to his *Fables* of 1700 (see Dryden, *The Poems and Fables,* ed. James Kinsley (London: Oxford University Press, 1962), 531, 528. For Patterson's comment, see *Negotiating the Past,* 17.

38. Nevill Coghill, *The Poet Chaucer* (London: Oxford University Press, 1949), 132, 134.

39. C. David Benson, "Chaucer's Unfinished Pilgrimage," *Christianity and Literature* 37 (1988): 12.

40. See, for example, Lounsbury, *Studies,* 2:494ff., 529.

41. W. B. Yeats, *Autobiographies* (London: Macmillan, 1955), 151.

42. G. K. Chesterton, "On Mr. Geoffrey Chaucer," in *"All I Survey": A Book of Essays* (London: Methuen, 1933), 174, 178. For a comparable medieval-modern contrast, see W. H. Auden, "Ode to the Medieval Poets," *Collected Poems,* ed. Edward Mendelson, rev. ed. (London: Faber, 1991), 863.

43. T. S. Eliot, "Dante," in *Selected Essays,* 3rd ed. (London: Faber, 1951), 262.

44. Ezra Pound, *ABC of Reading,* new ed. (London: Faber, 1961), 98–114, and "A Retrospect," in *Literary Essays of Ezra Pound,* edited and with an introduction by T. S. Eliot (London: Faber, 1954), 7.

45. The four-page program is held in the City of Birmingham Reference Library, at classmark L p22.41.

46. A contemporary American "Chaucer pageant," celebrated at Wheaton College on 23 May 1925, differs from its English counterpart in taking not the Tabard for its setting but the marketplace at Canterbury, where the pilgrims are just arriving in the pageant's opening scene. Thereafter they largely disappear from the action, giving way to a succession of "episodes" that includes the crowning of the May Queen, a mummers' play from the Chester cycle, and a display of medieval "sports and pastimes." The Chaucerian occasion returns in the form of the Pardoner telling a truncated version of his tale, but overall "Chaucer" is a misleading label for a congeries of medieval incidents that has little to do with him. See *May Day in Canterbury: A Chaucerian Festival,* arranged by Anne Fontaine Maury (Boston: Walter H. Baker, 1925)

47. Eleanor C. Smyth, *An Essay on Chaucer: Chiefly on the "Prologue" to the "Canterbury Tales"* . . . ([Bexhill-on-Sea]: n.p., 1924), 21–23. The Tabard's status as no less an object of interest than the pilgrims themselves is illustrated by George Dyson's decision to add an overture—*At the Tabard Inn* (produced in 1943)—to his earlier work for chorus, orchestra, and soloists, *The Canterbury Pilgrims* (1931). Both works were released on compact disc by Chandos in 1997 (Chan 9531[2]).

48. Thompson, *Chaucer and His Times,* 69–73, 134–35.

49. Manly, *Some New Light,* 77–83.

50. G. G. Coulton, *Chaucer and His England* (London: Methuen, 1908), 11, 71.

51. Chesterton, *Chaucer,* 184, 75, 183.

3. Spoken Chaucer

1. *The Letters of W. B. Yeats,* ed. Allan Wade (London: Rupert Hart-Davis, 1954), 456; hereafter cited in text as *Letters.*

2. The route by bicycle to Canterbury was a well-established trip. For an amusing Victorian instance, see *A Canterbury Pilgrimage: Ridden, Written, and Illustrated* by Joseph and Elizabeth Robins Pennell (1885; reprint, Canterbury: Yorick Books, 1990).

3. Ronald Schuchard, "'The Minstrel in the Theatre': Arnold, Chaucer, and Yeats's New Spiritual Democracy," *Yeats Annual* 2, ed. Richard J. Finneran (London: Macmillan, 1983), 15.

4. Yeats's narrative poem *The Shadowy Waters* first appeared in the *North American Review* in May 1900 and was extensively revised during 1905 before being included in *Poems 1899–1905* (1906). In Yeats's words, it "had once again to be condensed and altered" before its production as a play at the Abbey Theatre in November 1906, resulting in the "Acting version" of the poem. See appendix 4 to vol. 2 of the *Collected Works* (1908), in *The Variorum Edition of the Plays of W. B. Yeats,* ed. Russell K. Alspach and Catherine C. Alspach (London: Macmillan, 1966), 342; hereafter cited in the text as *Plays.*

5. Schuchard, "'Minstrel in the Theatre,'" 8.

6. *The Variorum Edition of the Poems of W. B. Yeats,* ed. Peter Allt and Russell K. Alspach (New York: Macmillan, 1957), 227–28; hereafter cited in the text as *Poems.*

7. W. B. Yeats, *Later Poems* (London: Macmillan, 1922), 108; *Variorum Poems,* 227.

8. W. B. Yeats, "Literature and the Living Voice," in *Explorations,* selected by Mrs. W. B. Yeats (London: Macmillan, 1962), 220–21.

9. W. B. Yeats, "Modern Poetry: A Broadcast," in *Essays and Introductions* (London: Macmillan, 1961), 491–92; hereafter cited in the text as *Essays.*

10. Yeats, "Literature and the Living Voice," 221.

11. John Stevens, *Music and Poetry in the Early Tudor Court* (1961; reprint, Cambridge: Cambridge University Press, 1979), 158. The illustration is in Cambridge Corpus Christi College MS 61, reproduced many times, as for example in Derek Pearsall, "The *Troilus* Frontispiece and Chaucer's Audience," *Yearbook of English Studies* 7 (1977): opp. 70.

12. Yeats, "Literature and the Living Voice," 205.

13. W. B. Yeats, "Gitanjali," in *Essays,* 390–91.

14. Yeats, *Plays,* 1296. In the note on *The Unicorn from the Stars* that Yeats included in vol. 3 of the *Collected Works* of 1908, the desired unity is envisaged as "the day when Quixote and Sancho Panza long estranged may once again go out gaily into the bleak air" (*Plays,* 712).

15. Yeats, preface to *Poems 1899–1905,* in *Poems,* 850; *Plays,* 1293.

16. Yeats, preface to *Poems 1899–1905,* 849.

17. Richard Ellmann, *The Identity of Yeats* (1954; reprint, London: Faber, 1964), 90.

18. Joseph Hone, *W. B. Yeats, 1865–1939* (1943; reprint, Harmondsworth: Penguin, 1971), 131. Hone is referring here to Yeats's "predilection" in the mid-1890s, though there is little evidence that Yeats was much acquainted with Chaucer before 1905. There are a few inconsequential references to him in a lecture of 1893, "Nationality and Literature," but Yeats's talk here of "the simple thought of Chaucer" indicates the limits of his engage-

ment. See *Uncollected Prose by W. B. Yeats,* ed. John P. Frayne, vol. 1 (London: Macmillan, 1970), 272. For Yeats's address to the Whitefriars Club Chaucer dinner of November 1900, see chapter 2.

19. Yeats, *Autobiographies,* 191.

20. Yeats, "Literature and the Living Voice," 207.

21. The phrase "dumb as a stone" or "the dumb stone" (cf. line 656 of the *House of Fame*) is scattered through Yeats's work, for instance in *The Wanderings of Oisin,* line 96, and in "The Two Kings," lines 94, 96v, 179 (*Poems,* 53, 281, 284).

22. Yeats refers to Cupid's upbraiding Chaucer for his "defamation" of Criseyde in the prologue to the *Legend of Good Women* in "*Samhain:* 1905," in showing how the Abbey Theatre writers are not the first to have to contend with the conventional moralizing of their day. See *Explorations,* 186–87.

23. Yeats, "*Samhain:* 1904: First Principles," in *Explorations,* 158, 148–49. Chaucer's "praise of trees" is also mentioned in the Spenser essay (*Essays,* 377). The reference is presumably to the *Parliament of Fowls,* lines 172–82. Perhaps the lines from the play *Deirdre* (1907), "Praise the redness of the yew; / Praise the blossoming apple-stem," are therefore another Chaucerian echo. See *Plays,* 353.

24. Yeats, letter to Farr, 1906, in *Letters,* 469.

25. For a useful review of the complex question of Chaucer's audience, see "Chaucer's Audience: A Symposium," *Chaucer Review* 18 (1983): 137–81.

26. Hone, *Yeats,* 253–54.

27. Yeats, *Autobiographies,* 129.

28. W. B. Yeats, *A Vision* (London: Macmillan, 1962), 289. Yeats may have read the monograph on Chaucer by Emile Legouis, recorded in both its original French version (1910) and in the translation by L. Lailavoix (1913), in the 1920s catalog of Yeats's library printed by Edward O' Shea in *Yeats Annual* 4, ed. Warwick Gould (Basingstoke: Macmillan, 1986), 285. Legouis's sensible and (for its day) judicious account of Chaucer's work would certainly have disabused Yeats of his rather simplified 1905–6 assessment, and his complaints at the "slow-moving" nature of *Troilus and Criseyde* anticipate Yeats's remark that the poem "robbed verse of its speed." See Emile Legouis, *Geoffrey Chaucer,* trans. L. Lailavoix (London: Dent, 1913), 133.

29. Yeats, *A Vision,* 144.

30. Francis Lee Utley, "Stylistic Ambivalence in Chaucer, Yeats, and Lucretius—the Cresting Wave and Its Undertow," *University Review* 37 (1970–71): 193.

31. Schuchard, "'Minstrel in the Theatre,'" 22.

32. Yeats, "A People's Theatre," in *Explorations,* 258, 253, 250.

33. The Yeats-Dante relationship is considered in chapter 5 of my *Dante and English Poetry: Shelley to T. S. Eliot* (Cambridge: Cambridge University Press, 1983), 140–70.

34. Yeats, "A People's Theatre," 251–52.

35. Elizabeth Salter, *Fourteenth-Century English Poetry: Contexts and Readings* (Oxford: Clarendon, 1983), 42.

36. Yeats, *Autobiographies,* 151.

37. Roland Blenner-Hassett, "Yeats' Use of Chaucer," *Anglia* 72 (1954): 455–62. George Mills Harper records that George Yeats copied out the "Franklin's Tale" passage in

1917; see *The Making of Yeats's "A Vision": A Study of the Automatic Script,* 2 vols. (London: Macmillan, 1987), 1:54. Harper argues further (97) that Blake's essay on the Canterbury pilgrims, which sees them as permanent types ("nor can a child be born who is not one or other of these characters"), was an important stimulus for Yeats's classification of types in *A Vision.* See *Poems of William Blake,* ed. W. B. Yeats (London: Routledge, 1905), 244.

38. Yeats, "Speaking to the Psaltery," in *Essays,* 13–27; "Four Lectures by W. B. Yeats, 1902–4," ed. Richard Londraville, in *Yeats Annual* 8, ed. Warwick Gould (Basingstoke: Macmillan, 1991), 78–122.

39. Hone, *Yeats,* 335.

40. Yeats, "A Dialogue of Self and Soul," in *Poems,* 477–79.

4. Children's Chaucer

1. Ada Hales, *Stories from Chaucer* (London: Methuen, 1911). The edition's purpose and audience is indicated at the back of the book, where it is included in Methuen's "Complete Educational Catalogue."

2. F. J. Harvey Darton, *Tales of the Canterbury Pilgrims: Retold from Chaucer and Others,* introduction by F. J. Furnivall, illustrated by Hugh Thomson (London: Wells Gardner, Darton, 1904). This and each of the other children's versions discussed in this chapter will be cited by page number in the text, with the first full reference given in the notes.

3. The undated *Academy* review is quoted in an advertisement for Mrs. Haweis's *Chaucer for Children* printed opposite the title page of the 1881 *Chaucer for Schools.*

4. Examples of this treatment of the "Knight's Tale" include J. Walker McSpadden, adaptor, *Tales from Chaucer* (London: Harrap, [1909]), 51, and M. Sturt and E. C. Oakden, *The Canterbury Pilgrims: Being Chaucer's "Canterbury Tales" Retold for Children* (London: Dent, 1923), 30.

5. Janet Harvey Kelman, *Stories from Chaucer Told to the Children,* illustrated by W. Heath Robinson (London: T. C. and E. C. Jack, [1906]).

6. The illustrations to a range of children's Chaucer editions are discussed by Miriam Youngerman Miller, "Illustrations of the *Canterbury Tales* for Children: A Mirror of Chaucer's World?" *Chaucer Review* 27 (1992–93): 293–304.

7. Geraldine McCaughrean, adaptor, *Geoffrey Chaucer: The Canterbury Tales* (1984; reprint, London: Puffin, 1996), 102.

8. See Spurgeon, *Five Hundred Years,* 2:251–52, 3:3, 68. For more on this see the section "Chaucer the Child-Poet" in Carolyn P. Collette, "Chaucer and Victorian Medievalism: Culture and Society," *Poetica: An International Journal of Linguistic Literary Studies* 29–30 (1989): 118–20.

9. "The Cycle of English Song," pt. 2, *Temple Bar* 38 (April–July 1873): 324.

10. The phrase is Swinburne's, from his *Miscellanies* (1886), 152, quoted in Brewer, *Critical Heritage,* 2:225. Compare Meredith's poem "The Poetry of Chaucer," where the subject is described all-inclusively as "childlike, and manly, and motherly" (quoted in Spurgeon, *Five Hundred Years,* 3:3).

11. There is no wart in Clara L. Thomson, adaptor, *Tales from Chaucer,* illustrated by Marion Thomson (London: Horace Marshall, [1903]), 45, nor any ulcer in William Calder,

Chaucer's Canterbury Pilgrimage (Edinburgh: Blackwood, 1892), 78. In Eleanor Farjeon, adaptor, *Tales from Chaucer* (1930; reprint, London: Oxford University Press, 1959), the ulcer has become a harmless "lump" (7).

12. Mrs. H. R. Haweis, *Chaucer for Children: A Golden Key* (1877), xii; Mary Seymour, *Chaucer's Stories Simply Told,* illustrated by E. M. Scannell (1884), xii. Seymour attempts to "sell" Chaucer in her introduction as an idealized Lord Fauntleroy figure: "Though exceedingly small of stature, Geoffrey's appearance was noble and distinguished, the expression of his face calm and beautiful, his complexion fair and pale, his hair deeply golden of tint and very luxurious," and so forth. We are also told that in early manhood he was "the chief friend" of Edward III, and "though but thirty years of age, one of the most learned scholars of the day," and "a brave and fearless soldier" (ii–iii).

13. F. J. Furnivall, introduction to Darton's *Tales of the Canterbury Pilgrims,* xviii. Such idealizing at this time is not, of course, limited to a Chaucer aimed at children; witness Austin's quincentenary speech referred to in chapter 2, where the poet is held to inculcate "fidelity, hopefulness, charity, deference towards authority, manliness towards men, chivalry towards women, tenderness for children, loftiness of thought, the lifting up of the heart, the purifying of the soul, reverence, piety, and patriotism." This and other extracts from Austin's speech were reported in *Literature,* 27 October 1900, 313–14.

14. The absence of historical contextualization is indeed a striking feature of children's editions from recent decades. A. J. B. Dick's retellings are prefaced by a short introduction that ponders on the "usefulness" of stories from six hundred years ago, concluding that Chaucer's use lies in his "help[ing] us to understand other people, and also to understand ourselves. For however different we may all seem from one another at first, we come to realise that we are all very much the same underneath. . . . in the end, we all find that the most important thing in life is to be able to understand other people"; A. J. B. Dick, *Milestones: Eight Tales from Chaucer,* illustrated by H. C. McBeath (London: Nelson, 1965), viii. A disregard of history is if anything more marked in Dulan Barber, adaptor, *The Canterbury Tales,* illustrated by Geoffrey Fraser (London: Blackie, 1966), where an even skimpier introduction begins, "In the fifteenth century[!], when Geoffrey Chaucer wrote the *Canterbury Tales* . . ." (7).

15. As Percy Shelly commented, John Livingston Lowes's enthusiasm for the Miller's and Reeve's tales in his *Geoffrey Chaucer* of 1934 is something of a milestone in academic criticism. See Shelly, *The Living Chaucer,* 242; Lowes, *Geoffrey Chaucer: Lectures Delivered in 1932 on the William J. Cooper Foundation in Swarthmore College* (Oxford: Clarendon, 1934), 176–81. Lowes notes that "for pure virtuosity the 'Miller's Tale' . . . is perhaps [Chaucer's] masterpiece" (180).

16. Margaret C. Macaulay, *Stories from Chaucer: Retold from the "Canterbury Tales"* (Cambridge: Cambridge University Press, 1911), v.

17. Emily Underdown, *The Gateway to Chaucer: Stories Told . . . from the "Canterbury Tales"* . . . , illustrated by Anne Anderson (London: Nelson, [1912]), 99.

18. Ian Serraillier, adaptor, *The Road to Canterbury: Tales from Chaucer,* illustrated by John Lawrence (Harmondsworth: Penguin, 1979).

19. Selina Hastings, *A Selection from the Canterbury Tales* . . . , illustrated by Reg Cartwright (London: Walker, 1988), 33–35.

20. Lee Lorenz's retelling of the tale also omits any sexual trickery, with the effect that the motive for moving the cradle to the foot of a different bed is left unclear. See *Scornful Simkin: Adapted from the "Reeve's Tale,"* retold and illustrated by Lee Lorenz (London: Dent, 1980), n.p.

21. Francis Storr and Hawes Turner, *Canterbury Chimes; or, Chaucer Tales Retold for Children,* rev. ed. (London: Kegan Paul, Trench, Trübner, 1914). The authors are unusually condoning of the omitted fabliaux: "I must now skip several tales that you will read when you are older. They are all worth reading. . . . [Chaucer] was a poet who saw with clearer eyes than other men. To him nothing was common or unclean" (123). Even in the original 1878 edition the authors tell their audience that the Miller's and Reeve's tales "were good of their kind, but not such as you would care to hear" (85). The censoring of such tales is not, of course, confined to children's versions; thus Mrs. Haweis's *Tales from Chaucer* of 1887 in the Routledge's World Library series is aimed at an adult audience, the "Miller's Tale" being offered in a detailed prose paraphrase subject to what Mrs. Haweis calls "a very slight alteration" (64). This consists in a euphemistic treatment of Nicholas and Alison's relationship (the two are "pranking about the house" together when Absolon visits) and a misplaced kiss episode in which "the mischievous Alison rushed at [Absolon] with a broom of no great purity, which he received on his face with considerable force" (62–63).

22. Serraillier's, which is a surprisingly conservative edition for 1979, talks about the maiden being "seduced" (110). Dick talks about her being "taken by force" (16).

23. McCaughrean's "trivialized and emasculated" version of the "Clerk's Tale" is disparagingly discussed by Judith Bronfman, *Chaucer's "Clerk's Tale": The Griselda Story Received, Rewritten, Illustrated* (New York: Garland, 1994), 79–80.

24. For an account of these early continuations of the *Tales,* see John M. Bowers, "*The Tale of Beryn* and *The Siege of Thebes:* Alternative Ideas of the *Canterbury Tales,*" *Studies in the Age of Chaucer* 7 (1985): 23–50. Harvey Darton wrote his own account of these texts in "A Chapter of Flattery," *London Mercury* 18 (1928): 623–32.

25. Regina Z. Kelly, *Young Geoffrey Chaucer: His Boyhood Adventures, His Student Days at Oxford, His Romantic Training as a Page at Court,* illustrated by Warren Chappell (New York: Lothrop, Lee and Shepard, 1952), 26.

26. A common popularizing trope is the idea of a crucial impetus being given to the major writer by some casual observation from an "ordinary" man or woman; witness Bennett and Jackson's classroom play "Tomorrow We Ride!" based on the "General Prologue," where a Chaucer with writer's block is shown his way forward by a serving girl in the Tabard:

> CHAUCER: . . . I have the words to tell tales, but cannot find the tales to tell. . . . Sometimes I fear that inspiration will never steer my pen upon the voyage I would have it take.
> TESS: Tales needn't come out of your own head.
> LANDLORD: Keep out of this, wench.
> CHAUCER: Nay, Harry, let her speak. How else, Tess, should my tales be born?
> TESS: By listening to the pilgrims as they travel.

C. M. Bennett and C. V. Jackson, *Masters and Masterpieces: A Book of Classroom Plays Based on the Lives and Works of Five Great Writers* (London: John Murray, 1958), 19.

27. Lee Patterson, "'What Man Artow?' Authorial Self-Definition in 'The Tale of Sir Thopas' and 'The Tale of Melibee,'" *Studies in the Age of Chaucer* 11 (1989): 117–75. The citations are taken from page 164. For an account of the way tales like "Melibee" and "Sir Thopas" were served up as didactic children's literature in the fifteenth century, see Seth Lerer, "Reading Like a Child: Advisory Aesthetics and Scribal Revision in the *Canterbury Tales,*" chapter 3 of his *Chaucer and His Readers: Imagining the Author in Late-Medieval England* (Princeton, N.J.: Princeton University Press, 1993), 85–116. For Chaucer's depiction of childhood more generally, see Yvonne Truscott, "Chaucer's Children and the Medieval Idea of Childhood," *Children's Literature Association Quarterly* 23 (1998): 29–34.

5. English Chaucer

1. Matthew Browne, pseud. [William Rands], *Chaucer's England,* 2 vols. (1869), 1:45. Other nineteenth-century references to the "Englishness" of Chaucer not discussed in the present chapter can be found in Spurgeon, *Five Hundred Years,* 2:148, 3:3, and in John Ruskin's *Lectures on Art* (1870), quoted in Brewer, *Critical Heritage,* 2:106. See also Collette, "Chaucer and Victorian Medievalism," 121–23.

2. The chapter in question is entitled "Mediaeval Nuditarianism" (1:279–317). It includes such observations as "I do not want to incur the charge of man-millinerism, but I doubt if many men, even in rude health, could read the description of the Miller's bedroom in the middle of the night without a sense of nausea" (285). For another notable reader who twenty years later regarded parts of Chaucer as "needlessly filthy," see Theodore Roosevelt, *Letters,* ed. Elting E. Morison, vol. 1 (Cambridge, Mass.: Harvard University Press, 1951), 275–77 (commented on by Thomas A. Kirby, "Theodore Roosevelt on Chaucer and a Chaucerian," *MLN* 68 [1953]: 34–37).

3. F. D. Maurice, *On the Representation and Education of the People* (1866), 58; quoted in Spurgeon, *Five Hundred Years,* 3:83.

4. Green, *A Short History,* 221.

5. See chapter 2, note 27.

6. "Oddly enough," says Henry Dwight Sedgwick of the Prioress, "the description of her manners at table, which suits her so well and seems to bear Chaucer's personal mark, is copied almost word for word from the *Roman de la Rose*" (*Dan Chaucer,* 280). Noyes in his *Bookman* article suggests that the idea of the Prioress's table manners having a textual source, as in contemporary books of etiquette, reflects "the ludicrous concentration of some of the scholars on 'sources.' . . . such things are not found in books" ("Chaucer," 193).

7. Legouis, *Geoffrey Chaucer,* 56, 58–59.

8. See E. G. Sandras, *Étude sur G. Chaucer considéré comme imitateur des Trouvères* (Paris, 1859). Sandras's "impertinence" in presenting a Chaucer wholly dependent on his French sources is attacked by Lounsbury, *Studies,* 3:407–12; see also Furnivall's strictures in *Trial-Forewords,* 43–53. For Mario Praz, it was the heightened vivacity of Italy, encountered by Chaucer on his two trips there in the 1370s, that sharpened his perception of the

life later depicted in the *Canterbury Tales;* England may have been Chaucer's proper subject, but he had to go to Italy to find it. See "Chaucer and the Great Italian Writers of the Trecento," in *The Flaming Heart: Essays on Crawshaw, Machiavelli, and Other Studies* (1958; reprint, New York: Norton, 1973), 83–84. In a series of lectures given in Dublin in 1875, Furnivall spoke of the "versatile" and "mercurial" qualities of mind that linked Chaucer with the Irish and French rather than with the "slow dull English" (see Furnivall Collection, Kings College Library, London, ms 2/9, "Notes and Newspaper Clippings on Chaucer with Enclosures"). For Chaucer's enrollment by some critics as "an honorary American," see Pearsall, *Life,* 7.

9. Alfred Austin, quincentenary speech, 313 (see chapter 4, note 13).

10. Browne, *Chaucer's England,* 1:44–45.

11. Chesterton, *Chaucer,* 213.

12. Browne, *Chaucer's England,* 1:47, 49–50.

13. G. Wilson Knight, *This Sceptred Isle: Shakespeare's Message for England at War* (Oxford: Blackwell, 1940), 35.

14. Chesterton, *Chaucer,* 14.

15. Legouis, *Geoffrey Chaucer,* 31; Ames, "Life and Characteristics," 145, 168. For an alternative view of Chaucer's patriotism (as espoused in his political career, if not his poetry), see E. P. Kuhl, "Chaucer the Patriot," *Philological Quarterly* 25 (1946): 277–80.

16. "Chaucer's England," *Times Literary Supplement (TLS),* 20 April 1940, 195.

17. R. W. Chambers, "Geoffrey Chaucer: Spring-Tide of English Poetry," ibid., 194.

18. "Chaucer's England," *TLS,* 195.

19. Less "icy" springs than that of 1940 often call forth more routine appreciations of Chaucer in the press; see, for example, Richard Church, "Poet of Spring," *John O' London's Weekly,* 22 March 1946, 252; Ernest Hauser, "Geoffrey Chaucer, Bard of Spring," *Reader's Digest,* April 1972, 154–61.

20. *Punch,* 18 October 1944, 330. Vallins's figures began with "The Warden" on 26 January 1944, 70. A list (up until 1952) can be found in Henry Bosley Woolf, "Chaucer *Redivivus,*" *MLN* 62 (1947): 258–60, and "Chaucer and Vallins Again," *MLN* 67 (1952): 502, though the series continued into 1953. The wartime pilgrims were collected in Vallins's *Sincere Flattery: Parodies from "Punch"* (London: Epworth Press, 1954), 23–35.

21. *Punch,* 26 June 1946, 548; 6 July 1949, 24.

22. *A Canterbury Tale* is available on video from Carlton Home Entertainment (cat. no. 30370 60123).

23. See Hilaire Belloc, *The Old Road* (London: Constable, 1904). An earlier "restaging" of Chaucer along the Pilgrims' Way can be found in Maurice Hewlett, *New Canterbury Tales* (London: Constable, 1901), where a medieval party including a Prioress and a Shipman assembles in Winchester (in 1450), telling six tales in prose along the way.

24. As Peter Conrad notes in his perceptive discussion of the film's debt to Chaucer, *A Canterbury Tale* "suffuses the Chaucerian subject with an incongruous Wordsworthian pantheism." See "Arrival at Canterbury," chapter 1 of his *To Be Continued: Four Stories and Their Survival* (Oxford: Clarendon, 1995), 29. Versions of modern pastoral are discussed in my *The English Eliot: Design, Language, and Landscape in "Four Quartets"* (London: Routledge, 1991), 77–122, and in Simon Featherstone, "The Nation as Pastoral in British Literature of the Second World War," *Journal of European Studies* 16 (1986): 155–68.

25. On this, see Graham Holderness, "Agincourt 1944: Readings in the Shakespeare Myth," in *Popular Fictions: Essays in Literature and History*, ed. Peter Humm et al. (London: Methuen, 1986), 173–95.

26. Sedgwick, *Dan Chaucer,* 21, 358.

27. Noyes, "Chaucer," pt. 2, *Bookman* 78 (April–September 1930): 216; "Chaucer," pt. 1, 195, 192–93.

28. Brenda R. Silver, ed., "'Anon' and 'The Reader': Virginia Woolf's Last Essays," *Twentieth Century Literature* 25 (1979): 357. These two unfinished essays represent what survives of *Reading at Random*.

29. Virginia Woolf, "The Pastons and Chaucer," in *The Essays of Virginia Woolf,* vol. 4, 1925–28, ed. Andrew McNeillie (London: Hogarth Press, 1994), 33.

30. Silver, "Anon," 391.

31. Woolf, "The Pastons and Chaucer," 30.

32. See McNeillie, in *Essays of Virginia Woolf,* 36 n. 1, who also lists Coulton's *Chaucer and His England* (1908) among Woolf's reading. Arnold's brief but well-known appraisal of Chaucer salutes his "largeness, freedom, shrewdness, benignity," but insists that he lacks the "high seriousness" that characterizes "the great classics" like Dante, and which is "altogether beyond Chaucer's reach." See his introduction to *The English Poets . . . ,* ed. Thomas Humphry Ward (1880), xxxi–vi. From Lowell's essay in *My Study Windows* (1871), Woolf would have been encouraged to see Chaucer as at the opposite pole to modern self-consciousness and self-absorption, "escaping from the fixed air of self into the brisk atmosphere of universal sentiments" and "turning frankly and gaily to the actual world, and drinking inspiration from sources open to all . . . turning away from a colourless abstraction to the solid earth and to emotions common to every pulse." James Russell Lowell, "Chaucer," in *My Study Windows,* introduction by Richard Garnett (London: Walter Scott, n.d.), 206, 260.

33. Silver, "The Reader," 427–29.

34. Woolf, "The Pastons and Chaucer," 29.

35. The quotation is from a draft of "Anon" included in Silver's commentary (404). Woolf's change of date from 1478 to 1477 indicates the precedence she gave to Caxton's printing of the *Morte D'Arthur* over his edition of the *Canterbury Tales* (1478). Woolf held that the former work was printed in 1477, though it actually appeared in 1485. See "Anon," 384.

36. Silver, "The Reader," 427; "Anon," 389.

37. Woolf, "The Pastons and Chaucer," 28–29.

38. Virginia Woolf, *Pointz Hall: The Earlier and Later Typescripts of "Between the Acts,"* ed. Mitchell A. Leaska (New York: New York University, 1983), 49.

39. Virginia Woolf, *Between the Acts,* introduction by Quentin Bell, Definitive Collected Edition (London: Hogarth Press, 1990), 119.

40. Chesterton, *Chaucer,* 15.

41. The "tight hermeneutic circle" arising from Chaucer's putative status as at once both originator and inheritor, in this case of the English language itself, has been traced in detail by Christopher Cannon, "The Myth of Origin and the Making of Chaucer's English," *Speculum* 71 (1996): 646–75.

42. Chesterton's interest in landscape figures as representations of the nation also features in one of his best-known poems, *The Ballad of the White Horse* (1911); see my *English Eliot*, 120–21.

43. Sir Arthur Quiller-Couch, "A Gossip on Chaucer, 2," in his *Studies in Literature*, second series (Cambridge: Cambridge University Press, 1934), 225. Lee Patterson discusses pertinently how a liberal humanist tradition of Chaucer scholarship (represented by the work of Charles Muscatine) also works to "dehistoricize history . . . by reading it as the external reflection of a determining Chaucerian selfhood. Muscatine tells us, in other words, not how Chaucer is a fourteenth-century poet, but rather how the fourteenth century is Chaucerian" (*Negotiating the Past*, 26). The idea here of an originary and transcendental Chaucer (as Patterson says, "a poet who is in but not of his time") parallels the incarnational theme discussed in Chesterton.

44. Chesterton, *Chaucer*, 183.

45. John Masefield, "Chaucer," 32.

46. John Masefield, *Reynard the Fox; or, The Ghost Heath Run*, in *Collected Poems*, new ed. (London: Heinemann, 1932), 525.

47. Woolf, "The Pastons and Chaucer," 28.

6. Writers Chaucer

1. Harriet Monroe, "Chaucer and Langland," *Poetry* 6 (April–September 1915): 301, quoted in Brewer, *Critical Heritage*, 2:337.

2. Pound, *ABC of Reading*, 99–103.

3. Ezra Pound, "Cavalcanti," in *Literary Essays*, 181; quoted in Brewer, *Critical Heritage*, 2:334. For Pound's essay "The Serious Artist," see *Literary Essays*, 41–57.

4. On Chaucer and Pound, see Georg M. Gugelberger, "Zum Mittelaltereinfluss in der modernen Dichtung: Ezra Pounds Chaucerbild," *Orbis Litterarum* 35 (1980): 220–34. Pound's comment on Chaucer's "exquisite" lyrics comes from "The Hard and Soft in French Poetry," in *Literary Essays*, 287, quoted in Brewer, *Critical Heritage*, 2:330. Pound's encomium on Chaucer in *ABC of Reading* (98–114) is inexplicably omitted from Brewer's compilation of Pound's comments in the *Critical Heritage* volume (2:329–34) and from any consideration in Shelly's survey of significant modern writing on Chaucer by "a poet or a critic" (*The Living Chaucer*, 19–20). According to Marshall McLuhan, it is "the only appreciation [Chaucer] has received since Dryden that relates him to the mind of Europe." See McCluhan, "Pound's Critical Prose," in *The Interior Landscape: The Literary Criticism of Marshall McLuhan, 1943–1962*, ed. Eugene McNamara (New York: McGraw-Hill, 1969), 78.

5. Brewer, *Critical Heritage*, 2:489.

6. T. S. Eliot, "Chaucer's *Troilus*," *TLS*, 19 August 1926, 547.

7. Eliot, "Dante," *Selected Essays*, 275.

8. Robert Kilburn Root, ed., *The Book of Troilus and Criseyde* (Princeton, N.J.: Princeton University Press, 1926), l.

9. T. S. Eliot, *The Clark Lectures*, in T. S. Eliot, *The Varieties of Metaphysical Poetry*, ed. Ronald Schuchard (London: Faber, 1993), 228.

10. Eliot, "Dante," 252. As Seamus Heaney puts it, Eliot's insistence on the decorous uniformity of Dante's style "underplays the swarming, mobbish element in the Italian." See Heaney, "Envies and Identifications: Dante and the Modern Poet," in *Dante Readings,* ed. Eric Haywood (Dublin: Irish Academic Press, 1987), 37. On Eliot's neglect of the polyvocal qualities in Dante, see also my *English Eliot,* 8–12, 63–65.

11. Strohm, *Social Chaucer,* 168.

12. Two deeply unconvincing claims for the significance of the Chaucer-Eliot relationship can be found in Linda Tarte Holley, "Chaucer, T. S. Eliot, and the Regenerative Pilgrimage," *Studies in Medievalism* 2 (1982): 19–33, and Dansby Evans, "Chaucer and Eliot: The Poetics of Pilgrimage," *Medieval Perspectives* 9 (1994): 41–47.

13. William Carlos Williams, *Paterson* (New York: New Directions, 1963), 112; Gale C. Schricker, "The Case of Cress: Implications of Allusion in *Paterson,*" *William Carlos Williams Review* 11 (1985): 21. Schricker quotes as Williams's manifesto the famous statement from the opening of book 1 of *Paterson,* "no ideas but in things" (14; Schricker, 17).

14. See Williams, preface to *Selected Essays* (New York: Random House, n.d.), xvii: "Chaucer, Villon and Whitman were contemporaries of mind with whom I am constantly in touch—through the art of writing. They are worthy rivals—whom I am proud and have been proud to honor as I can."

15. See Williams, *Selected Letters,* ed. John C. Thirwall (New York: McDowell, Obolensky, 1957), 263.

16. Williams, *Paterson,* 208.

17. For reference to an early draft in which Williams talks of basing his poem on the "general structure" of the *Canterbury Tales* (though he does little to clarify what he has in mind), see Charles Doyle, *William Carlos Williams and the American Poem* (London: Macmillan, 1982), 109.

18. Dolores Palomo, "Alpha and Omega: Of Chaucer and Joyce," *Mosaic* 8, no. 2 (winter 1975): 20, 23.

19. Helen Cooper, "Chaucer and Joyce," *Chaucer Review* 21 (1986–87): 143.

20. An early statement of the position was Robert M. Jordan's "Lost in the Funhouse of Fame: Chaucer and Postmodernism," *Chaucer Review* 18 (1983–84): 100–115, where Chaucer's act of "writing about writing" in the *House of Fame* is related to the procedure of novelists like Joyce and John Barth. This was followed by Jordan's full-length study *Chaucer's Poetics and the Modern Reader* (Berkeley: University of California Press, 1987). On Barth, see also Robert P. Winston, "Chaucer's Influence on Barth's *The Sot-Weed Factor,*" *American Literature* 56 (1984): 584–90. For a general account of the critical argument over Chaucer and postmodernism, see my introduction to *Chaucer: The Canterbury Tales,* Longman Critical Readers (London: Longman, 1998), 1–22.

21. Cooper, "Chaucer and Joyce," 143–44.

22. James Joyce, *Ulysses,* ed. Hans Walter Gabler, rev. ed. (London: Bodley Head, 1986), 642.

23. John H. Lammers, "The Archetypal Molly Bloom, Joyce's Frail Wife of Bath," *James Joyce Quarterly* 25 (1987–88): 497–98.

24. Helen Cooper, more purely concerned with levels of style and textual effects, relates Molly's discourse rather to the "Parson's Tale," as a final monologue "incapable of admitting any point of view but [its] own" that threatens to halt the "play of voices." She argues, however, that Molly's voice is far more sympathetic to the rest of Joyce's novel than the Parson's severe homily is to the viewpoints of the other pilgrims, and that it therefore "does justice to the rest of the work" (149–50). In this, Molly might be said to be rather less "isolated": if Chaucerian community harbors rigidly opposed positions, then the sense of collectivity might be something of an illusion, compared with a modern stream-of-consciousness scenario where sympathetic telepathy is at least an undercurrent. Joyce did in fact write an essay on "The Good Parson of Chaucer" for an Italian public examination in 1912; see Richard Ellmann, *James Joyce,* rev. ed. (Oxford: Oxford University Press, 1982), 321.

25. In particular, Lewis M. Schwartz, "Eccles Street and Canterbury: An Approach to Molly Bloom," *Twentieth Century Literature* 15 (1969): 155–62, and Joseph Voelker, "Molly Bloom and the Rhetorical Tradition," *Comparative Literature Studies* 16 (1979): 146–64.

26. For a comparison of Joyce's story "The Dead" in *Dubliners* with Chaucer's *Book of the Duchess,* see Milton Miller, "Definition by Comparison: Chaucer, Lawrence, and Joyce," *Essays in Criticism* 3 (1953): 377–81. A common interest in the mendacities of oral tradition (centering on the *House of Fame, Ulysses,* and *Finnegans Wake*) is the subject of Willi Erzgraber, "Common Traits of Chaucer's and Joyce's Narrative Art," in *Telling Stories: Studies in Honour of Ulrich Broich . . . ,* ed. Elmar Lehmann and Bernd Lenz (Amsterdam: Gruner, 1992), 188–204.

27. Elizabeth Steele, "Chaucer and Henry James: Surprising Bedfellows," *Henry James Review* 13 (1992): 126–42.

28. Henry James, "A Tragedy of Error," in *The Tales of Henry James,* vol. 1, 1864–1869, ed. Maqbool Aziz (Oxford: Clarendon, 1973), 1–19.

29. W. R. Martin and Warren U. Ober, "The Provenience of Henry James's First Tale," *Studies in Short Fiction* 24 (1987): 57–58.

30. Steele, "Chaucer and Henry James," 139, 129.

31. On Madame de Cintré's habitual fearfulness, see Henry James, *The American,* introduction by Malcolm Bradbury (London: Dent, 1997), 265–66, 283–84.

32. Steele, "Chaucer and Henry James," 23, 116, 165.

33. James notes of *The American* that "the interest of everything is all that it is [Newman's] vision, *his* conception, *his* interpretation" (preface, 17). The quality of the "leads" on which Steele builds her case can be judged from the following: "Troilus and his counterpart Newman are both described as having risen from the 'dead' early in each work; and Pandarus' description of his niece as a 'bounteous' woman [is] echoed in Valentin's insistence that Claire is 'generosity itself'" (139).

34. Steele, "Chaucer and Henry James," 126.

35. Adeline R. Tintner, "*Daisy Miller* and Chaucer's 'Daisy' Poem: The 'Prologue' to the *Legend of Good Women,*" *Henry James Review* 15 (1994): 20.

36. Ibid., 22; Henry James, "Daisy Miller: A Study," in *The Tales of Henry James,* vol. 3, 1875–1879, ed. Maqbool Aziz (Oxford: Clarendon, 1984), 194.

37. Henry James, *The Spoils of Poynton,* ed. David Lodge (Harmondsworth: Penguin, 1987), 166–67.

38. Lawrence refers to Chaucer most frequently in his essay "Introduction to These Paintings," where Chaucer's "lovely" and "fearless" recognition of the body is contrasted with "a horror of sexual life" that overtakes English culture at the time of the Renaissance. See *Phoenix: The Posthumous Papers of D. H. Lawrence,* ed. Edward D. McDonald (London: Heinemann, 1936), 551–52, 555.

39. See Marijane Osborn, "Complexities of Gender and Genre in Lawrence's *The Fox,*" *Essays in Literature* 19 (1992): 86: The name and location of Bailey Farm (in Lawrence's words "a little homestead . . . lying just one field removed from the edge of the wood") "make one think of the farm 'biside a grove, stondynge in a dale' in the tale that Chaucer's Nun's Priest tells at Harry Bailly's request." See D. H. Lawrence, *The Fox; The Captain's Doll; The Ladybird,* ed. Dieter Mehl (Cambridge: Cambridge University Press, 1992), 9.

40. Banford is referred to as "a little fighting cock" in *The Fox,* 51.

41. Lawrence, *The Fox,* 70.

42. Osborn, "Complexities of Gender," 94.

43. Miller, "Definition by Comparison," 376.

44. F. T. Flahiff, "*The Great Gatsby:* Scott Fitzgerald's Chaucerian Rag," in *Figures in a Ground: Canadian Essays on Modern Literature Collected in Honor of Sheila Watson,* ed. Diane Bessai and David Jackel (Saskatoon: Western Producer Prairie, 1978), 97–98.

45. Nancy Y. Hoffman, "*The Great Gatsby: Troilus and Criseyde* Revisited?" in *Fitzgerald/Hemingway Annual 1971,* ed. Matthew J. Bruccoli and C. E. Frazer Clark Jr. (Dayton, Ohio: NCR Microcard Editions), 148–58.

46. F. Scott Fitzgerald, *The Great Gatsby* (1926; reprint, Harmondsworth: Penguin, 1950), 103, 118.

47. The most explicit reworking of *Troilus and Criseyde* in modern fiction is Andrea Newman's novel *An Evil Streak* (London: Michael Joseph, 1977), in which an elderly academic, working on a translation of Chaucer's poem, orchestrates an affair involving his niece so that he can spy on the couple's lovemaking in his flat through a trick mirror. His grubby cast of mind is reflected in his own understanding of Chaucer's poem as a text solely concerned with sexual intrigue.

48. Margaret Atwood, *The Handmaid's Tale* (1986; reprint, London: Virago, 1987), 313.

49. Deborah S. Ellis, "*The Color Purple* and the Patient Griselda," *College English* 49 (1987): 188–201.

50. Alice Walker, *The Color Purple* (1983; reprint, London: Women's Press, 1992), 177–82.

51. Ellis, *"Color Purple,"* 199.

52. See Elaine Tuttle Hansen, "The Powers of Silence: The Case of the Clerk's Griselda," chapter 7 of her *Chaucer and the Fictions of Gender* (Berkeley: University of California Press, 1992), 188–207.

53. Walker, *The Color Purple,* 240.

54. Ellis, *"Color Purple,"* 199.

55. Strohm, *Social Chaucer,* 168. Neither *The Handmaid's Tale* nor *The Color Purple* is considered in Judith Bronfman's study of the rewritings of the "Clerk's Tale" *(Chaucer's "Clerk's Tale"),* which keeps cautiously to those versions where Griselda is featured by name.

56. Attention to the relation of "Just Meat" with Chaucer was first raised by Whitney Wells, "A New Analogue to the 'Pardoner's Tale,'" *MLN* 40 (1925): 58–59.

57. Jack London, "Just Meat," in *When God Laughs and Other Stories* (London: Mills and Boon, 1911), 116.

58. Dave Godfrey, "River Two Blind Jacks," in *Canadian Short Stories,* second series, selected by Robert Weaver (Toronto: Oxford University Press, 1968), 301–17; see Lorraine M. York, "'River Two Blind Jacks': Dave Godfrey's Chaucerian Allegory," *Studies in Canadian Literature* 9 (1984): 206–13. The "Pardoner's Tale" is also reworked into Sarah J. Curry's "The Devil's Gold," in a collection tellingly entitled *A Treasury of Plays for Men,* ed. Frank Shay (London: Little, Brown, 1928), 25–38.

59. The correspondence was first traced in an anonymous article "Kipling and Chaucer," *Atlantic Monthly* 84 (1899): 714–16.

60. D. Maureen Thum, "Frame and Fictive Voice in Chaucer's 'The Pardoner's Tale' and Kipling's 'The King's Ankus,'" *Philological Quarterly* 71 (1992): 274–75; Rudyard Kipling, "The King's Ankus," in *The Second Jungle Book* (1895; reprint, Ware: Wordsworth, 1994), 173.

61. Kipling returned briefly to Chaucer in several other works, particularly in the Wife of Bath figure Mrs Ashcroft in the short story "The Wish House" (1924); this doughty reminiscer nevertheless takes on a quasi-Alcestis role in rescuing from death the man she terms her "master," Harry Mockler. See Rudyard Kipling, *Short Stories: 2: Friendly Brook and Other Stories,* selected by Andrew Rutherford (Harmondsworth: Penguin, 1971), 163–81. In the same volume is "Dayspring Mishandled" (1928), in which a Chaucer scholar is fooled by a forged manuscript purporting to contain "a fragment of a hitherto unknown Canterbury Tale." Kipling highlights the patronizing attitudes this discovery evokes in the Press: "The lighter-minded journals disport[ed] themselves according to their publics; for 'our Dan,' as one earnest Sunday editor observed, 'lies closer to the national heart than we wot of'" (219–20). For an overview of Kipling and Chaucer, as well as a brilliant reading of the eponymous protagonist of Kipling's story "Mary Postgate" (1915) as a conflation of the Prioress and the Wife of Bath, see Nora Crook, "Kipling and Chaucer: 'Mary Postgate,'" chapter 6 of her *Kipling's Myths of Love and Death* (London: Macmillan, 1989), 111–47.

62. Wolfgang E. H. Rudat, "Jake Barnes, Chaucer's Pardoner, and the Restaurant Scene in Ernest Hemingway's *The Sun Also Rises,*" *Cithara* 26, no. 2 (1987): 51.

63. Allen Barnett, "Philostorgy, Now Obscure," in *The Body and Its Dangers and Other Stories* (New York: St. Martin's Press, 1990), 47.

64. Steven F. Kruger, "Claiming the Pardoner: Toward a Gay Reading of Chaucer's 'Pardoner's Tale,'" *Exemplaria* 6 (1994): 138.

65. See Dominic Manganiello, *T. S. Eliot and Dante* (London: Macmillan, 1989); James J. Wilhelm, *Dante and Pound: The Epic of Judgement* (Orono: University of Maine Press, 1974); Mary T. Reynolds, *Joyce and Dante: The Shaping Imagination* (Princeton, N.J.: Princeton University Press, 1981).

66. One notes, however, the recent book on the Chaucer-Fitzgerald relationship by Deborah Davis Schlacks, *American Dream Visions: Chaucer's Surprising Influence on F. Scott Fitzgerald* (New York: Peter Lang, 1994).

67. Velma Bourgeois Richmond, "Chaucer's Religiosity and a Twentieth-Century Analogue, Muriel Spark," *Modern Language Quarterly* 51 (1990): 445.

68. Pearsall, *Life,* 218.

69. Peter Conrad goes further than I would in arguing that the very act of speaking out by the unnamed protagonist in Atwood's novel is founded in Chaucer's recognition of the rights of the individual to have a voice against collective orthodoxy. The novel is thus a "tribute to the subversiveness of Chaucer" and can be compared with "the scandalous reminiscences of the Wife of Bath." It will be clear from my discussion of the novel above that I regard such a reading as crucially ignoring *The Handmaid's Tale*'s protestations about male appropriation of female voices, of which indeed the Wife's reminiscences are, some would argue, a signal example. See Conrad, *To Be Continued*, 32–35.

7. Translated Chaucer

1. Review of Nevill Coghill, "Chaucer: *The Canterbury Tales* Translated into Modern English," *Listener*, 7 February 1952, 236.

2. Frank Ernest Hill, "Unknown Poet," introduction to his *The Canterbury Tales: The "Prologue" and Four Tales with the "Book of the Duchess" and Six Lyrics . . . Translated into Modern English Verse* (London: Longmans, Green, 1930), xii.

3. Derek Pearsall, review of David Wright, trans., *The Canterbury Tales*, *Studies in the Age of Chaucer* 9 (1987): 200; hereafter cited by page number in the text.

4. David Wright, trans., *The Canterbury Tales* (1985; reprint, Oxford: Oxford University Press, 1986), xxi; hereafter cited by page number in the text.

5. "Chaucer Modernized," *TLS*, 24 July 1930, 610.

6. Hill, "Unknown Poet," 104; Nevill Coghill, trans., *The Canterbury Tales: Translated into Modern English*, rev. ed. (Harmondsworth: Penguin, 1977), 77; hereafter cited by page number in the text. Chesterton takes Hill to task for his changes to this line in *Chaucer*, 220–21.

7. Dryden, preface to *Poems and Fables*, 533 (see chap. 2, n. 37).

8. W. W. Skeat, trans., *The "Man of Law's Tale," the "Nun's Priest's Tale," the "Squire's Tale" . . . Done into Modern English* (London: De La More, 1904), preface, xxi, 53.

9. Hill, "Unknown Poet," xiii.

10. W. W. Skeat, trans., *The "Knight's Tale" or "Palamon and Arcite" . . . Done into Modern English* (London: De La More, 1904), 1.

11. Other versions by Skeat in the King's Classics series included a one-volume compilation of the Prioress's, Pardoner's, Clerk's, Second Nun's, and Canon's Yeoman's tales (1904), a one-volume "General Prologue," part of the *Romance of the Rose* and some minor poems (1907), the *Legend of Good Women* (1907), and a one-volume *House of Fame* and *Parliament of Fowls* (1908).

12. J. U. Nicolson, *The Canterbury Tales: Rendered into Modern English*, introduction by Gordon Hall Gerould (1934; reprint, London: W. H. Allen, 1949), 1, 4.

13. See Richard Church, "Tittivating Chaucer," *Spectator*, 5 April 1935, 576–77.

14. See R. H. Llewellyn's review of Coghill in *Speculum* 27 (1952): 540.

15. The most frequently used modern parallel text version of Chaucer is that by A. Kent Hieatt and Constance Hieatt, eds., *The Canterbury Tales . . . Selected, with Translations, a Critical Introduction, and Notes by the Editors* (1964; reprint, New York: Bantam, 1981). Al-

though this claims to be a verse translation, the emphasis on solely clarifying the content of the original leads to considerable neglect of rhyme or rhythm: "By course of time and elapse of a certain number of years / the mourning and tears wholly ceased. / Then, it seems to me, there was, by a general agreement, / a meeting of the Greeks / at Athens on certain questions and affairs" ("Knight's Tale," 139). The selection amounts to eight tales and the "General Prologue."

16. John S. P. Tatlock and Percy Mackaye, trans., *The Modern Reader's Chaucer: The Complete Poetical Works . . . Now First Put into Modern English,* illustrated by Warwick Goble, new ed. (New York: Macmillan, 1938), vii; hereafter cited by page number in the text.

17. R. M. Lumiansky's prose version of the *Tales* of 1948 justifies its procedure in an introduction by constantly referring to the *Tales* as "a collection of short stories" (though the "Knight's Tale" might be better seen as a "modern novelette") of particular interest to the twentieth century as the "age of the short story." In his preface to the translation, Mark Van Doren abets this excision of Chaucer's poetry by insisting on the "absolute plainness" of the original; this renders a prose retelling "natural" and a way of reproducing Chaucer's poetic self-effacement: "Mr Lumiansky keeps himself out of sight as well as Chaucer does. It is merely the stories that we get, as clear as sunlight and as live as human speech." R. M. Lumiansky, *The Canterbury Tales . . . a New Modern English Prose Translation,* preface by Mark Van Doren (1948; reprint, New York: Washington Square, 1960), xix–xx, vii–viii. In 1952 Lumiansky brought out a prose *Troilus and Criseyde,* written in "semi-formal conversational Modern English, such as might be heard at a somewhat relaxed official function": *Geoffrey Chaucer's Troilus and Criseyde: Rendered into Modern English Prose,* illustrated by H. Lawrence Hoffman (Columbia: University of South Carolina Press, 1952), xi.

18. Arthur Burrell, ed., *Chaucer's Canterbury Tales for the Modern Reader* (London: Dent, 1908), 1, viii.

19. Frank Ernest Hill, trans., *The Canterbury Tales . . . Rendered into Modern English Verse,* 2 vols. (London: Limited Editions Club, 1934), I.xxii.

20. All future references to Hill's version of the *Tales* are to *The Canterbury Tales . . . Translated into Modern English Verse* (London: Longmans, 1935). An anonymous *TLS* reviewer found Hill's a "straightforward, spirited and sensitive modern version" ("Chaucer for the Multitude: A Translation into Modern English," *TLS,* 15 August 1936, 661), while of his 1930 selection, Mabel Day's review, in the *Review of English Studies* 7 (1931): 112, suggested that some of Hill's lines were "more vigorous" than their rather "flat" originals.

21. In line 7 of the passage Hill seems simply to have mistranslated "sewed" as "saw," rather than the correct "pursued."

22. H. L. Hitchins, ed., *Canterbury Tales: Chaucer for Present-Day Readers,* new ed. (London: John Murray, 1949), 1.

23. See the headnote in Coghill's introduction to the second series of broadcasts, "Chaucer, the Master Storyteller," *Radio Times,* 1 July 1949, 6. The first series went out on the BBC Third Programme in seven installments between 21 October 1946 and 16 April 1947, with a weekly repeat. The series was further repeated daily between 4 and 10 May 1947. In 1949 seven further installments were added, the series beginning with the "General Prologue" (4 July) and ending with the "Canon's Yeoman's Tale" (3 October), with a weekly repeat. This series was then repeated on the Home Service (London Region only) starting on 2 November 1949. The broadcasts are held in the National Sound Archives at the British Library.

24. Letters criticizing and supporting the original review can be found in the *Listener* for 14 February 1952 (268) and 21 February (310). The Internet discussion dates from August to September 1997 (e-mail: CHAUCER@LISTSERV.UIC.EDU).

25. See, for example, Gillian Evans, *Chaucer* (Glasgow: Blackie, 1977), an introductory study suddenly brought to life in its final pages, where the author fulminates against "the work of vulgarization" represented by Coghill's translation and musical and by Pasolini's film of the *Tales:* "It is to the shame of our present desire for instant results for the minimum expense of effort and engagement that Coghill has been substituted for Chaucer in the experience of many" (138). It is difficult, however, to square this decrying of our "desire for instant results" with her then recommending David Wright's *prose* version two pages later (140).

26. David Wright, trans., *Chaucer: The Canterbury Tales: A Modern Prose Rendering* (1964; reprint, London: Panther, 1965), 19, 20, 25; hereafter cited by page number in the text.

27. For such a comparative review, see that by Malcolm Andrew in *Speculum* 62 (1987): 498–99.

28. While Andrew in his *Speculum* review ends up giving the preference to Wright over Coghill, he himself notes other examples in the former work of "tonal infelicity, crass modernization, or a tendency to crudify" (498).

29. Coghill, "Master Storyteller," 6. Coghill's original scripts for the broadcasts are held on microfiche at the BBC Written Archives Centre, Caversham Park, Reading. Some paper scripts also survive there, together with other production material and correspondence relating to both the 1946 and 1949 broadcasts (Files R19/142/1, 2). Many of the revisions Coghill made on individual scripts and between the two series are a response to worries about "offensive" language and episodes; see, for example, the letter from the acting controller to the producer, Stephen Potter (7 February 1947), complaining about the unsuitability for transmission of the then current version of the "Merchant's Tale." Some of the original offending phrases have been reinstated in the present printed text.

30. Theodore Morrison, trans. and ed., *The Portable Chaucer,* rev. ed. (Harmondsworth: Penguin, 1977).

31. See Albert C. Salzberg, "The 'Prologue' to the *Canterbury Tales* and the Morrison Version," *Translation Review* 42–43 (1993): 19.

32. Ronald L. Ecker and Eugene J. Crook, *The Canterbury Tales . . . Translated into Modern English* (Palatka, Fla.: Hodge and Braddock, 1993), ix. Ecker is responsible for the poetry and Crook for the prose tales.

33. For an estimate of the Ecker-Crook version that chimes with my own, see Malcolm Andrew's review in *English Studies* 76 (1995): 480–81.

34. Margaret Stanley-Wrench, *Troilus and Criseyde . . . Translated into Modern English* (London: Centaur, 1965), 25.

35. Nevill Coghill, *Troilus and Criseyde: Translated into Modern English* (Harmondsworth: Penguin, 1971), 12.

36. George Philip Krapp, *Troilus and Cressida . . . Rendered into Modern English Verse* (1932; reprint, London: Limited Editions Club, 1939).

37. Classic examples of wholesale condemnation laced with satisfied self-regard would be Marvin Mudrick's two pieces, "Chaucer and What We Make of Him," *Hudson Review* 6 (1953–54): 124–30, and "Chaucer as Librettist," *Philological Quarterly* 38 (1959): 21–29. See also Salzberg's critical piece on Theodore Morrison, "Morrison Version," 19–22. An honorable exception to this routine dismissal is Giles Sinclair, "Chaucer—Translated or Obliterated?" *College English* 15 (1953–54): 272–77.

38. One or two less accessible twentieth-century versions of the *Tales* have not been referred to in the present chapter, nor have space constraints made it possible to consider translations of Chaucer's shorter poems. Versions of these include James J. Donohue, trans., *Chaucer's Lesser Poems Complete, in Present-Day English* (Dubuque, Iowa: Loras College Press, 1974); Ann McMillan, trans., *Legend of Good Women* (Houston, Tex.: Rice University Press, 1987); and Brian Stone, trans., *Chaucer: Love Visions* (Harmondsworth: Penguin, 1983). One curiosity worth mentioning is J. Barlow Brooks's translation of the "Nun's Priest's Tale" into Lancashire dialect. This opens: "A widow, gerrin rayther owd, / Lived in a cottige, so awm towd, / Near some threes as stood in a dale. / If ye durnt mind awl tell er tale. / Sin th day oo stopt bein a wife / An started t live a simple life / Oo little ownt, or ad comin in; / A dairy an a poulthry run / Fer ersel an er dowther's fun." See *Chaucer's Cock and Other Fables (in Lancashire Dialect)* (Oxford: n.p., 1951), 7.

39. Peter G. Beidler, "Chaucer and the Trots: What to Do about Those Modern English Translations," *Chaucer Review* 19 (1984–85): 300.

8. Performance Chaucer

1. "Chaucer's Bawdy Pantomime," *Radio Times,* 16 October 1969, 10.

2. Five of the seven episodes (see note following) that made up the 1969 *Tales* were in fact repeated on BBC 2 between 18 August and 15 September 1971, with episodes 3 and 6 omitted. There have been a handful of other television transmissions of Chaucer, as, for example, the "Miller's Tale" in eighteenth-century costume, broadcast in the "Screenplay Firsts" series, BBC 2, 8 September 1993. I have not been able, unfortunately, to consult *Ribald Tales of Canterbury,* originally released on video and broadcast on the adult channel Fantasy X, 4 September 1997.

3. The episodes (all broadcast on BBC 2) consisted of "General Prologue" and "Knight's Tale" (23 October 1969); "Miller's Tale" and "Reeve's Tale" (30 October); "Shipman's Tale," "Sir Thopas," "Melibee," and "Nun's Priest's Tale," the latter preceded by the Prioress singing a psalm (6 November); "Wife of Bath's Prologue," "Friar's Tale," "Summoner's Tale," and "Pardoner's Tale" (13 November); "Wife of Bath's Tale," "Clerk's Tale," and "Monk's Tale" (20 November); "Merchant's Tale" and "Manciple's Tale" (27 November); and "Canon's Yeoman's Tale," "Squire's Tale," "Franklin's Tale," Parson's sermon, and "Retraction" (4 December). Obviously some of the tales were much truncated and others merely referred to in passing for the sake of completeness. Thus "Sir Thopas" is interrupted by the Host after only five stanzas, and Chaucer is asked to save "Melibee" till the return to the Tabard so that the Host's wife can have the benefit of hearing it, too. The episodes can be seen in the BBC Broadcast Archives at Brentford.

4. The original scripts and production files for the series are on microfilm in the BBC Written Archives Centre at Caversham. These are particularly useful for the 20 November episode, where the Brentford copy has only the prerecorded studio tales and is missing the pilgrimage framework; the script, however, indicates that the Monk told his interminable series of "tragedies" as the pilgrims fell asleep on their night's stopover.

5. See file T5/948/1, Caversham.

6. Quoted in "Chaucer's Bawdy Pantomime."

7. Henry Raynor, "A Tolerable Compromise," *Times*, 24 October 1969, 13. Other reviews published on the same date were less welcoming—see Sylvia Clayton, "Pilgrimage to Canterbury," *Daily Telegraph*, 15, and Peter Black's review in the *Daily Mail* headlined "Forsooth, ye herald's panto poems do try me too far" (3).

8. At the time of writing (1998), a video of the Italian version is available from Vivivideo (Cat. DPHS 020009).

9. Pier Paolo Pasolini, script of *I racconti di Canterbury*, in *Trilogia della vita*, ed. Giorgio Gattei (Milan: Mondadori, 1990), 127.

10. Pier Paolo Pasolini, "Abiura dalla *Trilogia della vita*," in ibid., 7 ("that fight for the democratization of the 'right to self-expression' and for sexual liberalization, which were two fundamental elements in the struggle for progress in the fifties and sixties").

11. For an interesting comparison between Pasolini's "Abiura" and Chaucer's "Retraction," see Patrick Allen Rumble, *"La Trilogia della vita": Pier Paolo Pasolini's "schermo eloquio"* (Ph.D. diss., University of Toronto, 1991). Rumble sees both men as making a formulaic recantation in order to satisfy ecclesiastical officialdom and to "protect potentially transgressive material from the forces of moral conformity by *conceding* some ground to those very forces" (4, 223–47). At the end of the film itself Pasolini had already exposed Chaucer's "Retraction" in his insistence on the *Tales* as told "per il solo piacere di raccontare" and in the "hilariously parodic" "Amen" that is Pasolini-Chaucer's last word (241).

12. Pasolini's "vision" of both the negative and positive "possibilities of sexuality" is discussed in Martin Green, "The Dialectic of Adaptation: *The Canterbury Tales* of Pier Paolo Pasolini," *Literature/Film Quarterly* 4 (1976): 46–53.

13. See the series of interviews with Pasolini featuring the *Tales* and reprinted in *Pier Paolo Pasolini*, ed. P. Willemen (London: British Film Institute, 1977), 69–74. Pasolini also notes here his difficulties in incorporating into the film the links, which he originally began to shoot but then eliminated, and his inability to explain his own sequence of tales, "why the first tale is first rather than seventh" (73).

14. "Passionate Ideologue," *TLS*, 12 October 1973, 1253; Dilys Powell, review of *The Canterbury Tales*, *Sunday Times*, 17 June 1973, 37. For one recent critic, Pasolini's "contempt for the flesh and truculent anality dominate [the film]"; see Maurizio Viano, *A Certain Realism: Making Use of Pasolini's Film Theory and Practice* (Berkeley: University of California Press, 1993), 282.

15. Stanley Reynolds, "Prologue," *Guardian*, 24 October 1969, 8.

16. The phrase on the billing was taken from Harold Hobson's review of the musical (in a theater roundup headed "A Ritual of Despair") in the *Sunday Times*, 24 March 1968, 48.

17. Although the book of the musical has never been published, a *Canterbury Tales: Song Album* featuring the overture and six songs (music by Richard Hill and John

Hawkins) has been published by Chappell (London, n.d.). This also includes cast photos and a synopsis of the story. A cassette of the score and songs, recorded by the original London cast, was brought out by That's Entertainment Records in 1984 (ZC TER 1076).

18. Coghill, *Poet Chaucer,* 179.

19. Julia Fitzsimmons's master's dissertation, "The *Canterbury Tales* in Performance" (University of Birmingham, 1993), contains further useful information about some of the versions discussed in this chapter. For Kittredge's argument, see "Chaucer's Discussion of Marriage," *Modern Philology* 9 (1911–12): 435–67.

20. Coghill, *Chaucer,* 45.

21. Phil Woods with Michael Bogdanov, *Canterbury Tales: Chaucer Made Modern* (North Shields: Iron Press, 1992), p. v; hereafter cited by page number in the text.

22. B. A. Young, "Canterbury Tales," *Financial Times,* 2 January 1979, 9.

23. Arnold Wengrow, *Canterbury Tales: A Contemporary Theatrical Adaptation of the Works of Geoffrey Chaucer* (Colorado Springs: Meriwether, 1983), 41, 51, 92.

24. The episodes were broadcast on BBC Radio 4 on 13, 20, and 27 March and 3 April 1991. They were later issued on cassette in the BBC Radio Collection (ZBBC 1302, 1993).

25. Kenneth Pickering, *Some Canterbury Tales: Freely Adapted from Geoffrey Chaucer,* music by Derek Hyde (London: Samuel French, 1988), 1.

26. Jim Sperinck, *The Canterbury Tales Panto: A Pantomime,* rev. ed. (Hemel Hempstead: Jasper, 1994).

27. See, for example, the reference to E. L. Blanchard's pantomime of 1863, *Harlequin Chaucer and Grim John of Gaunt,* in Clement Scott and Cecil Howard, *The Life and Reminiscences of E. L. Blanchard* (1891), 1:243; see also Spurgeon, *Five Hundred Years,* 2(2):67.

28. Olena S. Bunn, "A Bibliography of Chaucer in English and American Belles-Lettres since 1900," *Bulletin of Bibliography and Dramatic Index* (ed. Anne Sutherland) 19 (September 1946–December 1949): 205–6.

29. Percy Mackaye, *The Canterbury Pilgrims: A Comedy* (New York: Macmillan, 1903), 35–36.

30. The animations were broadcast in two episodes on BBC 2 on 21 and 22 December 1998 at 7:30 P.M., with in both cases a repeat Middle English version broadcast at 12:00 noon the following day, the first episode containing the Nun's Priest's, Knight's, and Wife of Bath's tales, the second the Merchant's, Pardoner's, and Franklin's. The pilgrims were represented by animated puppets, the tales being presented in two-dimensional cartoon format, apart from the Pardoner's. Although the second episode concluded with the arrival at Canterbury, publicity has been issued promising a third installment in the year 2000, featuring the "ride back to London" and the tales of the Miller, Reeve, and Squire.

31. *Start the Week,* broadcast on BBC Radio 4, 14 December 1998, at 9:00 A.M.

9. Novel Chaucer

1. Emily Richings, *In Chaucer's Maytime* (London: Fisher Unwin, 1902), 3.

2. Alfred W. Pollard, *Chaucer* (1893), 76.

3. There is still some uncertainty as to whether Chaucer's wife Philippa was the daughter of Sir Paon de Roet (and thus the sister of the Katherine de Roet who later married Hugh Swynford), but the relationship is now, as Pearsall says, "generally accepted." See Pearsall, *Life*, 50–51.

4. Anya Seton, *Katherine* (1954; reprint, London: Coronet, 1961), 31, 35.

5. Wallace B. Nichols, *Deputy for Youth* (London: Ward, Lock, 1935), 14.

6. For an account of Chaucer's wardship of Staplegate, see Pearsall, *Life*, 101–2. That Staplegate had any connection with Cecilia is entirely Nichols's fiction.

7. See Ezra Pound, "Chaucer Was Framed?" chapter 50 of his *Guide to Kulchur* (London: Faber, 1938), 280–83 (the chapter is far too oblique and desultory to provide any answer). The deed of release has been an embarrassment to Chaucer's reputation ever since its discovery was announced in the *Athenaeum* on 29 November 1873 (698). Although many Chaucerians have been keen to side with Furnivall's interpretation of the case ("I think it certain that Chaucer committed no felony in his 'raptus' of Cecilia Chaumpaigne," *Trial-Forewords*, 142), more recent investigation has indeed inclined to lay the charge of rape at Chaucer's door. See P. R. Watts, "The Strange Case of Geoffrey Chaucer and Cecilia Chaumpaigne," *Law Quarterly Review* 63 (1947): 419–515, and Christopher Cannon, "*Raptus* in the Chaumpaigne Release and a Newly Discovered Document concerning the Life of Geoffrey Chaucer," *Speculum* 68 (1993): 74–94.

8. C. E. D. Phelps, *The Accolade; or, The Canon and His Yeoman* (Philadelphia: Lippincott, 1905), 16–17.

9. Vera Chapman, *The Wife of Bath* (London: Rex Collings, 1978), 134–38.

10. In Geraldine McCaughrean's children's version, as we saw in chapter 4, the Wife ends the pilgrimage engaged to Harry Bailly, while in Mackaye's *Canterbury Pilgrims* (see chapter 8) she weds the Miller (202). William Scott Durrant's "playlet" of 1912 opens with the male pilgrims in flight from the husband-chasing Wife, whom Harry Bailly again agrees to marry. See *Chaucer Redivivus: A Playlet for the Open Air or Hall* (London: George Allen, 1912). Susan Swan's novel *The Wives of Bath* is set in the 1960s in Bath Ladies College outside Toronto. The girls of the college, which is "only a fiefdom in the kingdom of men," are governed by a lesbian headmistress who "looked the way Chaucer's Wife of Bath might have looked if she had stepped into the twentieth century: broad in the behind and out for herself, and the rest of the world could go hang." Although this figure "lived outside the rules of men," the principal action concerns a pupil whose desire to be male leads her to murder the school janitor and cut off his penis, which she then tries to glue onto herself. Susan Swan, *The Wives of Bath* (1993; reprint, London: Granta, 1994), 217, 22.

11. P. C. Doherty, *An Ancient Evil: The Knight's Tale of Mystery and Murder as He Goes on Pilgrimage from London to Canterbury* (London: Headline, 1994), 4.

12. Another recent exponent of the medieval whodunit is Candace Robb. In the third volume of her Owen Archer Mystery series, Chaucer makes a guest appearance, imparting some crucial information to Archer in his investigations. Chaucer is portrayed in traditional novelistic guise as "round and plain," comically self-effacing and inept, and unhappily married, though Owen does condescend to regard him as a "complex little man." See Candace Robb, *The Nun's Tale: An Owen Archer Mystery* (1995; reprint, London: Arrow, 1998), 203–11.

13. P. C. Doherty, *A Tapestry of Murders: The Man of Law's Tale . . .* (London: Headline, 1994), 152–53.

14. P. C. Doherty, *Ghostly Murders: The Poor Priest's Tale . . .* (London: Headline, 1997), 6.

15. Doherty, *Tapestry*, 1, and *Ghostly Murders*, 1. Doherty's "black" Chaucer is perhaps anticipated in turn by a recent series of poems on the "General Prologue" by Andrew Crozier, Roy Fisher, Keith Please, and Kevin Power, offering portaits of the pilgrims that stress their sinister or alienated qualities. See *Riders and Horses: Poems Written on the Theme of Geoffrey Chaucer's the "Prologue" to the "Canterbury Tales"* (Guildford: Circle Press, 1982), in particular Please's versions of the Reeve (10–11) and the Doctor (13), who is a corpse-robber. With no affable Chaucerian narrator and no Host, the assembly is presented in a series of terse, stark vignettes in a general climate of "no love and nothing / in the air but rain," as the final poem's concluding lines (Kevin Power on the Franklin) have it (21).

16. Doherty, *Ancient Evil*, 248, and *A Tournament of Murders: The Franklin's Tale . . .* (London: Headline, 1996), 249.

17. Bunn, "Bibliography of Chaucer," 208.

18. See Pearsall's review of Donald R. Howard's *Chaucer: His Life, His Works, His World*, *Studies in the Age of Chaucer* 13 (1991): 200.

10. Concluding Chaucer

1. Hugh Holman, *Up This Crooked Way: A Sheriff Macready Detective Story* (1946; reprint, London: Foulsham, 1951), 132, 92.

2. There is a tradition of incidental reference to Chaucer in the modern detective novel, either to the handy phrase "mordre wol out" from the "Nun's Priest's Tale" (VII.3052) or to the lines from the "Knight's Tale" describing the decoration of Mars's temple: "the smylere with the knyf under the cloke," and so forth (I.1995–2008). See the listings in B. J. Whiting, "Some Chaucer Allusions, 1923–42," *Notes and Queries* 187 (1944): 288–91, to which may be added Edmund Crispin, *Holy Disorders* (London: Gollancz, 1946), which uses the "Knight's Tale" lines as epigraph. In Crispin's novel the protagonist, suggestively called Geoffrey Vintner, is an amiable but rather obtuse individual playing second fiddle to the sleuth Gervase Fen and may owe something to the characterization of Chaucer in the *Tales*. In Vernon Hall Jr.'s "Sherlock Holmes and the Wife of Bath," *Baker Street Journal* 3 (1948): 84–93, Holmes undertakes to deduce from the Wife's "Prologue" that she murdered her fourth husband and that in writing it Chaucer "anticipated the methods of the writers of *romans policiers*" (91). In Robert Robinson's *Landscape with Dead Dons* (London: Gollancz, 1956), an Oxford academic fakes the discovered manuscript of the lost "book of the Leoun" Chaucer refers to in the *Canterbury Tales* "Retraction," and then has to commit murder to keep his secret intact.

3. Chesterton, *Chaucer*, 15.

4. Mrs. X, *The Barmaid's Tale*, ed. James Morton (London: Little, Brown, 1996). I take the subtitle from the book's dust jacket rather than the title page.

5. Nora Naish, *The Magistrate's Tale* (1995; reprint, London: Mandarin, 1996), 231.

6. Woolf, "The Pastons and Chaucer," 27; see chapter 5 in this volume.

7. Vance Bourjaily, *Now Playing at Canterbury* (New York: Dial Press, 1976), 518. The only individual story in the novel that bears much resemblance to anything in the *Canterbury Tales* is chapter 9, "The Fastest Jeep in the World," where a reckless bravado, after a

night's drinking, takes on the challenge of a beautiful female driver in a car chase in the Mexican mountains and plummets to his death. His companion, recounting the tale, suggests that the challenger was no less than pursuing Death herself, a personification that contributes to the general evocation of the "Pardoner's Tale" (225–39).

8. Journeys by vehicle of one sort or another are often the locus of corporate tale-telling in modern fiction, from Thomas Hardy's party traveling by carrier's van in "A Few Crusted Characters" (in *Life's Little Ironies,* 1894) to Dan Simmons's *Hyperion* (1989; reprint, London: Headline, 1991), set on board a spacecraft in the twenty-ninth century, and in which at least one of the tellers evokes the Chaucerian pilgrimage as a parallel (23). Two works that feature journeys by bus and that make more of the connection with Chaucer are Alan Plater's *Trinity Tales,* broadcast in six installments on BBC 2 television between 21 November and 26 December 1975, and Karen King-Aribisala's *Kicking Tongues* (Oxford: Heinemann, 1998), set in present-day Nigeria.

9. Graham Swift, *Last Orders* (London: Picador, 1996).

10. Joseph Conrad, *Heart of Darkness* (1902; reprint, Harmondsworth: Penguin, 1973), 39.

11. Helen Storm Corsa, *Chaucer: Poet of Mirth and Morality* (Notre Dame, Ind.: University of Notre Dame Press, 1964); Ruth M. Ames, *God's Plenty: Chaucer's Christian Humanism* (Chicago: Loyola University Press, 1984).

12. John Gardner, *The Life and Times of Chaucer* (1977; reprint, St. Albans: Granada, 1979), 3–4, 192, 312–14.

13. Jay Breckenridge, "A Visit with Geoffrey Chaucer: The Medieval Poet Characterized for a Modern Audience" (Ph.D. diss., Carnegie-Mellon University, 1984), 2.

14. Jay Breckenridge, "At Last, Geoffrey Chaucer in Person," *Pennsylvania English* 15 (1990): 46.

15. Breckenridge, "A Visit," 5–6.

16. A notable instance of exasperated aggression toward academic "ownership" of Chaucer is Thomas Laughlin Halliburton, "Why Do English Professors Say Such Crazy Things about the *Canterbury Tales?* An Investigation of the Rhetoric, Logic, Method, and History of Academic Exegesis of Chaucer's Tales in America, 1900–1984" (Ph.D. diss., University of Texas at Austin, 1985). Halliburton objects to the claims for detailed, objective analysis on a "scientific" model that underwrite much scholarly commentary, arguing that the competitive professionalization of the academy has led to a spurious quest for originality and complexity in interpretation: "Tales like the Franklin's, which seem so ordinary and in the main so unproblematic, turn out to be underlaid and driven by occult mechanisms" (318). As an alternative, he occasionally offers accounts of the "ordinary" or "vulgarly interesting" readings he would like to reinstate, as when he takes us through the "Knight's Tale" (257–59): "The reader . . . will be moved by pity and sympathy and curiosity of the ordinary make-believe literary sort. . . . 'Those poor boys, locked away in prison forever!' she will say to herself in pity, and things will only get worse for her when the knights fall in love with Emelye and fall out with one another" (257), and so on. More convincing in some of its denunciations than its remedies, Halliburton's thesis concludes with a philippic against the entire scholarly profession: "Literary scholars are, almost all of them, a menace to education"; no one would willingly choose to enter "so dismal a rat-race" (350).

17. Recent endorsements of Chaucer by established writers include Francine Prose, "Naughty, Bawdy, and Wise: A Valentine for Chaucer," *New York Times Book Review,* 14 February 1988, 26, and that by Ian McEwan, who appeared on BBC Radio 4's *Today* program (18 December 1998) to propose Chaucer as the "person of the millennium" in the program's competition of that name (which was won by Shakespeare; Chaucer did not make the shortlist).

18. "In Praise of Tales and Their Teller," *Kentish Gazette,* 24 April 1992, 9.

19. Hawkes's description of today's cultural and commercial Shakespeare industry as "Bardbiz" is outlined in chapter 7 of his *Meaning by Shakespeare* (London: Routledge, 1992), 141–53.

20. E. T. Donaldson, "Chaucer the Pilgrim," in his *Speaking of Chaucer* (London: Athlone: 1970), 10. As Donaldson notes at the outset of this essay, "Verisimilitude in a work of fiction is not without its attendant dangers, the chief of which is that the responses it stimulates in the reader may be those appropriate not so much to an imaginative production as to an historical one or to a piece of reporting" (1). For further reservations over Canterbury as the "real" destination of the *Tales,* see, for example, John Norton-Smith, *Geoffrey Chaucer* (London: Routledge and Kegan Paul, 1974), 83; Helen Cooper, *The Structure of the "Canterbury Tales"* (London: Duckworth, 1983), 69–72; and Traugott Lawler, *The One and the Many in the "Canterbury Tales"* (Hamden: Archon Books, 1980), 109–21.

21. For Muscatine's attack on the creation of an "almost puritanical Chaucer," see his essay "Chaucer's Religion and the Chaucer Religion," in *Chaucer Traditions: Studies in Honour of Derek Brewer* (Cambridge: Cambridge University Press, 1990), 249–62. See also Peter Conrad's critique of the "arrival-motif" of the film *A Canterbury Tale* in the light of his insistence on a *Canterbury Tales* "ruled by accident, by coincidence, mischance, and the unaccountable friction between individuals, which is why its constituent stories are often incomplete and why the collective journey is never completed" (*To Be Continued,* 11–12).

22. As, for example, in the Basingstoke production discussed in chapter 8 and the open-air production staged by the Cleveland Theatre Company at Preston Park, Stockton, 28 July–28 August 1993.

23. Hansen, *Chaucer and the Fictions of Gender,* 230–31.

24. Lee Patterson, *Chaucer and the Subject of History* (London: Routledge, 1991), 1–13, 423–25.

25. Strohm, *Social Chaucer,* 182.

26. James Norman Hall, "Escape de luxe: A Memory of 1918," *Harpers Magazine* 160 (December 1929–May 1930): 94.

27. Rita Copeland, *Rhetoric, Hermeneutics, and Translation in the Middle Ages: Academic Traditions and Vernacular Texts* (Cambridge: Cambridge University Press, 1991).

28. On Chaucer examining in the British school system, see Jean Simpson, "A Consideration of Chaucer Questions in A-Level Examinations from 1963 to 1995 . . ." (master's dissertation, University of Birmingham, 1998).

Medieval Cultures

Volume 21
Olivia Holmes
Assembling the Lyric Self: Authorship from Troubadour Song to Italian Poetry Book

Volume 20
Karen Sullivan
The Interrogation of Joan of Arc

Volume 19
Clare A. Lees
Tradition and Belief: Religious Writing in Late Anglo-Saxon England

Volume 18
David Matthews
The Making of Middle English, 1765–1910

Volume 17
Jeffrey Jerome Cohen
Of Giants: Sex, Monsters, and the Middle Ages

Volume 16
Edited by Barbara A. Hanawalt and David Wallace
Medieval Crime and Social Control

Volume 15
Kathryn Kerby-Fulton and Denise L. Despres
Iconography and the Professional Reader: The Politics of Book Production in the Douce "Piers Plowman"

Volume 14
Edited by Marilynn Desmond
Christine de Pizan and the Categories of Difference

Volume 13
Alfred Thomas
Anne's Bohemia: Czech Literature and Society, 1310–1420

Volume 12
Edited by F. R. P. Akehurst and Stephanie Cain Van D'Elden
The Stranger in Medieval Society

Volume 11
Edited by Karma Lochrie, Peggy McCracken, and James A. Schultz
Constructing Medieval Sexuality

Volume 10
Claire Sponsler
Drama and Resistance: Bodies, Goods, and Theatricality in Late Medieval England

Volume 9
Edited by Barbara A. Hanawalt and David Wallace
Bodies and Disciplines: Intersections of Literature and History in Fifteenth-Century England

Volume 8
Marilynn Desmond
Reading Dido: Gender, Textuality, and the Medieval "Aeneid"

Volume 7
Edited by Clare A. Lees
Medieval Masculinities: Regarding Men in the Middle Ages

Volume 6
Edited by Barbara A. Hanawalt and Kathryn L. Reyerson
City and Spectacle in Medieval Europe

Volume 5
Edited by Calvin B. Kendall and Peter S. Wells
Voyage to the Other World: The Legacy of Sutton Hoo

Volume 4
Edited by Barbara A. Hanawalt
Chaucer's England: Literature in Historical Context

Volume 3
Edited by Marilyn J. Chiat and Kathryn L. Reyerson
The Medieval Mediterranean: Cross-Cultural Contacts

Volume 2
Edited by Andrew MacLeish
The Medieval Monastery

Volume 1
Edited by Kathryn L. Reyerson and Faye Powe
The Medieval Castle

INDEX

Steve Ellis is professor of English literature at the University of Birmingham. He has written extensively on the modern reception of Chaucer and of Dante. Among his books are *Dante and English Poetry: Shelley to T. S. Eliot,* a verse translation of Dante's "Hell," two volumes on Chaucer, and two volumes of poetry.